PRINCIPAL COINS
OF THE ROMANS

PRINCIPAL COINS OF THE ROMANS

VOLUME II
THE PRINCIPATE
31 BC–AD296

R.A.G.CARSON

Published for
The Trustees of the British Museum by
British Museum Publications Limited

British Library Cataloguing in Publication Data

Carson, Robert Andrew Glendinning
   Principal coins of the Romans
   Vol. 2: The Principate, 31BC–AD 296
   1. Coins, Roman
   1. Title 11. British Museum
  737.4'9'37   CJ833

ISBN 0 7141 0839 1 *the set*
ISBN 0 7141 0844 8 *Volume 1*
ISBN 0 7141 0852 9 *Volume 2*
Published by British Museum Publications Ltd
6 Bedford Square, London WC1B 3RA

Designed by Harry Green
Set in 10 on 11pt Bembo
Printed in Great Britain by Balding and Mansell,
London and Wisbech

Contents

1	The Julio-Claudians, 31 BC–AD 68	7
2	The Civil War, AD 68–69	28
3	The Flavians, AD 69–96	35
4	The Adoptive Emperors, AD 96–138	45
5	The Antoninines, AD 138–192	57
6	The Civil War and the Severans, AD 192–235	72
7	The Military Emperors, AD 235–270	89
8	The Gallic Empire, AD 260–274	115
9	The Recovery of the Empire, AD 270–294	124
10	The British Empire, AD 287–296	153
Concordance		158
Indexes		163
	Emperors and their Relatives	
	Mints	
	Types	
	General	

1 The Julio-Claudians 31BC–AD68

After Actium in 31 BC Octavian, or Augustus as he was entitled in 27 BC, was left as sole ruler of the Roman world. His reorganisation of the State included a re-modelling of the coinage to provide a complete system in three metals. The major unit, the gold aureus, struck at a standard of 42 to the pound, comprised 25 silver denarii struck at 84 to the pound. Both aureus and denarius also had a less common half-piece or quinarius. In bronze new denominations were introduced in orichalcum, the sestertius, tariffed at four to a silver denarius and the dupondius valued at half a sestertius, while in copper were issued a coin worth half a dupondius, the *as*, together with its half, the semis, and quarter, the quadrans. The coinage in precious metals was controlled by the emperor, but some role was left to the Senate in the production of the bronze coinage which is consistently marked on the reverse with the letters SC (*senatus consulto*). On the precious metal coinage the obverse almost invariably carries an imperial portrait, but on the bronze coinage initially the imperial portrait appears only on the obverse of the *as*. On Tiberian bronze a portrait begins to appear also on the dupondius, and, from Caligula on, the sestertius also regularly has an obverse portrait.

At the beginning of the reign of Augustus coinage in gold and silver continued to be struck in Italy, presumably at Rome, and at times from mints in the East where mints at Ephesus and Pergamum also issued series of the silver cistophoric tetradrachms, as well as bronze coinages. In North Africa a coinage of denarii was issued for Octavian by the governor of Cyrenaica, Scarpus, immediately after Actium. A new series in all three metals, signed with the names of the *tresviri monetales* was struck at Rome, from about 20 BC down to c.6 BC. In the western provinces the legate Carisius issued aurei, denarii, and bronze *asses* at Emerita in Spain. Other coinages in gold and silver are attributed to Spanish mints at Caesaraugusta and Colonia Patricia from 25 BC. From 15 BC coinage in gold and silver was produced only by a new mint at Lyons, and bronze coinage with its distinctive reverse of the altar of Rome and Augustus at Lyons was also issued there from 10 BC. For the latter part of Augustus' reign only the Gallic mint issued gold and silver, and this practice was continued by Tiberius, though the Rome mint struck the distinctive SC bronze. In the East Tiberius issued a new series of silver drachms from a mint at Caesarea in Cappadocia. Early in the reign of Gaius (Caligula) the production of gold and silver appears to have been transferred from Lyons to Rome which remained the sole mint in the West also under Claudius (another view has it that the change may not have taken place until Nero's reform in AD 64). Caesarea continued to mint for Caligula and for Claudius, who also introduced a new cistophoric tetradrachm coinage at Ephesus. The first ten years of Nero's coinage was in gold and silver only, and the brief span of senatorial influence is marked by the inclusion of EX SC on the reverse. After the reform of AD 64, which removed this formula and lowered the standard of gold to 45 to the pound (and of silver to 96 to the pound), a plentiful coinage in *aes* was struck at Rome, and bronze coinage was resumed at Lyons – its issues marked by a distinctive globe at the point of the obverse bust. A brief experimental issue of Neronian bronze was produced in orichalcum only, the denominations from dupondius downwards bearing the appropriate mark of value.

Although the overwhelming proportion of coinage is in the name of and, most frequently, bears the portrait of the emperor himself, issues for, or honouring, other members of the imperial family are a feature of Julio-Claudian coinage. In the Augustan coinage this reference is usually confined to the reverse-portraits of Agrippa, Tiberius, or the standing figures of Augustus' heirs, Gaius and Lucius, but, at Lyons, Tiberius' portrait appears on bronze coins towards the end of the reign of Augustus. In subsequent coinages some distinctive issues carry the portraits of other imperial personages on the obverse.

Augustus, 31BC–AD14

320　Denarius Rome, 29 BC

Obv.　Victory standing r. on prow, holding wreath and palm.
Rev.　IMP CAESAR. Emperor standing in quadriga r., holding branch and reins.
　　　Æ, 3.98 gm. ↖.
The reverse depicts the triumph celebrated by Augustus in this year for the victory at Actium alluded to by the obverse.

321　Denarius Rome, 29 BC

Obv.　Head, laureate, r., IMP CAESAR.
Rev.　Column ornamented with prows and anchors, and surmounted by statue of Augustus holding spear and parazonium.
　　　Æ, 4.10 gm. ↖.
The reverse continues the allusion to the victory at Actium.

322　Quinarius East, 29 BC

Obv.　CAESAR IMP VII Head, bare, r.
Rev.　ASIA RECEPTA. Victory standing l., holding wreath and palm on a *cista mystica* between two serpents. Æ, 1.91 gm. →.
A specific recording of the recovery of the province from Antony.

323　Aureus East, 27 BC

Obv.　CAESAR DIVI F COS VII. Head, bare, r.; below, small capricorn.
Rev.　AEGVPT CAPTA. Crocodile r. Ν, 8.08 gm. ↘.
The crocodile symbolises Egypt seized from Cleopatra.

324　Aureus Spain, 19–16 BC

Obv.　AVGVSTVS. Head, bare, r.
Rev.　S·P·Q·R. Victory flying r., placing wreath on shield leaning against column and inscribed CL·V. Ν, 7.77 gm. ↘.
The reverse refers to the *clypeus virtutis*, one of the honours accorded to Augustus in 27 BC.

325　Denarius Rome, 27–20 BC

Obv.　Head, bare, r.
Rev.　AVGVSTVS. Capricorn l, holding globe with rudder attached; above cornucopiae.
　　　Æ, 3.78 gm. ↙.
The honorific, Augustus, was accorded to the princeps in 27 BC. Augustus's natal sign was the capricorn.

326　Denarius Rome, 27–20 BC

Obv. Head, laureate, r.
Rev. CAESAR AVGVSTVS. Two laurel branches.
    R, 3.72 gm. ↙.
The laurels are those planted on either side of the portico of the house of Augustus by order of the Senate.

327 **Denarius** Spain, 22–19 BC

Obv. CAESAR AVGVSTVS. Head, bare, r.
Rev. S·P·Q·R CL·V inscribed on round shield.
    R, 3.67 gm. ↙.
For the reverse, see No. 324.

328 **Denarius** Spain, 19–16 BC

Obv. CAESAR AVGVSTVS. Head, laureate, r.
Rev. DIVVS IVLIVS. Comet with eight rays and tail.
    R, 3.78 gm. ↘.
A comet, the *sidus Iulium*, was observed shortly after Caesar's death in 44 BC.

329 **Aureus** Spain, 21–19 BC

Obv. CAESARI AVGVSTO. Head, laureate, r.
Rev. MAR VLT. Round temple with domed roof, showing six columns, and containing a legionary eagle flanked l. and r. by a standard. N, 7.90 gm. ↙.
This temple, erected by Augustus on the Capitol as a repository for the standards returned by the Parthians, was dedicated on 12 May, 20 BC.

330 **Aureus** Rome, 19 BC

Obv. Q. RVSTIVS FORTVNAE. Heads of Fortuna Felix in stephane l., and FORTVNA VICTRIX in prow-ornamented helmet r.
Rev. CAESARI AVGVSTO. Victory l., placing shield inscribed S·C· on cippus. N, 8.95 gm. ←.
The types are probably associated with the return of Augustus from the East in this year. On this first issue of the series with magistrates' names Rustius does not style himself moneyer.

331 **Denarius** Rome, 19 BC

Obv. TVRPILIANVS III VIR FERO. Bust of Feronia, draped and with stephane, r.
Rev. CAESAR AVGVSTVS SIGN RECE. Parthian kneeling r., holding standard with vexillum attached. R, 3.81 gm. ↘.
Augustus' successful diplomacy in 20 BC, secured the return by Phraates of Parthia of standards captured in the earlier defeats of Cassius, Decidius Saxa and Antony.

332 **Aureus** Rome, 17 BC

Obv. AVGVST·DIVI·F·LVDOS SAE. Herald, helmeted, draped, standing l., holding caduceus and shield with six-pointed star.
Rev. M SANQVINIVS III VIR. Head of deified Julius Caesar, laureate, r.; above, comet with four rays and tail. N, 7.89 gm. ↗.
The obverse figure is the herald who announced the Saecular Games recorded in the inscription. The comet on reverse is the *sidus Iulium* which appeared after Caesar's death.

333 Denarius Rome, 16 BC

Obv. S·C·O·B·R·P·CVM·SALVT·IMP·CAESAR·AVGVS·CONS.
Bust of Augustus, three-quarters facing, on
round shield within laurel-wreath.

Rev. L·MESCINIVS·RVFVS III VIR. Mars, helmeted,
holding spear and parazonium, standing l.
on pedestal inscribed S P Q R V P S P R S ET
RED AVG. Æ, 4.02 gm. ↖.

The date is confirmed by other coins of this
moneyer with Augustus' tribunician year 8. The
dedications on obverse and reverse are for the
emperor's recovery from illness and for his safe
return from his visit to Gaul.

334 Denarius Rome, 13 BC

Obv. AVGVSTVS. Head, bare, r.; to l., lituus.

Rev. C MARIVS TRO III VIR. Bust of Diana,
diademed, r., with quiver on back.
Æ, 3.81 gm. ↙.

The personification of Diana is traditionally
identified as a portrait of the emperor's daughter,
Julia.

335 Aureus Rome, 13 BC

Obv. CAESAR AVGVSTVS. Head in oak-wreath, r.

Rev. M·AGRIPPA PLATORINVS·III·VIR. Head of
Agrippa, wearing mural and rostral crown, r.
Λ, 8.01 gm. ←.

Agrippa's unusual crown commemorates his
victories as both general and admiral.

336 Sestertius Rome, 22 BC

Obv. OB CIVIS SERVATOS. Oak-wreath between
laurel-branches.

Rev. C·GALLVS·C·F·LVPERCVS·III·VIR·A·A·A·F·F·SC.
Æ, 27.73 gm. ↗.

An early example of the new sestertius denomination in orichalcum. This is the last series on
which the magistrates responsible for coining
record their names and office. The formula after the
name designates the magistrate as *tresvir aere argento
auro flando feriundo*, that is, one of the college of three
responsible for casting and striking bronze, silver
and gold.

337 Dupondius Rome, 18 BC

Obv. AVGVSTVS TRIBVNIC POTEST. Oak-wreath.

Rev. C·ASINIVS·GALLVS·III·VIR·A·A·A·F·F·SC.
Æ, 13.61 gm. →.

The new dupondius denomination in orichalcum.

338 As Rome, 22 BC

Obv. CAESAR·AVGVSTVS TRIBVNIC POTEST. Head
bare, r.

Rev. C·CASSIVS·CELER·III·VIR·A·A·A·F·F·SC.
Æ, 11.14 gm. ↑.

The new copper *as* was the only Augustan bronze
denomination to carry the imperial portrait.

339　Quadrans Rome, 5 BC

Obv. GALLVS·MESSALA·III·VIR. Altar hung with garland.
Rev. APRONVS·SISENNA·A·A·A·F·F·SC.
　　Æ 2.88 gm. ↖.
The smallest Augustan bronze denomination.

340　As Rome, 7 BC

Obv. CAESAR·AVGVST·PONT·MAX·TRIBVNIC·POT.
　　Head, laureate, l.; to l., Victory, standing l.,
　　holding cornucopiae and touching
　　emperor's laurel-wreath.
Rev. M·SALVIVS·OTHO·III·VIR·A·A·A·F·F·SC.
　　Æ, 14.6 gm. ↑.
The occasion for this special series may be the triumph celebrated by Tiberius in this year.

341　Aureus East, 21–19 BC

Obv. CAESAR. Head, bare, r.
Rev. AVGVSTVS Heifer walking l. ᴬⱽ, 7.97 gm. ↖.
Unusually fine style. Probably struck during Augustus' visit to Samos in these years.

342　Denarius East, 21–19 BC

Obv. Head, laureate, r.
Rev. AVGVSTVS. Capricorn r., holding globe with
　　rudder attached; above, cornucopiae.
　　Æ, 3.80 gm. ↑.
The capricorn was Augustus' natal sign.

343　Aureus East, 21–19 BC

Obv. AVGVSTVS. Head, bare, r.
Rev. ARMENIA CAPTA. Victory, kneeling on and
　　slaying recumbent bull, r. ᴬⱽ, 7.84 gm. ↘.
An expedition under Tiberius in 20 BC brought Armenia under Roman control as a client kingdom under Tigranes.

344　Cistophorus East, c.27 BC

Obv. IMP·CAESAR. Head bare, r.
Rev. AVGVSTVS. Sphinx seated r. Æ, 12.16 gm. ↗.
Uncertain mint. Augustus in his early years used a signet ring with a sphinx device.

345　Cistophorus East, c.19 BC

Obv. IM·IX·TR·PO·V. Head, bare, r.
Rev. COM ASIAE. Hexastyle temple with ROM ET
　　AVGVST on entablature. Æ, 11.92 gm. ↗.
The temple of Rome and Augustus at Pergamum identifies the mint of this series.

346 Dupondius East, *c*.19 BC

Obv. AVGVSTVS. Head, bare, r.
Rev. C.A in circle of dots within wreath of laurels
and prows. Æ, 15.36 gm. ↑.
The C(*ommune*) A(*siae*) reverse suggests mintage at
Pergamum, and perhaps association with the
cistophoric issue (No. 345).

347 Denarius Emerita, *c*.25–23 BC

Obv. IMP CAESAR AVGVST. Head, bare, r.
Rev. P CARISIVS LEG PRO PR. Bird's-eye view of
town with gateway of two doors; above
doors, IMERITA. Æ, 3.95 gm. ↖.
Coinage for Augustus by Carisius, his legate in
further Spain. The reverse type identifies the mint
with certainty.

348 Quinarius Emerita, *c*.25–23 BC

Obv. AVGVST. Head, bare, r.
Rev. P CARISI LEG I. Victory standing r., placing
wreath on trophy. Æ, 1.81 gm. ↙.

349 As Emerita, *c*.25–23 BC

Obv. CAESAR·AVG·TRIB·POTEST. Head, bare, r.
Rev. P CARISIVS/LEG/AVGVSTI. Æ, 11.40 gm. ↘.

350 Aureus Lyons, *c*.15 BC

Obv. AVGVSTVS DIVI·F. Head, bare, l.
Rev. IMP X. Augustus, seated l. on platform,
receiving branches from two figures in
military dress, standing r. Ν, 7.90 gm. ✓.
The figures with triumphal branches are Tiberius
and Nero Drusus who conquered Rhaetia in 15 BC.

351 Aureus Lyons, 15–12 BC

Obv. As No. 350, but head r.
Rev. IMP X. Bull butting r. Ν, 7.97 gm. ✓.
The bull was the familiar reverse type on earlier
coins of Massilia.

352 Aureus quinarius Lyons, 11–10 BC

Obv. As No. 351.
Rev. TR·POT·XIII. Victory seated r. on globe.
Ν, 3.16 gm. ↘.
Victory was the conventional type on both gold and
silver quinarii.

353 Denarius Lyons, 11–9 BC

Obv. As No. 351.
Rev. IMP XII ACT. Apollo standing front, head l.,
holding plectrum and lyre. Æ, 3.89 gm. ←.
Actian Apollo recalls the defeat of Antony at the
battle of Actium.

354 Aureus Lyons, *c.*8 BC

Obv. As No. 351.
Rev. C·CAES·AVGVS·F. Caius Caesar galloping r.,
holding sword and shield; behind, legionary
eagle between two standards. Aɴ, 7.87 gm. ✓.
The reverse celebrates the prince's introduction to
military service in this year.

355 Denarius Lyons, 2 BC–AD 4

Obv. CAESAR AVGVSTVS DIVI F PATER PATRIAE.
Head, laureate, r.
Rev. C L CAESARES AVGVSTI F COS DESIG PRINC
IVVENT. Gaius and Lucius Caesar standing
facing, resting hand on shield; behind, two
crossed spears, point downward; between
spears, simpulum and lituus. Æ, 3.84 gm. ✓.
Augustus was accorded the honorific title *pater
patriae* in 2 BC. Gaius and Lucius, the emperor's
grandsons were regarded as his heirs, and to them
the title *princeps iuventutis* is given, the first use of the
title that came to denote the heir apparent.

356 Aureus Lyons, AD 13–14

Obv. As No. 353.
Rev. TI CAESAR AVG F TR POT XV. Head of
Tiberius, bare, r. Aɴ, 7.81 gm. ↓.
After the death of Gaius and Lucius, Tiberius was
adopted as Augustus' heir. In this year he shared in
the coinage to mark his triumph for the victories in
Germany in AD 12.

357 Sestertius Lyons, *c.*AD 10–14.

Obv. As No. 353.
Rev. ROM ET AVG. Altar of Rome and Augustus at
Lyons, between two columns surmounted
by Victory. Æ, 24.77 gm. ↓.
The altar is that set up as the central point of the
Concilium Galliarum in 10 BC.

358 As Lyons, AD 9–11

Obv. TI CAESAR AVGVST F IMPERAR V. Head,
laureate, r.
Rev. As No. 357. Æ. 10.63 gm. ↖.
Only late in the reign of Augustus, and only in
bronze, is there coinage with the portrait and titles
of Tiberius on the obverse.

Tiberius, AD14-37

359 Aureus Lyons, *c.*AD 14

Obv. T CAESAR DIVI AVG F AVGVSTVS. Head,
laureate, r.
Rev. DIVOS AVGVST DIVI F. Head, bare, r.; above,
star. Aɴ, 7.79 gm. ↓.
The Senate decreed the deification of Augustus on
17 September, AD 14, and he is portrayed as *divus* on
this early issue of Tiberius.

360 Aureus Lyons, AD 15–16

Obv. As No. 359.
Rev. IMP VII TR POT MAX. Tiberius in quadriga, holding branch and eagle-tipped sceptre. *N*, 7.89 gm. ↖.
The reverse recalls the triumph accorded to Tiberius for his German victories in AD 12.

361 Aureus quinarius Lyons, AD 32–33

Obv. TI DIVI F AVGVSTVS. Head, laureate, r.
Rev. TR POT XXXIIII. Victory seated r. on globe and holding a wreath. *N*, 3.78 gm. ↑.
This Victory quinarius was struck with frequency in this reign.

362 Denarius Lyons, *c.* AD 16–21

Obv. As No. 359.
Rev. PONTIF MAXIM. Female figure, draped, seated r. on chair, holding branch and sceptre. *R*, 3.58 gm. ↖.
The reverse figure represents Livia as Pax. The so-called 'tribute penny', cf. Matthew, 12, 13–17.

363 Sestertius Rome, AD 22–23

Obv. TI CAESAR DIVI AVG F AVGVST P M TR POT XXIIII S C.
Rev. CIVITATIBVS ASIAE RESTITVTIS. Tiberius, laureate, togate, seated l; on curule chair, feet on stool, holding patera and sceptre. *Æ*, 27.41 gm. ↓.
Tiberius promised two million sestertii and remitted tax liability for five years to twelve cities in Asia which suffered from an earthquake in AD 17, and two further cities which suffered in 23 were granted similar remissions.

364 Sestertius Rome, AD 22–23

Obv. As No. 363.
Rev. DIVVS AVGVSTVS PATER. Augustus, radiate, togate, seated l. on throne, feet on stool, holding branch and sceptre; to l., altar. *Æ*, 27.32 gm. ↑.
The reverse reproduces the statue of Augustus erected by Tiberius and Livia near the theatre of Marcellus.

365 Sestertius Rome, AD 22–23

Obv. As No. 363.
Rev. S P Q R / IVLIAE / AVGVST. Carpentum drawn r. by two mules. *Æ*, 26.78 gm. ←.
A *supplicatio*, in which a carpentum was used, was decreed by the Senate in AD 22 in honour of Livia's recovery from illness. Under the will of Augustus Livia was adopted into the Julian gens with the name Julia.

366 Dupondius Rome, AD 22–23

Obv. TI CAESAR DIVI AVG F AVG P M TR POT XXIIII S C.
Rev. IVSTITIA. Bust of Justitia, draped, and with
         stephane, r. Æ, 15.15 gm. ↘.
The personification here and on the following two
coins may represent a portrait of the empress Livia.

367 Dupondius Rome, AD 22–23

Obv. As No. 366.
Rev. SALVS AVGVSTA. Bust of Salus, draped, r.
         Æ, 14.48 gm. ↑.
See No. 366.

368 Dupondius Rome, AD 22–23

Obv. DRVSVS CAESAR TI AVGVSTI F TR POT ITER S C.
Rev. PIETAS. Bust, draped, veiled, and with
         stephane, r. Æ, 14.96 gm. ↓.
See No. 366.

369 Dupondius Rome, AD 22–23

Obv. TI CAESAR DIVI AVG F AVGVST IMP VIII. Head,
         laureate, l.
Rev. CLEMENTIAE S C. Small bust of Tiberius,
         draped, facing within concentric circles of
         laurel-wreath, raised band of petals, and
         ornamented border. Æ, 17.25 gm. ↑.
An early instance of the imperial portrait on the
obverse of the dupondius. *Clementia* is perhaps the
mildness with which Tiberius dealt with political
offenders. For the unusual reverse, cf. No. 333 *Obv.*

370 As Rome, AD 22–23

Obv. As No. 369, but head bare l.
Rev. PONTIF MAXIM TRIBVN POTEST XXIIII S C.
         Æ, 11.21 gm. ↓.
Unusually fine obverse portrait.

371 As Rome, AD 22–23

Obv. DRVSVS CAESAR TI AVG F DIVI AVG N. Head of
         Drusus, bare, l.
Rev. PONTIF TRIBVN POTEST ITER S C.
         Æ, 10.75 gm. ↓.
Drusus, now his father's sole and obvious heir, has a
share in the official coinage.

372 Sestertius Rome, AD 22–23

Obv. DRVSVS CAESAR TI AVG F DIVI AVG V PONT TR
  POT II S C.
Rev. Winged caduceus upright between two
  crossed cornucopiae; on top of each, bust of
  a little boy facing inwards. Æ, 27.73 gm. ↘.
The reverse refers to the twin sons of Drusus –
Tiberius Gemellus and Germanicus – born in AD 19.

373 Sestertius Rome, AD 36–37

Obv. TI CAESAR DIVI AVG F AVGVST P M TR POT
  XXXIX S C.
Rev. DIVO / AVGVSTO / S P Q R. Augustus, radiate,
  togate, holding branch and sceptre, seated l.
  on throne, placed on car, drawn l. by four
  elephants, each with mahout on neck.
  Æ, 29.12 gm. ↑.
The precise circumstances of this honour to
Augustus are unknown.

374 As Rome, *c.*AD 15–16

Obv. DIVVS AVGVSTVS PATER. Head, radiate, l; in
  front, thunderbolt; above, star.

Rev. S C on either side of female figure, veiled,
  draped, seated right, holding patera and
  sceptre. Æ, 10.65 gm. ↑.
Of the extensive coinage by Tiberius in honour of
Divus Augustus this early group forms a real
consecration issue. The unidentified figure on the
reverse is probably Livia.

375 As Rome, *c.*AD 22–30

Obv. DIVVS AVGVSTVS PATER. Head, radiate, l.
Rev. PROVIDENT S C. Altar with panelled door;
  above, flames. Æ, 11.17 gm. ↓.
The more finished style of obverse portraiture,
comparable with that of Nos. 369 and 370, suggests
a date for this group.

376 Quadrans Lyons, *c.*AD 14

Obv. TI CAESAR DIVI AVG F AVGVSTVS. Head,
  laureate, r.
Rev. ROM ET AVG. Altar of Rome and Augustus at
  Lyons, cf. No. 357. Æ, 3.32 gm. ←.
Only very rare bronze was struck at this mint for
Tiberius.

377 As Bilbilis in Spain, AD 31

Obv. TI CAESAR DIVI AVGVSTI F AVGVSTVS. Head,
  laureate, r.
Rev. MVN AVGVSTA BILBILIS TI CAESARE V L AELIO
  SEIANO. around an oak wreath containing
  COS. Æ, 12.3 gm. ↖.

The status and influence of Tiberius' prefect, Sejanus, is apparent in his association with the emperor as an honorary duovir of Bilbilis. COS presumably refers to the consulship of Sejanus in AD 31, and the numeral V after the emperor's name similarly records Tiberius' fifth consulship in the same year.

Caligula, AD37-41

378   **Aureus** Lyons, AD 37–38

Obv. C CAESAR AVG GERM P M TR POT COS. Head, bare, r.
Rev. Head, radiate, r; l. and r., a star.
    N, 7,71 gm. ←.
The reverse portrait, though anonymous is clearly Tiberius.

379   **Aureus** Lyons, AD 37–38

Obv. As No. 378.
Rev. As No. 378. *N*, 7.66 gm. ↑.
The anonymous portrait here on the reverse is that of Augustus.

380   **Aureus** Rome, AD 37–38

Obv. As No. 378, but head laureate.
Rev. AGRIPPINA MAT C CAES AVG GERM. Bust of
    Agrippina, draped, r. *N*, 7.69 gm. ↖.
Caligula is thought to have transferred the minting of precious metal coinage from Lugdunum to Rome after his initial coinage. The evidence for this view is slight – the use of a laureate portrait, and

somewhat improved style and lettering. A notable feature of the coinage of Caligula is the honour paid to members of the emperor's family – in this instance his mother Agrippina.

381   **Denarius** Rome, AD 37–38

Obv. As No. 380.
Rev. GERMANICVS CAES P C CAES AVG. Head, bare,
    r. *R*, 3.81 gm. ↖.
Here the emperor's father is honoured.

382   **As** Rome, AD 37–38

Obv. GERMANICVS CAESAR TI AVGVST F DIVI AVG N.
    Head, bare, r.
Rev. C CAESAR AVG GERMANICVS PON M TR POT S C.
    Æ, 11.80 gm. ↓.
The portrait of Germanicus here takes pride of place on the obverse.

383   **Sestertius** Rome, *c.*AD 37–38

Obv. AGRIPPINA M F MAT C CAESARIS AVGVSTI. Bust, draped, r.
Rev. S P Q R / MEMORIAE / AGRIPPINAE.
    Æ, 27.53 gm. ↓.
Decorated carpentum drawn l. by two mules; the tilt of the carriage is supported by standing female figures. Caligula appointed an annual day of remembrance when Agrippina's image would be paraded in a covered carriage.

384 **Sestertius** Rome, AD 37–38

Obv. C CAESAR AVG GERMANICVS PON M TR POT.
  Head, laureate, l.
Rev. AGRIPPINA DRVSILLA IVLIA S C. Æ, 27.28 gm. ↓.
Caligula's three sisters standing front in the guise
respectively of Securitas, holding cornucopiae and
leaning on column, Concordia holding patera and
cornucopiae, and Fortuna holding rudder and
cornucopiae.

385 **Dupondius** Rome, AD 40–41

Obv. CAESAR DIVI AVG PRON AVG P M TR P IIII P P S C.
Rev. NERO ET DRVSVS CAESARES. The two princes
  riding r. Æ, 17.23 gm. ↓.
The reverse honours the emperor's two elder
brothers who died as the result of Sejanus'
machinations.

386 **As** Rome, AD 37–38

Obv. C CAESAR AVG GERMANICVS PON M TR POT.
  Head, laureate, r.
Rev. VESTA S C. Vesta, veiled, draped, seated l. on
  throne, holding patera and sceptre.
  Æ, 10.84 gm. ↓.
The state cult of Vesta had an association with the
emperor as Pontifex Maximus.

387 **Sestertius** Rome, AD 40–41

Obv. C CAESAR DIVI AVG PRON AVG P M TR P IIII P P.
  Head, laureate, l.
Rev. ADLOCVT COH. Emperor standing l. on
  platform, haranguing five soldiers, each
  holding shield and parazonium, and four
  carrying an aquila; to r. low chair.
  Æ, 28.06 gm. ↓.
The reverse, with its absence of S C, reflects
Caligula's reliance on the support of the Praetorian
guard.

388 **Quadrans** Rome, AD 40

Obv. C CAESAR DIVI AVG PRON AVG SC. A pileus.
Rev. PON M TR P III P P COS TERT R C C.
  Æ, 3.27 gm. ↓.
RCC (*remissa ducentesima*) refers to the abolition by
Caligula of the sales tax of a half per cent.

389 **Dupondius** Rome, *c.*AD 37

Obv. DIVVS AVGVSTVS S C. Head, radiate, l.
Rev. CONSENSV SENAT ET EQ ORDIN P Q R.
  Augustus, laureate, seated l. on curule chair,
  holding branch in r. hand. Æ, 16 gm. ↓.
The reverse represents a statue dedicated to
Augustus.

390 As Rome, AD 37–41

Obv. M AGRIPPA L F COS III. Head, wearing rostral
crown, l.
Rev. S C. Neptune, naked, except for cloak over
shoulder and arm, standing l., holding
dolphin and trident. Æ, 11.51 gm. ↓.
The rostral crown and the Neptune reverse allude to
the naval success at Naulochus in 36 BC of Agrippa,
Caligula's grandfather.

Claudius, AD41–54

391 Aureus Rome, AD 41

Obv. TI CLAVD CAESAR AVG P M TR P. Head,
laureate, r.
Rev. PRAETOR RECEPT. Claudius, bare-headed and
togate, standing r., clasping hands with
Praetorian, holding shield and aquila,
standing l. Æ, 7.77 gm. ↖.
A clear allusion to the part played by the Praetorian
guard in the proclamation of Claudius as emperor.

392 Aureus Rome, AD 44–45

Obv. As No. 391, but TI CLAVD CAESAR AVG P M TR
P IIII.
Rev. IMPER RECEPT. View of the Praetorian camp;
above the front wall stands a soldier holding
spear; to his l., an aquila. N, 7.73 gm. ↘.
On his proclamation Claudius was escorted by the
guard to the Praetorian camp. This type, as No. 391,
formed part of the first coinage in AD 41, and was
repeated, as here, in subsequent issues.

393 Denarius Rome, AD 46–47

Obv. As No. 391, but TI CLAVD CAESAR AVG P M TR
P VI IMP XI.
Rev. PACI AVGVSTAE. Female figure, winged,
draped, advancing r., holding in l. hand
caduceus pointing down at snake gliding r.,
and with r. hand pulling fold of her drapery.
Æ, 3.86 gm. ↘.
This remarkable syncretic type combines the
characteristics or attributes of Pax, Victoria,
Felicitas, Salus and Pudor.

394 Sestertius Rome, AD 41

Obv. TI CLAVDIVS CAESAR AVG P M TR P IMP. Head,
laureate, r.
Rev. SPES AVGVSTA S C. Spes, advancing l., holding
flower and raising skirt. Æ, 29.74 gm. ↓.
The reference is to the birth in this year of the emperor's son, later called Britannicus. This is the first
instance of this type which was to become almost a
standard dynastic type for the imperial heir.

395 Dupondius Rome, AD 41–42

Obv. DIVVS AVGVSTVS S C. Head, radiate, l.
Rev. DIVA AVGVSTA. Livia, draped, and with
wreath of corn-ears, seated l. on throne,
holding corn-ears and long torch.
Æ, 16.28 gm. ↓.

Augustus was deified immediately on his death, but only in AD 42 was the same honour accorded to Livia by Claudius.

396 As Rome, AD 41–42

Obv. TI CLAVDIVS CAESAR AVG P M TR P IMP. Head, bare, l.
Rev. S C. Minerva, helmeted, draped, advancing r., brandishing javelin and holding shield. Æ, 9.26 gm. ↓.

Minerva, an apt type for the scholarly Claudius, has here the military attributes appropriate to an emperor.

397 As *c.*AD 50

Obv. As No. 396.
Rev. As No. 396. Æ, 11.51 gm. ↓.

A contemporary copy of No. 396. *Asses* of Claudius, especially those with Minerva reverse, were extensively copied in the western provinces, not least in Britain.

398 Quadrans Rome, AD 41

Obv. TI CLAVDIVS CAESAR AVG. Modius on three legs.
Rev. PON M TR P IMP COS DES IT S C. Æ, 3.46 gm. ↓.

The obverse type reflects the imperial concern for Rome's corn supply.

399 Quadrans Lugdunum, AD 41

Obv. TI CLAVDIVS CAESAR AVG P M TR P IMP. Head, laureate, r.
Rev. ROM ET AVG. The altar of Rome and Augustus at Lugdunum. Æ, 3.59 gm. ↓.

A rare coinage from this mint celebrating the fiftieth anniversary of the altar and of the birth of Claudius at Lugdunum.

400 Aureus Rome, AD 46–47

Obv. TI CLAVD CAESAR AVG P M TR P VI IMP XI. Head, laureate, r.
Rev. DE BRITANN. Triumphal arch surmounted by equestrian statue between two trophies. N, 7.63 gm. ↓.

The successful conquest of Britain in AD 43 was not celebrated on the coinage until the issue of AD 46–47.

401 Didrachm Caesarea in Cappadocia, *c.*AD 46

Obv. TI CLAVD CAESAR AVG GERM P M TR P. Head, laureate, l.
Rev. DE BRITANNIS. Claudius in quadriga r., holding eagle-tipped sceptre in r. hand. Æ, 7.48 gm.

The celebration of the conquest of Britain was extended to the provincial coinage also.

402 Aureus Rome, AD 41–45

Obv. NERO CLAVDIVS DRVSVS GERMANICVS IMP.
Head, laureate, l.
Rev. DE GERMANIS. Triumphal arch surmounted
by equestrian statue l., between two
trophies. N, 7.85 gm. →.
This coinage in honour of the emperor's father
commemorates his German victories in BC 12–9.

403 Sestertius Rome, AD 41–45

Obv. NERO CLAVDIVS DRVSVS GERMANICVS IMP.
Head, bare, l.
Rev. TI CLAVDIVS CAESAR AVG P M TR P IMP S C.
Claudius, bare-headed, togate, seated l., on
curule chair holding branch in r. hand;
around chair, scattered arms. Æ, 29.36 gm. ↑.
Claudius is shown on the reverse as sharing in the
reflected glory of his father's military success.

404 Aureus Rome, AD 41–45

Obv. ANTONIA AVGVSTA. Bust, draped, r., and
wearing wreath of corn-ears.
Rev. CONSTANTIAE AVGVSTI. Constantia standing
facing, holding long torch and cornucopiae.
N, 7.40 gm. ↓.
The emperor's mother, Antonia, posthumously
made an Augusta, was also honoured on his
coinage.

405 Dupondius Rome, AD 41–45

Obv. ANTONIA AVGVSTA. Bust, draped, head bare, r.
Rev. TI CLAVDIVS CAESAR AVG P M TR P IMP S C.
Claudius, togate, veiled, standing l. holding
simpulum in r. hand. Æ, 16.12 gm. ↓.
The priestly attributes of Claudius here presumably
reflect the fact that Antonia had been priestess of the
cult of the deified Augustus.

406 As Rome, AD 42

Obv. GERMANICVS CAESAR TI AVG F DIVI AVG N.
Head, bare, r.
Rev. TI CLAVDIVS CAESAR AVG GERM P M TR P IMP
P P S C. Æ, 11.34 gm. ↓.
The series honouring members of the imperial
family included the emperor's brother,
Germanicus.

407 Sestertius Rome, AD 42

Obv. AGRIPPINA M F GERMANICI CAESARIS. Bust,
draped, head bare, r.
Rev. As No. 406. Æ, 30.67 gm. ↓.
Coinage honours extended to include even the
emperor's late sister-in-law.

408 Aureus Rome, AD 50–54

Obv. TI CLAVD CAESAR AVG GERM P M TRIB POT P P.
Head, laureate, r.
Rev. AGRIPPINAE AVGVSTAE. Bust of Agrippina II,
draped, r. wearing wreath of corn-ears.
N, 7.70 gm. ✓.
Agrippina, given the title of Augusta in AD 50, was
the first Roman empress to appear on coins in her
lifetime.

409 Cistophoric tetradrachm Ephesus, AD 50

Obv. TI CLAVD CAES AGRIPP AVGVSTA. Heads of
Claudius, laureate and Agrippina, bare,
jugate, l.
Rev. DIANA EPHESIA. Cult statue of Diana Ephesia
facing. Æ, 10.81 gm. ↓.
Agrippina has the unusual honour of sharing the
obverse with the emperor.

410 Aureus Rome, AD 51–54

Obv. NERONI CLAVDIO DRVSO GERM COS DESIGN.
Bust, draped, head bare, r.
Rev. EQVESTER ORDO PRINCIPI IVVENT in four lines
on shield behind which is a vertical spear.
N, 7.65 gm. ↘.
Nero, adopted by Claudius in AD 50, was given the
title, *princeps iuventutis* in AD 51.

Nero, AD 54–68

411 Denarius Rome, AD 54

Obv. DIVVS CLAVDIVS AVGVSTVS. Head, laureate, l.
Rev. EX S C. Ornamented quadriga, r; on top of
car, four small horses, flanked by Victories.
Æ, 3.65 gm. ↓.
Claudius was consecrated immediately after his
death, but his cult had little permanence.

412 Aureus Rome, AD 54

Obv. AGRIPP AVG DIVI CLAVD NERONIS CAES MATER.
Busts of Nero, bare-headed, r, and of
Agrippina, draped, l, facing one another.
Rev. NERONI CLAVD DIVI F CAES AVG GERM IMP TR P.
EX S C in oak-wreath. N, 7.60 gm. ↑.
Agrippina's dominant influence is shown by the fact
that her portrait shares the obverse with the
emperor and her title alone appears on the obverse.
The formula EX S C on this and subsequent early
issues is evidence for the extension of senatorial
prerogative to the precious metal coinage.

413 Aureus Rome, AD 55

Obv. NERO CLAVD DIVI F CAES AVG GERM IMP TR P
COS. Busts, jugate, r. of Nero, bare-headed,
and Agrippina draped.
Rev. EX S C AGRIPP AVG DIVI CLAVD NERONIS CAES
MATER. Chariot drawn l. by four elephants;
Divus Claudius, radiate, and holding eagle-
tipped sceptre, and Divus Augustus, radiate
and holding patera and sceptre, seated left on
two chairs on chariot. N, 7.61 gm. ↑.

The less prominent position given to Agrippina's portrait, and the relegation of her title to the reverse indicates the beginning of the erosion of her influence.

414 Denarius Rome, AD 56–57

Obv. NERO CAESAR AVG IMP. Head, bare, r.
Rev. PONTIF MAX TR P III P P. EX S C in oak-wreath. Æ, 3.55 gm. ↖.
With the issue of this year Agrippina disappears from the coinage.

415 Didrachm Caesarea in Cappadocia, *c.*AD 59

Obv. NERO CLAVD DIVI CLAVD F CAESAR AVG GERMANI. Head, laureate, r.
Rev. ARMENIA. Victory, advancing r; holding wreath and palm. Æ, 7.39 gm. ↑.
The allusion is to the conquest of Armenia by Corbulo.

416 Aureus Rome, AD 60–61

Obv. As No. 413.
Rev. PONTIF MAX TR P VII COS IIII P P. In field, EX S C. Roma, helmeted, in military dress, r., inscribing shield held on l. knee, l. foot set on helmet; to r. of helmet, dagger and bow. Ν, 7.71 gm. ↓.

417 Aureus Rome, AD 64–65

Obv. NERO CAESAR AVGVSTVS. Head, laureate, r.
Rev. AVGVSTVS AVGVSTA. Nero, radiate, togate, standing l., holding patera and sceptre; beside him, empress, veiled, draped, standing l., holding patera and cornucopiae. Ν, 7.31 gm. ↓.
Nero's empress here is most probably Poppaea.

418 Aureus Rome, AD 64–65

Obv. As No. 417.
Rev. ROMA. Roma, helmeted, draped, seated r. on cuirass, r. foot set on helmet, holding Victory and parazonium; behind, round and oblong shields and greave. Ν, 7.39 gm. ↓.
The reference of this type is to the rebuilding of the city after the great fire in AD 64.

419 Aureus Rome, AD 64–65

Obv. As No. 417.
Rev. VESTA. On podium of four steps, round temple, with domed roof and six columns, containing figure of Vesta, seated front, head l., holding patera and sceptre. Ν, 7.35 gm. ↘.
This type suggests that the temple, destroyed in the great fire, was rebuilt by Nero.

420 **Aureus** Rome, AD 65

Obv. As No. 417.
Rev. IVPPITER CVSTOS. Jupiter, bare to waist, seated l. on throne, holding thunderbolt and sceptre. N, 7.25 gm. ↓.
The reverse celebrates Nero's deliverance from the conspiracy of Piso.

421 **Denarius** Rome, AD 65

Obv. As No. 417.
Rev. SALVS. Salus, draped, seated l. on throne, holding patera in r. hand. R, 3.31 gm. ↓.
A further commentary on the emperor's safe survival of the conspiracy. The personification of Salus appears here for the first time on imperial coins.

422 **Sestertius** Rome, AD 64–66

Obv. NERO CLAVD CAESAR AVG GER P M TR P IMP P P. Bust, laureate, r., with aegis.
Rev. AVGVSTI S·POR·OST·C. View of harbour of Ostia; to l. and r., crescent-shaped pier or breakwater; above, figure on column, holding sceptre in l. hand; below, Neptune reclining l., holding rudder and dolphin; in centre, seven ships. Æ, 29.84 gm. ↓.
The construction of the harbour, begun by Claudius, was completed under Nero.

423 **Sestertius** Rome, AD 64–66

Obv. As No. 422, but . . . CLAVDIVS GERM.
Rev. CON II DAT POP S C. Nero, bare-headed, togate, seated l. on platform on r.; behind him, *praefectus annonae* standing facing; in front, attendant, standing l. holding out tessera to citizen standing r., holding fold of toga to receive it; in centre, Minerva, standing l., holding owl and spear; behind, building with four pillars. Æ, 22.72 gm. ↓.
The reverse may be connected with measures taken to relieve distress caused by the great fire.

424 **Sestertius** Rome, AD 64–66

Obv. As No. 422, but bust l.
Rev. DECVRSIO S C. Nero, bare-headed, cuirassed, on horse prancing r., carrying spear in r. hand; behind, mounted soldier, with vexillum in r. hand. Æ, 28.20 gm. ↓.

425 **Sestertius** Rome, AD 64–66

Obv. As No. 422, but CLAVDIVS.
Rev. s c. Ornamented triumphal arch with wreath hung on front; above, emperor in facing quadriga between Victory on r., holding wreath and palm, and Pax on l., holding caduceus and cornucopiae; in niche on l., Mars, holding spear and shield. Æ, 27.20 gm. ↓.

This arch was decreed in honour of the victories in the East in AD 58.

426 Dupondius Rome, AD 64

Obv. As No. 422, but head, radiate, r.
Rev. VICTORIA AVGVSTI s c. Victory, draped, advancing l., holding wreath and palm; below, II. Æ, 15.25 gm. ↓.

The new coinage initially included a series of the smaller bronze denominations, all in orichalcum, and marked with signs of value.

427 As Rome, AD 64

Obv. As No. 422, but without aegis.
Rev. GENIO AVGVSTI s c. Genius, naked above waist, standing l., sacrificing out of patera in r. hand over altar, and holding cornucopiae in l.; below, I. Æ, 8.79 gm. ↓.

The *as* in orichalcum.

428 Semis Rome, AD 64

Obv. NERO CAES AVG IMP. Head, laureate, r.

Rev. CER QVIN Q ROM CO s c; in field l., s. Urn and wreath on table with decorated panel. Æ, 2.95 gm. ↓.

The mark of value, s, indicates the semis, also in orichalcum. The urn is for the votes of the judges and the wreath for the victor in the *certamen quinquennale Romae constitum*, the games founded by Nero in AD 60.

429 Quadrans Rome, AD 64–66

Obv. NERO CLAV CAE AVG. Owl on altar.
Rev. GER P M TR P IMP s c. Laurel-branch.
This, the smallest denomination in orichalcum, lacks a mark of value. Æ, 2.03 gm. ↓.

430 Dupondius Rome, AD 64–66

Obv. NERO CLAVD CAESAR AVG GER P M TR P IMP P P. Head, radiate, r.
Rev. MAC AVG s c. Building of two storeys, with two wings and domed roof; in front, five steps; in centre, male figure, standing l. holding sceptre in l. hand. Æ, 14.16 gm. ↙.

The building is the *Macellum Augusti*, the vegetable market constructed in AD 56–57.

431 As Rome, AD 64–66

Obv. NERO CLAVDIVS CAESAR AVG GERMA. Head, laureate, l.
Rev. PONTIF MAX TR P IMP P P. Apollo-Citharoedus, standing r., playing lyre. Æ, 11.99 gm. ↓.
Undoubtedly the artist-emperor is here represented in the guise of Apollo.

432   Semis Rome, AD 64–66

Obv.   As No. 431, but GERM.
Rev.   PON MAX TR P IMP P P. Roma, helmeted,
draped, seated l. on cuirass, r. foot on
helmet, holding wreath and parazonium.
Æ, 7.13 gm. ↓.
A heavyweight semis.

433   Quadrans Rome, AD 64–66

Obv.   NERO CLAVD CAE AVG GER. Helmet placed on
column against which leans a shield.
Rev.   P M TR P IMP P P S C. Laurel-branch.
Æ, 3.03 gm. ↑.

434   Sestertius Rome, AD 66–67

Obv.   IMP NERO CLAVD CAESAR AVG GERM P M TR P
XIII P P. Bust, laureate, r., with aegis.
Rev.   Roma, helmeted, draped, seated l. on
cuirass, r. foot on stool holding spear and
shield at side; below and to r, shield and
helmet. Æ, 27.55 gm. ↓.

435   Sestertius Lyons, AD 64–66

Obv.   IMP NERO CAESAR AVG PONT MAX TR POT P P.
Head, laureate, r; small globe at point of
bust.
Rev.   PACE P R TERRA MARIQ PARTA IANVM CLVSIT
S C. Temple of Janus. Æ, 27.05 gm. ↓.
Resumed bronze coinage at this mint is distin-
guished by the small globe on the obverse. Peace
everywhere throughout the Roman world was
marked by the closing of the temple of Janus.
Historical tradition places this in AD 66 when
Tiridates of Parthia came to Rome, but dated coins
attest it as early as AD 64.

436   Dupondius Lyons, AD 64–66

Obv.   IMP NERO CAESAR AVG P MAX TR P P P. Head,
laureate, r.; small globe at point of bust.
Rev.   SECVRITAS AVGVSTI S C. Securitas, bare to the
waist, seated r. on throne, holding sceptre in
l. hand and resting head on r.; to r., altar
and torch resting on bucranium.
Æ, 14.03 gm. ↓.

437 As Lyons, AD 64–66

Obv. NERO CLAVD CAESAR AVG GER P M TR P IMP P
  P. Head, bare, r; small globe at point of bust.
Rev. ARA PACIS S C. Decorated front wall of altar
  enclosure. Æ, 10.78 gm. ↓.
The absence of the type at the Rome mint suggests
that this was an altar set up at Lugdunum in honour
of the Parthian victory.

438 As Lyons, AD 64–66

Obv. IMP NERO CAESAR AVG P MAX TR P P P. Head,
  bare, r; small globe at point of bust.
Rev. S C. Victory, draped, advancing l., holding
  in both hands shield inscribed S P Q R.
  Æ, 9.95 gm. ↓.

2 The Civil War AD68-69

A series of revolts in the provinces of Gaul, Spain, and Africa in the spring of AD 68 ended in the collapse of Nero's authority, and his suicide on 9 June, 68. The revolt of Vindex in Gaul in March encouraged that of Galba in Spain, and coinage was struck to meet the rebels' needs, mostly of silver denarii with the addition of a few rare issues of aurei, but with no complementary bronze coinage. Initially the uncertainty as to who or what system was to succeed Nero is reflected in the coinage in the absence of the portrait or name of any individual, and in a choice of types which are largely borrowings from earlier coinages.

In North Africa Clodius Macer, legate of Numidia, was the first to strike out an independent line. He refused to support Galba, invaded the province of Africa, and captured Carthage where he struck a coinage of denarii. Though he placed his name and portrait on his coins, he made no claim to empire, and shortly after the recognition of Galba the revolt of Macer was suppressed. The revolt of Vindex in Gaul was quickly put down by the German legions, but in Spain, Galba, following his acclamation, produced a coinage, probably at Taracco, using simply his title of imperator but without portrait. Following on the Senate's recognition of Galba as emperor on 9 June the mint at Rome began to strike coinage in his name in all three metals. In the West, probably at the mint of Lyons, re-opened in the last years of Nero's reign, a parallel series, also in all three metals, was issued for Galba.

In early January AD 69, however, Galba was murdered in a revolt by the Praetorian guard which proclaimed Otho as emperor. For Otho the Rome mint struck gold and silver coinage, but no bronze had been issued when in April Otho in turn was ousted by a new claimant, Vitellius, who had been proclaimed by his legions in Germany in January. Coinage for the new emperor was struck in Gaul, some of it recognisable as the work of the mint of Lyons, and after the defeat of Otho the mint at Rome initiated a coinage for Vitellius as well. In July 69, however, the legions in the eastern provinces declared for Vespasian, and by the end of the year Vespasian's forces had invaded Italy and taken Rome. The succession was finally settled and the new Flavian dynasty established.

Revolt Coinage, AD68

439   Aureus Gaul, AD 68

Obv. Bust of Minerva, helmeted, r., in cuirass with aegis ornament.
Rev. SECVRITAS P R. Securitas, draped, seated r. on throne, holding sceptre in l. hand and resting head on r.; to r., altar. *N*, 7.13 gm. ↓.

440   Denarius Gaul, AD 68

Obv. [SALVS GENE] RIS HUMANI. Victory, standing r. on globe, holding wreath and palm.
Rev. S P Q R in oak-wreath. *R*, 3.58 gm. ←.

441   Denarius Spain, AD 68

Obv. LIBERTAS P R Bust of Libertas, head bare, draped, r.
Rev. RESTITVTA. Pileus flanked by two daggers. *R*, 3.40 gm. ↓.
The reverse is copied from a coin of Brutus, cf. Vol. I No. 274.

442 Denarius Spain, AD 68

Obv. Head of Augustus, bare, r.
Rev. AVGVSTVS. Capricorn r., holding, between paws, globe and rudder; above, cornu-copiae. Æ, 3.69 gm. ↖.
The types are borrowed from the Augustan coinage, cf. No. 325 above.

443 Denarius Spain, AD 68

Obv. CONCORDIA HISPANIARVM ET GALLIARVM. Busts, bare-headed, of Hispania r. and Gallia l.; between them, Victory on globe; above, star in crescent; below, cornucopiae and shield.
Rev. VICTORIA P R. Victory in biga r. Æ, 3.15 gm. ↓.

444 Denarius Rhineland, AD 68

Obv. FIDES EXERCITVVM. Clasped hands.
Rev. FIDES PRAETORIAORVM. Clasped hands. Æ, 3.44 gm. ↓.
This is one of a series probably associated with the early stages of the revolt of the legions in Germany before the proclamation of Vitellius.

Clodius Macer, AD68

445 Denarius Carthage, AD 68

Obv. L CLODIVS MACER S C. Head of Macer, bare, r.
Rev. PRO PRAE AFRICAE. Galley r. Æ, 3.81 gm. ↖.
The formula S(*enatus*) C(*onsulto*) suggests that Macer in theory at any rate regarded himself as acting constitutionally on behalf of the Senate.

446 Denarius Carthage, AD 68

Obv. L CLODI MACRI CARTHAGO S C. Bust of Carthage, turreted, draped, r.; behind her, cornucopiae.
Rev. SICILIA. Triskelis with Medusa head at centre; in angles, corn-ears. Æ, 2.47 gm. ↑.
The types confirm Macer's occupation of Carthage and his threat to seize Sicily.

Galba, AD68-69

447 Denarius Africa, AD 68

Obv. SER GALBA IMP AVG. Bust of Galba, laureate, r.; small globe below bust.
Rev. VICTORIA P R S C. Victory standing front on globe, head l., holding wreath and palm. Æ, 3.76 gm. ↓.
The style, fabric and the presence of S C reminiscent of coins of Clodius Macer suggest that this is part of the coinage of Galba's supporters in North Africa who suppressed Macer in the autumn of AD 68.

448   Denarius Lyons, AD 68

Obv. SER GALBA IMP AVG. Galba on horseback r.,
brandishing javelin.
Rev. TRES GALLIAE. Three female busts r.; small
globe at point of busts. Æ, 2.97 gm. ↓.
An explicit recognition of Gaul's support of Galba.
The absence of portrait suggests an issue early in the
revolt, but the use of the title Augustus before the
Senate's recognition on 9 June is anomalous.

449   Denarius Lyons, AD 68

Obv. GALBA IMP. Head of Galba, laureate, r.; small
globe under bust.
Rev. GALLIA HISPANIA. Gallia standing r., holding
boar-tipped sceptre, clasping hands with
Hispania, standing l., holding shield,
parazonium, and spear. Æ, 3.38 gm. ↓.
Personifications of the two provinces which
supported Galba's revolt.

450   Aureus Lyons, AD 68

Obv. GALBA IMPERATOR. Head of Galba, laureate,
r.; small globe under bust.
Rev. ROMA RENASC. Roma, helmeted, in military
dress, advancing r., holding Victory on
globe and spear. N, 7.70 gm. ↓.
Until his recognition by the Senate on 9 June the
only title used by Galba was *imperator*.

451   Sestertius Lyons, AD 68

Obv. SER GALBA IMP CAES AVG TR P. Bust of Galba,
laureate, r; marked point to bust.
Rev. ROMA RXL S C. Roma, helmeted, in military
dress, standing l., holding Victory and eagle-
tipped sceptre, resting l. arm on trophy and l.
foot on helmet; to l. shield. Æ, 25.83 gm. ↓.
The addition of Caesar to Galba's titles probably
dates from his meeting with the senatorial
commission in July. The formula RXL (*remissa
quadragessima*) refers to Galba's remission of the
import and export duty of 2½ per cent.

452   As Lyons, AD 68

Obv. As No. 451.
Rev. S C. Aquila between two standards, each set
on prow, and ornamented with wreath.
Æ, 11.15 gm. ↓.

453   Aureus Lyons, AD 68

Obv. SER GALBA IMP CAESAR AVG P M TR P. Head of
Galba, laureate, r.; globe under bust.
Rev. ROMA VICTRIX. Roma, helmeted, in military
dress, standing l., r. foot on globe, holding
branch and spear. N, 7.63 gm. ↓.
The title of Pontifex Maximus was assumed some
time after the emperor's arrival in Rome.

454 Sestertius Lyons, AD 68

Obv. SER SVLPI GALBA IMP CAESAR AVG P M TR P.
Bust of Galba, laureate, draped, l.
Rev. HONOS ET VIRTVS S C. Honos, bare to waist,
standing r., holding cornucopiae and
sceptre, facing Virtus, helmeted, in military
dress, standing l., r. foot on boar's head,
holding parazonium and spear.
Æ, 29.71 gm. ↓.

This reverse, complimentary to the military forces,
was used later by both Vitellius and Vespasian.

455 Aureus Rome, AD 68

Obv. IMP SER GALBA AVG. Head of Galba, bare, r.
Rev. S P Q R OB C S in two lines in oak-wreath.
Ν, 7.32 gm. ↙.

The *corona civica* reverse is an appropriate type for
the first coinage at Rome after the Senate's
recognition of Galba.

456 Sestertius Rome, AD 68

Obv. IMP SER GALBA AVG TR P. Bust of Galba,
laureate, draped, r.
Rev. Roma, helmeted, draped, seated l. on
cuirass, r. foot on helmet, holding spear and
resting l. hand on shield; below, helmet.
Æ, 26.76 gm. ↓.

457 Aureus Rome, AD 68

Obv. IMP SER GALBA CAESAR AVG. Head of Galba,
laureate, r.
Rev. DIVA AVGVSTA. Livia, draped, standing l.,
holding patera and sceptre. Ν, 6.32 gm. ↓.

The empress Livia had been Galba's patron in his
earlier career.

458 Denarius Rome, AD 68

Obv. As No. 457.
Rev. HISPANIA. Hispania, draped, advancing l.,
holding in r. hand poppy and two corn-ears,
and in l., shield and two spears.
Æ, 3.09 gm. ↓.

The reverse honours the first province to support
Galba.

459 Denarius Rome, AD 68

Obv. As No. 457.
Rev. SALVS GEN HVMANI. Female figure, draped,
standing l., r. foot on globe, sacrificing out
of patera in r. hand, and holding rudder in l.
Æ, 3.40 gm. ↓.

A type featured on the early revolt coinage in the
West is now adopted by the Rome mint.

460   Sestertius Rome, AD 68

Obv. IMP SER GALBA CAE AVG TR P. Head of Galba,
laureate, l.
Rev. CONCORD AVG S C. Concordia, draped, seated
l., holding branch and sceptre.
Æ, 23.57 gm. ↓.

461   As Rome, AD 68

Obv. IMP SER SVLP GALBA CAES AVG TR P. Head of
Galba, laureate, r.
Rev. LIBERTAS PVBLICA S C. Libertas, draped,
standing l., holding pileus and cornucopiae.
Æ, 11.10 gm. ↓.

462   Aureus Rome, AD 68

Obv. IMP SER GALBA CAESAR AVG P M. Head of
Galba, laureate, r.
Rev. IMP. Galba, bare-headed, on horse galloping
r. N, 7.00 gm. ↓.
Though the horseman reverse recalls types used in
the early revolt coinage, the inclusion of the title
Pontifex Maximus places the coin in the later part of
AD 68.

Otho, AD69

463   Aureus Rome, AD 69

Obv. IMP M OTHO CAESAR AVG TR P. Head of Otho,
bare, r.
Rev. PAX ORBIS TERRARVM. Pax standing l., holding
branch and caduceus. N, 7.30 gm. ↓.

464   Denarius Rome, AD 69

Obv. As No. 463.
Rev. VICTORIA OTHONIS. Victory advancing l.,
holding wreath and palm. Æ, 3.41 gm. ↓.

Vitellius, AD69

465   Aureus Cologne?, AD 69

Obv. A VITELLIVS IMP GERMAN. Head of Vitellius,
laureate, r.; small globe below neck.
Rev. FIDES EXERCITVM. Clasped hands.
N, 5.91 gm. ↓.
This is one of an early group of coins repeating the
themes of the revolt coinage (cf. No. 444) perhaps
struck at Cologne.

466 Aureus Lyons, AD 69

Obv. A VITELLIVS IMP GERMANICVS. Head of
Vitellius, laureate, l.; small globe below
neck.
Rev. CLEMENTIA IMP GERMAN. Clementia seated l.,
holding branch and sceptre. N, 7.40 gm. ↓.
This coin represents the main group of Vitellius'
coinage from a western mint which, from its
stylistic characteristics, is most probably to be
identified as Lyons (Lugdunum).

467 Denarius Lyons, AD 69

Obv. A VITELLIVS IMP GERMAN. Head of Vitellius,
laureate, l.; small globe below neck; to l.
palm-branch.
Rev. VICTORIA AVGVSTI. Victory advancing l.,
holding in r. hand shield inscribed S P Q R.
Æ, 3.69 gm. ↓.
The reverse repeats the type on an *as* of Nero (No.
438) from this mint.

468 As Lyons, AD 69

Obv. A VITELLIVS IMP GERMAN. Head of Vitellius,
laureate, l.; globe below neck.
Rev. CONSENSVS EXERCITVVM S C. Mars, helmeted,
naked except for cloak floating behind him,
holding spear and aquila with vexillum.
Æ, 10.21 gm. ↓.
In bronze only a series of *asses* was struck at this
mint.

469 Denarius Rome, AD 69

Obv. A VITELLIVS GERMANICVS IMP. Head of
Vitellius, bare, r.
Rev. XV VIR SACR FAC. Dolphin on tripod;
underneath, raven. Æ, 3.12 gm. ↓.
Vitellius before his elevation had been a member of
the college of *quindecimviri sacris faciundis* to which
the reverse alludes. In this first issue at Rome
Vitellius is not styled Augustus.

470 Aureus Rome, AD 69

Obv. A VITELLIVS GERMAN IMP TR P. Head of
Vitellius, laureate, r.
Rev. L VITELLIVS COS III CENSOR. Bust of
L. Vitellius, laureate, draped, r. in front
eagle-tipped sceptre. Æ, 7.09 gm. ↓.
The acclamation of Vitellius was undoubtedly due
in part to the reputation gained by his father as both
general and administrator.

471 Aureus Rome, AD 69

Obv. A VITELLIVS GERM IMP AVG TR P. Head of
Vitellius, laureate, r.
Rev. LIBERI IMP GERM AVG. Busts of the emperor's
two children vis-à-vis, the son facing r., the
daughter facing l. N, 7.32 gm. ↓.
The inclusion of the title Augustus probably dates
from the emperor's arrival at Rome in July.

Obv. A VITELLIVS GERMAN IMP AVG P M TR P. Bust of Vitellius, laureate, draped, r.

Rev. MARS VICTOR S C. Mars helmeted, in military dress, advancing l., holding Victory in r. hand, and trophy over l. shoulder; at side, parazonium. Æ, 25.50 gm. ↓.

Bronze coinage at Rome appears only in the last issue marked by the inclusion of the title pontifex maximus. The reverse is an obvious reference to the defeat of Otho near Cremona in April.

3 The Flavians AD69-96

The proclamation of Vespasian by the legions in Egypt, Syria and Palestine was soon followed by a declaration of support by the legions in Illyricum, and the stages by which the provinces went over to the new emperor are reflected in the coinage issued by provincial mints. From late summer AD 69 precious metal coinage was produced by several eastern mints and was continued in some cases up to AD 76. Not all these mints can be identified with certainty. From a range of differentiating marks only EPF for Ephesus and ⊕K for Byzantium are readily identifiable. For the legions in Illyricum a short-lived precious metal coinage was struck most probably at Poetovio, and when Vespasian's forces had secured north Italy the mint at Lyons in Gaul began issues for him also. Lyons coined in all three metals up to 73, but only bronze was issued for the remainder of the reign of Vespasian, for Titus' brief reign, and for Domitian up to 82. As Rome was not wrested from Vitellius until late December, coinage there began only in 70, but for the rest of the Flavian period Rome remained the principal mint.

The coinage system established by Augustus and reformed by Nero continued in this period, with only a few modifications in the coinage of Domitian. From AD 82 the aureus was struck slightly heavier at about 7.60 gm., and the denarius also at about 3.32 gm. A single gold multiple, a 5-aureus piece, is recorded for Domitian, and a few silver medallions, multiples by weight of 8, 5, or 4 denarii. The smaller bronze denominations, the semis and the quadrans, issued only infrequently under Vespasian and Titus, were produced more commonly, especially the quadrans, under Domitian.

The Flavian coinage has a much greater dynastic character than has the Julio-Claudian. Under Vespasian, alongside coinage in his own name, there were consistent issues in the name of both Titus and Domitian; and again, under Titus there was a considerable coinage for Domitian also. In addition there were smaller issues for less important members of the family. An unusually large proportion of the Flavian coinage, especially that of Domitian, is readily datable by the inclusion in the inscriptions of the imperial consulship and tribunician power, and of the successive imperatorial acclamations.

In this period appeared the first series of 'restored' coins. Presumably to emphasise the continuity between the new dynasty and its predecessor a series of bronze coins of selected imperial personages was issued by Titus, reproducing portraits and types together with an inscription *Titus rest(ituit)*. The series was continued by Domitian early in his reign, but only briefly.

Vespasian, AD69–79

473 Denarius Rome, AD 69–70

Obv. IMP CAESAR VESPASIANVS AVG. Head, laureate, r.
Rev. CAESAR AVG F COS CAESAR AVG F PR. Bare heads of Titus r. and Domitian l., confronted. Æ, 3.25 gm. ↓.
The use of this reverse in the first coinage makes clear from the outset Vespasian's intention of establishing a new imperial dynasty.

474 Denarius Rome, AD 69

Obv. Bust of Sol, radiate, draped, to front.
Rev. VESPASIANVS across field on either side of figure of Vespasian in military dress, standing l., raising r. hand, and holding transverse spear. Æ, 3.41 gm. ↓.
This unusual coin according Vespasian no specific title must be a very early issue at Rome, but the significance of the Sol portrait is not immediately obvious.

475 Aureus Rome, AD 69–70

Obv. IMP CAESAR VESPASIANVS AVG. Head, laureate, r.

Rev. IVDAEA. Judaea seated r. in mourning attitude; behind, trophy. N, 7.28 gm. ↓.

Vespasian's successful bid for empire stemmed from his success against the Jewish insurgents.

476 Sestertius Rome, AD 71

Obv. IMP CAES VESPASIAN AVG P M TR P P P COS III. Head, laureate, r.

Rev. IVDAEA CAPTA S C. Jewess seated r. on cuirass in mourning attitude to r. of palm-tree, with, to r., two shields; to l., Jew, with hands bound behind back, standing r.; to l., shield. Æ, 26.90 gm. ↓.

Vespasian's suppression of the Jewish revolt, successfully completed by Titus, is widely celebrated in the coinage of this year.

477 Sestertius Rome, AD 71

Obv. As No. 476.

Rev. IVDAEA CAPTA S C. Type as No. 476, but to l. of palm-tree, Titus standing r., in military dress, foot on helmet, and holding spear and parazonium. Æ, 25.62 gm. ↓.

The role of Titus in the Jewish campaign receives emphasis here.

478 Dupondius Rome, AD 71

Obv. IMP CAES VESPASIAN AVG COS III. Head, radiate, r.

Rev. PAX AVGVSTI S C. Pax standing l., with torch in r. hand, setting fire to arms, and holding cornucopiae in l. Æ, 13.05 gm. ↓.

The reverse symbolises the end of the turmoils of the Civil War as much as the conclusion of the Jewish campaign. It is from this point that the radiate crown on the obverse becomes the standard indication of the dupondius.

479 Aureus Rome, AD 72–73

Obv. IMP CAES VESP AVG P M TR P COS IIII. Head, laureate, r.

Rev. IMP. Vespasian standing in quadriga r. N, 7.49 gm. ↓.

Though Vespasian and Titus celebrated a triumph for the Jewish campaign in June 71, the occasion continued to be celebrated in the coinage of this year; cf. also No. 480.

480 Sestertius Rome, AD 72

Obv. T CAESAR VESPASIAN IMP III PON TR POT II COS II. Bust, laureate, r. in cuirass with aegis.

Rev. S C. Titus, laureate, holding sceptre tipped with human head, and branch, standing in quadriga r.; on side of quadriga, figure of Titus placing hand on captive, and palm. Æ, 25.56 gm. ↓. See No. 479.

481 Aureus Rome, AD 73

Obv. IMP CAES VESP AVG CEN. Head, laureate, r.
Rev. VESTA. Round temple showing four
columns on podium of four steps; within
temple, statue of Vesta standing l.; to l. and
r. of temple, statue on a base. A, 7.26 gm. ↑.
The temple may have required restoration after the
fire of December 69.

482 Denarius Rome, AD 73

Obv. CAES AVG F DOMIT COS II. Head, laureate, r.
Rev. Domitian on horse prancing l., extending r.
hand and holding vertical sceptre tipped
with human head. Æ, 3.42 gm. ↑.

483 Sestertius Rome, AD 76

Obv. CAESAR AVG F DOMITIANVS COS IIII. Head,
laureate, r.
Rev. S C. Spes advancing l., holding flower and
raising skirt. Æ, 26.98 gm. ↓.
The Spes type, first introduced by Claudius (cf. No.
394), is commonly associated with an imperial heir.

484 Aureus Rome, AD 77–78

Obv. T CAESAR IMP VESPASIANVS. Head, laureate, r.
Rev. COS VI. Roma, helmeted, in military dress,
seated r. on two shields, r. foot on helmet,
holding spear; to r. and l., eagle flying; to r.,
miniature wolf and twins. A, 7.35 gm. ↙.
The reverse is a close copy of a Republican denarius
of about 100 BC. cf. *BMCRR It.* 562.

485 Aureus Rome, AD 77–78

Obv. CAESAR AVG F DOMITIANVS. Head, laureate, r.
Rev. COS V. Parthian, wearing breeches and cloak,
kneeling r., holding standard with vexillum
attached. A, 7.34 gm. ↓.
The reverse is probably an allusion to a Parthian
request for Roman military aid against the Alani.

486 Aureus Rome, AD 79

Obv. IMP CAESAR VESPASIANVS AVG. Head,
laureate, r.
Rev. TR POT X COS VIIII. Victory l., placing shield
on trophy of arms below which is captive
seated l. A, 7.22 gm. ↓.
A victory of Agricola in Britain is probably the
event celebrated by this reverse.

487 Aureus quinarius Rome, *c.*AD 79

Obv. As No. 486.
Rev. VICTORIA AVGVST. Victory seated l., holding
wreath and palm. A, 3.70 gm. ↓.
Though undated, this coin may belong to the same
issue as No. 486.

488   Aureus Lyons, *c.*AD 69

Obv. IMP CAESAR AVG VESPASIANVS. Head,
    laureate, r.
Rev. MARS VLTOR. Mars, helmeted, naked but for
    cloak, advancing l., carrying spear and
    trophy. *N*, 7.19 gm. ↓.
In this early coinage the western mint had no
reliable portrait of the new emperor. The tall, thin
figure on the reverse is typical of earlier coinage at
this mint.

489   Denarius Lyons, AD 70

Obv. IMP CAESAR VESPASIANVS AVG. Head,
    laureate, l.
Rev. VICTOPIA IMR VESPASIANI. Victory standing r.
    on globe, holding wreath and palm. *R*,
    3.34 gm. ↑.
A very similar Victory representation was used on
coinage of both Otho and Vitellius. Despite the
unusual transposition of the letters R and P in the
reverse inscription the coin appears to be a regular
issue.

490   Aureus Lyons, AD 71

Obv. IMP CAESAR VESPASIANVS AVG TR P. Head,
    laureate, r.
Rev. TRIVMP AVG. Vespasian, holding branch and
    eagle-tipped sceptre, standing in quadriga r.,
    and being crowned by Victory; to r. a
    soldier escorting a bound captive; in
    background, a trumpeter. *N*, 7.30 gm. ↓.
The triumph of Vespasian and Titus, celebrated in
Rome, is depicted in more than usual detail here.

491   Sestertius Lyons, AD 71

Obv. IMP CAES VESPASIAN AVG P M TR P P P COS III.
    Head, laureate, r.
Rev. CAES AVG F DESIG IMP AVG F COS DESIG ITER
    S C. Domitian standing r., holding spear, and
    Titus standing l., holding spear and parazon-
    ium. Æ, 25.67 gm. ↓.
A dynastic type with representations of all three
members of the Flavian family.

492   Sestertius Lyons, AD 72

Obv. T CAES VESPAS IMP PON TR POT COS II. Head,
    laureate, r.
Rev. S C. Mars, helmeted, naked but for a cloak,
    advancing r., holding spear and trophy.
    Æ, 26.01 gm. ↓.
The reverse is a close copy of the type used on
sestertii of Vitellius.

493   Denarius Poetovio, AD 69

Obv. IMP CAESAR VESPASIANVS AVG. Head,
    laureate, r.
Rev. CONSENSVS EXERCIT. Two soldiers clasping
    r. hands, and holding legionary eagles.
    R, 3.54 gm. ↓.
Representative of the coinage struck for the legions
of Illyricum which declared for Vespasian and
seized Italy from Vitellius.

494   Denarius East, AD 69

Obv. IMP CAES VESPAS AVG. Head, laureate, r.
Rev. AVG in oak-wreath. Æ, 3.01 gm. ↑.
The earliest coinage for Vespasian was struck in the East after his proclamation there by the legions. The first issues carry no mint indication.

495   Denarius East, AD 69

Obv. IMP CAESAR VESPASIANVS AVG. Head, laureate, r.
Rev. LIBERI IMP AVG VESPAS. Heads of Titus and Domitian, bare, r. and l., confronted; below, σ. Æ, 2.62 gm. ↙.
As at Rome, the earliest opportunity is taken to represent the members of the new dynasty. The mint-mark is probably the more common ⊕ (see No. 496) of which part has been removed by tooling.

496   Denarius East, AD 70

Obv. IMP CAESAR VESPAS AVG COS II TR P P P. Head, laureate, r.
Rev. LIBERI IMP AVG VESPAS. Titus and Domitian, togate and veiled standing front, head l., each holding patera in r. hand; in ex. ⊕. Æ, 3.49 gm. ↓.

497   Denarius Byzantium, AD 71

Obv. As No. 497, but COS III.
Rev. PACI ORB TERR AVG. Female bust, draped, and wearing turreted crown; below, ⊟K. Æ, 2.52 gm. ↓.
The fact that this was the assembly place of Vespasian's naval forces adds weight to the interpretation of the mint monogram as Byzantium.

498   Aureus Ephesus, AD 71

Obv. IMPERATOR T CAESAR AVGVTI F. Head, laureate, r.
Rev. CONCORDIA AVG. Ceres, draped, veiled, seated l., holding corn-ears and poppy in r. hand and cornucopiae in l.; in ex. EPE. Ν, 7.34 gm. ↑.

499   Denarius Ephesus, AD 71

Obv. DOMITIANVS CAESAR AVG F. Bust, draped, cuirassed, with aegis, head bare, r.
Rev. PACI ORB TERR AVG. Female bust, draped and wearing turreted crown, r.; below EPE. Æ, 2.69 gm. ↓.

Titus, AD 79–81

500 **Aureus** Rome, AD 80

Obv. DIVVS AVGVSTVS VESPASIANVS. Head, laureate, r.
Rev. EX S C. Quadriga, in form of temple, l.; on front, standing figure; on side, two standing figures; on roof, small quadriga with Victory to l. and r. ЛV, 7.21 gm. ↓.
An unusually extensive coinage honoured the deified Vespasian.

501 **Denarius** Rome, AD 80

Obv. DIVA DOMITILLA AVGVSTA. Bust, draped, r.
Rev. FORTVNA AVGVST. Fortuna standing l., holding rudder and cornucopiae. Ꜫ, 3.20 gm. ↓.
The coinage commemorates the deification of Domitilla, wife of Vespasian and mother of Titus.

502 **Aureus** Rome, AD 80

Obv. IMP TITVS CAES VESPASIAN AVG P M. Head, laureate, l.
Rev. TR P IX IMP XV COS VIII P P. Pulvinar, of Jupiter and Juno in form of square seat surmounted by winged thunderbolt. ЛV, 7. 19 gm. ↓.
With the service of propitiation after the disastrous eruption of Vesuvius is associated a series showing the *pulvinaria* or sacred couches of the gods.

503 **Sestertius** Rome, AD 80–81

Obv. IMP T CAES VESP AVG P M TR P P P COS VIII. Head, laureate, l.
Rev. IVD CAP S C. Jewess, seated r. in mourning pose by palm-tree; to r. two shields; to l., Jew with bound hands standing l.; to l., two shields and a helmet. Ꜫ, 25.31 gm. ↓.
The reverse recalls the part played by Titus in the suppression of the Jewish revolt.

504 **Sestertius** Rome, AD 81

Obv. IMP T CAES VESP AVG P M TR P P P COS VIII S C. Titus, togate, seated l. on curule chair, holding branch and roll; to l., shield and helmet; beside chair, cuirass and helmet; to r., two shields and two spears.
Rev. Bird's eye view of the Colosseum: to l., obelisk on base; to r., porticoed building. Ꜫ, 23.36 gm. ↓.
The completion of the amphitheatre in this year is here recorded.

505 **Denarius** Rome, AD 80

Obv. CAESAR DIVI F DOMITIANVS COS VII. Head, laureate, r.
Rev. PRINCEPS IVVENTVTIS. Minerva, helmeted, draped, advancing r., brandishing javelin and holding shield. Ꜫ, 3.21 gm. ↓.

The reverse, according Domitian the title of heir, presents Minerva, the type which was to dominate his own coinage later.

506   Dupondius Rome, AD 80–81

Obv. IVLIA IMP T AVG F AVGVSTA. Bust, draped, r.
Rev. CERES AVGVST S C. Ceres standing l., holding corn-ears and sceptre. Æ, 13.19 gm. ↓.
The practice of honouring members of the imperial family, begun under the Julio-Claudians, was continued by the Flavians as in the coinage for Julia, daughter of Titus.

507   As Rome, AD 80

Obv. DIVVS AVGVSTVS PATER. Head, radiate, l.
Rev. IMP T VESP AVG REST S C. Eagle with spread wings, standing front on thunderbolt, head l. Æ, 11.74 gm. ↓.
The series of 'restored' coins emphasised the continuity between the Flavian dynasty and its predecessor.

508   Sestertius Rome, AD 80

Obv. TI CLAVDIVS CAESAR AVG F BRITANNICVS. Bust, draped, head bare, l.
Rev. S C. Mars, helmeted, advancing l., holding spear and shield. Æ, 24.39 gm. ↓.

Britannicus, the son of Claudius, was an intimate friend of Titus, and it has been suggested that the coinage in his name was issued by Titus in association with the 'restored' series.

509   Sestertius Lyons, AD 80–81

Obv. IMP T CAES VESP AVG P M TR P P P COS VIII. Head, laureate, r.
Rev. ANNONA AVGVST S C. Annona seated l., holding bunch of corn-ears on lap. Æ, 27.4 gm. ↓.
Only a series of bronze with its distinctive portrait was issued by the Gallic mint.

Domitian, AD 81-96

510   Aureus Rome, AD 83

Obv. IMP CAES DOMITIANVS AVG P M. Head, laureate, r.
Rev. TR POT II COS VIIII DES X P P. Minerva, helmeted, advancing r., poising javelin, and holding shield. N, 7.60 gm. ↓.
Domitian's devotion to the cult of Minerva is reflected in her appearance on successive coin issues. Here she is seen in her most familiar representation as 'Athene Promachos'.

511 **Aureus** Rome, AD 81–84

Obv. DOMITIA AVGVSTA IMP DOMIT. Bust, draped, r.
Rev. DIVVS CAESAR IMP DOMITIANI F. Naked baby boy seated on globe in surround of seven stars. N, 7.73 gm. ↓.

Coinage for the empress Domitia is linked with a reverse commemorating the imperial heir who died in infancy and was consecrated.

512 **Tetradrachm** Ephesus, AD 82

Obv. IMP CAES DOMITIAN AVG P M COS VIII. Head, laureate, r.
Rev. CAPIT RESTIT. Temple of four columns on podium of four steps; within, Jupiter flanked by Juno and Minerva. R, 10.13 gm. ↓.

The Capitol was restored in 82 after damage by fire.

513 **As** Rome, AD 84

Obv. IMP CAES DOMITIAN AVG GERM COS X. Bust, laureate, r., with aegis.
Rev. MONETA AVGVST S C. Moneta standing l., holding scales and cornucopiae.
$\mathit{Æ}$, 10.58 gm. ↓.

The personification of Moneta appears now for the first time in the imperial coinage. The suggestion that the occasion was some rebuilding of mint premises on the Capitol after the fire of AD 80 assumes that the *aes* coinage continued to be produced in the traditional mint premises associated with Juno Moneta on the Capitol, and not in the new premises for the precious metal coinage.

514 **Aureus** Rome, AD 85

Obv. IMP CAES DOMITIANVS AVG GERMANIC. Head, laureate, r.
Rev. P M TR POT IIII IMP VIII COS XI P P. Minerva, helmeted, standing l., holding vertical spear. N, 7.64 gm. ↓.

Another version of the continuing representations of Minerva.

515 **Silver medallion** Rome, AD 85

Obv. IMP CAES DOMIT AVG GERM P M TR POT V. Bust, laureate, r., with aegis
Rev. IMP VIIII COS XI CENS POT P P. Minerva, helmeted, with aegis on breast, seated l., holding Victory on globe and spear, and resting l. arm on shield supported by figure seated l. in boat; on shield, four figures before two shrines. R, 26.08 gm. ↓.

The large flan of the piece, by weight eight denarii, permits an elaborate representation of Minerva Victrix.

516 **Aureus** Rome, AD 88

Obv. IMP CAES DOMIT AVG GERM P M TR P VII. Head, laureate, r.
Rev. IMP XIIII COS XIIII CENS P P P. Germania seated r. on shield; below, broken spear. N, 7.35 gm. ↓.

Domitian's German triumphs were celebrated by this type from AD 85 onwards.

517 Semis Rome, AD 85

Obv. IMP DOMIT AVG GERM COS XI. Bust of Apollo, laureate, draped r.; in front, branch.
Rev. S C. Lyre. Æ, 4.67 gm. ↓.
An infrequently struck denomination at this period.

518 Quadrans Rome, AD 81–96

Obv. IMP DOMIT AVG GERM. Bust of Minerva, helmeted, draped, r.
Rev. S C. Olive-branch. Æ, 2.90 gm. ↓.
The quadrans, struck fairly commonly in this reign, usually carries no specific date of issue.

519 Aureus Rome, AD 88

Obv. DOMITIANVS AVGVSTVS GERMANICVS. Head, laureate, r.
Rev. COS XIIII LVD SAEC FEC. Herald advancing l., carrying wand and shield adorned with helmeted bust of Minerva. N, 7.55 gm. ↓.
This is part of the special issue commemorating the *Ludi saeculares* celebrated in this year.

520 Sestertius Rome, AD 88

Obv. IMP CAES DOMIT AVG GERM P M TR P VIII CENS PER P P. Head, laureate, r.
Rev. COS XIIII LVD SAEC A POP FRVG S C. Domitian, bare-headed, togate, seated r. on platform; in front, two citizens standing l., the one in front pouring *fruges* from sack; behind, temple of four columns. Æ, 25.60 gm. ↓.
The reverse shows one of the ceremonies connected with the *Ludi saeculares*, with Domitian receiving *fruges* – wheat, oats, and beans – from the people.

521 Dupondius Rome, AD 88

Obv. As No. 520, but radiate.
Rev. COS XIIII LVD SAEC FEC S C. Domitian, bare-headed, togate, standing l., sacrificing out of patera over altar; to l., victimarius bending over sheep and goat; behind altar, two flute-players; in the background, temple with six columns. Æ, 13.99 gm. ↓.
The sacrifice of a black sheep and a goat to the Moirae on the first night of the games is here pictured.

522 Sestertius Rome, AD 89

Obv. IMP CAES DOMIT AVG GERM COS XIIII CENS PER P P. Head, laureate, r., with aegis.
Rev. S C. Domitian standing l., holding thunderbolt and spear, crowned by Victory. Æ, 27.22 gm. ↓.
In this year Domitian celebrated a triumph at Rome for the defeat of the revolt of Saturninus, and for victories over the Dacians and Marcomanni.

523 **Silver medallion** Rome, AD 92

Obv. IMP CAES DOMIT AVG GERM P M TR P XI. Head, laureate, r.
Rev. IMP XXI COS XVI CENS P P P. Minerva, helmeted, flourishing javelin and holding spear, standing r. on prow; at feet, an owl. Æ, 17.51 gm. ↓.
This represents by weight a five denarius piece.

524 **Aureus** Rome

Obv. IVLIA AVGVSTA. Bust, draped, r.
Rev. DIVI TITI FILIA. Peacock standing front, with tail spread. ᴺ, 7.60 gm. ↓.
Coinage by Domitian for his niece, Julia, is undated but this issue appears to be quite late in the reign.

525 **Sestertius** Lyons, AD 81

Obv. IMP DOMITIAN CAES DIVI VESP F AVG P M TR P P P COS VIII. Head, laureate, r.
Rev. S C. Mars, helmeted, naked but for cloak, advancing l., holding spear and trophy. Æ, 25.48 gm. ↓.
This mint struck only bronze for Domitian, and only in the first two years of the reign. Mars is one of the reverse types consistently used at this mint from the Civil War on.

4 The Adoptive Emperors AD96–138

Civil war following the assassination of Domitian was avoided by the Senate's proclamation as emperor of the elderly Nerva who secured his position by adopting as his heir the army's most popular and able general, Trajan. This practice of adopting an heir, irrespective of any family claim was continued by Trajan and by Hadrian. In a series of campaigns of conquest Trajan added new provinces to the empire in Dacia, Armenia, and Mesopotamia but, despite the great military activity and consequent coin requirements, Rome continued to be the sole mint with the exception of a mint possibly in Cyprus producing a restricted series of *asses* and semisses in orichalcum. Similarly, though Hadrian's care for the provinces and his frequent journeys of inspection are amply illustrated in a number of coin series, only one series of denarii and rare gold appears to have been issued outside Rome, by a mint in the East, possibly at Antioch. The series of 'cistophoric' silver tetradrachms from a mint in Asia was continued by Nerva, Trajan, and more extensively by Hadrian.

The denominational system continued essentially unchanged with only minor modifications. The aureus which Domitian had issued from about AD 82 at the pre-Neronian reform weight of about 7.60 gm. was continued on this standard by Nerva but was abandoned in his first year by Trajan who reverted to striking the aureus at about 7.20 gm. In silver, rare multiples are on record, approximating to 5 and 7 denarii by weight for Trajan, and to 7, 8 and 12 denarii for Hadrian. The denarius, whose fineness had been raised to about 90% by Domitian, slipped by stages to a fineness of 80% and to a weight of 3.20 gm. by AD 107, when, according to Dio Cassius, Trajan took steps to recall precious metal coinage of pre-Neronian standard. The silver quinarius also continued to be issued but now as a somewhat rare denomination. In bronze the last semisses with imperial portrait and title or imperial title only were issued by Hadrian.

Two series of 'restored' coins were issued in this period; the first by Nerva, limited to the denominations of sestertius and *as* and to coins of Augustus, and the second by Trajan in gold and silver only. This latter series included a selection of Republican denarii and aurei of some of the previous emperors. The intention, it has been suggested, was to commemorate earlier coin types, particularly of the Republic, which disappeared in the coin withdrawal of AD 107.

Nerva, AD96–98

526 Aureus Rome, AD 96

Obv. IMP NERVA CAES AVG P M TR P COS II P P. Head, laureate, r.
Rev. CONCORDIA EXERCITVVM. Clasped hands holding legionary eagle set on prow.
N̸, 7.55 gm. ↓.
In the circumstances of Nerva's election the message of the reverse is more an appeal rather than a statement of fact.

527 Denarius Rome, AD 97

Obv. As No. 526, but COS III.
Rev. IVSTITIA AVGVST. Justitia, draped, seated r., feet on stool, holding sceptre and branch.
Æ, 3.56 gm. ↓.
The reverse type may refer to the emperor's earlier eminence as a lawyer.

528 Denarius Rome, AD 97

Obv. As No. 527.
Rev. LIBERTAS PVBLICA. Libertas, draped, standing l., holding pileus and sceptre. Æ, 3.37 gm. ↓.

The contrast with the tyranny of Domitian's final years is emphasised by the reverse.

529   Sestertius Rome, AD 97

Obv. As No. 527.
Rev. FISCI IVDAICI CALVMNIA SVBLATA S C. Palm-tree. Æ, 26.07 gm. ↓.

Vespasian had required the payment by Jews to Jupiter Capitolinus of the didrachm formerly paid to the temple at Jerusalem. Nerva put an end to the abuses which had attended the execution of this legislation.

530   Sestertius Rome, AD 97

Obv. As No. 527.
Rev. PLEBEI VRBANAE FRVMENTO CONSTITVTO S C. Modius containing poppy between corn-ears. Æ, 27.54 gm. ↓.

The reference is to measures taken by Nerva for the supply of corn to the populace of Rome.

531   Sestertius Rome, AD 97

Obv. As No. 527.

Rev. VEHICVLATIONE ITALIAE REMISSA S C. Two mules grazing, one r., one l.; behind, cart, with pole and harness, tipped up. Æ, 24.35 gm. ↓.

The cost of the imperial post which fell particularly heavily on Italy was now remitted.

532   Tetradrachm Pergamum, AD 97

Obv. IMP NERVA CAES AVG P M TR POT P P COS III. Head, laureate, r.
Rev. COM ASI l. and r. of temple showing two columns on podium of four steps; within, Nerva standing l., holding globe and spear, and crowned by female figure, standing l., holding cornucopiae; on entablature, ROMA ET AVG. Æ, 10 gm. ↙.

The earlier representation of the temple of Rome and Augustus at Pergamum (No. 345) is here modified to show the cult-statues within the temple.

533   Sestertius Rome, AD 96–97

Obv. DIVVS AVGVSTVS. Head, laureate, r.
Rev. IMP NERVA CAESAR AVGVSTVS REST S C. Æ, 29.26 gm. ↓.

Since Nerva's 'restored' series ignores the Flavians in favour of the Julio-Claudians, especially Augustus, the issue was presumably early in the reign. There is no precise prototype for this Divus Augustus coin.

Trajan, AD98–117

534 Aureus Rome, AD 98

Obv. IMP CAES NERVA TRAIAN AVG GERM. Head, laureate, r.
Rev. PONT MAX TR POT COS II. Germania seated l. on shields, holding branch in r. hand, and resting l. arm on shields; below, helmet. A⁄, 7.49 gm. ↓.
The reverse type recalls Trajan's military successes in Germany before his succession.

535 Denarius Rome, AD 100

Obv. As No. 534.
Rev. P M TR P COS III P P. Concordia seated l., sacrificing out of patera over altar and holding double-cornucopiae. Æ, 3.17 gm. ↓.

536 Denarius Rome, AD 101–102

Obv. As No. 534.
Rev. P M TR P COS IIII P P. Trajan on horseback l., raising r. hand; in front, kneeling Dacian raising l. hand. Æ, 3.20 gm. ↓.
The first Dacian war began in AD 102.

537 Aureus Rome, AD 103

Obv. IMP NERVA TRAIANVS AVG GER DACICVS. Head, laureate, r.
Rev. P M TR P COS V P P. Trajan standing l. in triumphal quadriga, holding branch and eagle-tipped sceptre. A⁄, 7.07 gm. ↓.
Coinage celebrating Trajan's triumph on the successful conclusion of the first Dacian war in 102 was continued into the next year.

538 Denarius Rome, c.AD 107

Obv. Bust of Hercules, laureate, l., with lion-skin over breast and r. shoulder and club over l.
Rev. IMP CAES TRAIAN AVG GER DAC P P REST. Two horses galloping l., with naked and laureate rider on nearer; below, a rat and TI – Q; to r., S; in ex., D S S incuse on tablet. Æ, 2.95 gm. ↓.
This series of 'restored' Republican denarii is probably connected with the melting down of worn-out coinage in AD 107.

539 Aureus Rome, c.AD 107

Obv. DIVVS VESPASIANVS. Head, laureate, r.
Rev. IMP CAES TRAIAN AVG GER DAC P P REST. Above star of eight rays confronted busts of Mercury, draped and with caduceus, r. and Jupiter l. A⁄, 7.26 gm. ↓.
A series of earlier aurei were 'restored' at the same time as the Republican denarii (cf. No. 538).

540 **Sestertius** Rome, AD 104

Obv. IMP CAES NERVAE TRAIANO AVG GER DAC P M
TR P COS V P P. Bust, laureate, r., with
drapery on l. shoulder.
Rev. S P Q R OPTIMO PRINCIPI S C. Arched bridge
over river on which a boat is moored.
Æ, 28.42 gm. ↓.
Almost certainly a representation of the Trajan's
bridge over the Danube at Drobetae, completed by
105.

541 **Sestertius** Rome, c.AD 106

Obv. As No. 540.
Rev. As No. 540 but Dacian seated l. on round
shield by trophy, at foot of which oblong
shield, spear and curved sword.
Æ, 27.53 gm. ↓.
This version of 'Dacia Victa' is one of the types
celebrating the successful conclusion of the second
Dacian War.

542 **Sestertius** Rome, c.AD 106

Obv. As No. 540, but no drapery.

Rev. As No. 540 but Danuvius, with cloak
floating behind head, pressing down Dacia
seated r. Æ, 28.70 gm. ↓.
Another of the types commented on under No. 541.

543 **Denarius** Rome, AD 106

Obv. IMP TRAIANO AVG GER DAC P M TR P. Bust,
laureate, r., with drapery on l. shoulder.
Rev. COS V P P S P Q R OPTIMO PRINC DAC CAP.
Dacian seated r., hands bound behind back,
on pile of shields; to l., two swords; to r.,
two spears. Æ, 3.27 gm. ↓.
cf. Nos. 541–2.

544 **Denarius** Rome, c.AD 106

Obv. As No. 543.
Rev. As No. 543, but DANVIVS. River-god
reclining l., placing r. hand on prow of ship.
Æ, 2.79 gm. ↓. cf. No. 542.

545 **Sestertius** Rome, c.AD 106

Obv. As No. 540.
Rev. As No. 540 but Trajan as priest, veiled,
togate, ploughing r. with two oxen.
Æ, 25.09 gm. ↓.
The first furrow being ceremonially ploughed may
be that of Trajan's new colony at Saranizegethusa in
Dacia.

546 **Aureus** Rome, *c.*AD 109

Obv. As No. 543, but bust, laureate, draped, cuirassed, r.
Rev. As No. 543, but in ex., ALIM ITAL. Trajan, togate, standing l., holding roll in l. hand, and extending r. to boy and girl standing l. N, 7. 11 gm. ↓.

Trajan's measures to revive prosperity in Italy included an extension of the monthly corn-dole to children.

547 **Aureus** Rome, *c.*AD 109

Obv. As No. 546.
Rev. As No. 543, but in ex., REST ITAL. Trajan standing l. as on No. 546 but clasping hands with kneeling Italia; between them, two children. N, 7.34 gm. ↓.

A more general reference to Trajan's economic measures for the benefit of Italy.

548 **Sestertius** Rome, AD 107–111

Obv. As No. 542.
Rev. As No. 540, but view of the Circus Maximus. Æ, 28.51 gm. ↓.

A commemoration of Trajan's rebuilding of the Circus.

549 **Sestertius** Rome, AD 107–111

Obv. As No. 540.
Rev. As No. 540, but temple of eight columns enclosing seated figure, on podium of five steps; on roof, figure holding spear, and, at corners, Victories holding trophy; to r. and l. of temple, colonnade of five columns. Æ, 25.50 gm. ↓.

The representation may be that of Trajan's temple for Divus Nerva.

550 **Sestertius** Rome, AD 112–114

Obv. As No. 542 but COS VI.
Rev. As No. 540, but in ex., AQVA TRAIANA. River-god reclining l. under arched grotto supported on two columns. Æ, 27.89 gm. ↓.

A commemoration of the new aqueduct for Rome's water supply constructed by Trajan.

551 **Aureus** Rome, AD 112–114

Obv. IMP TRAIANO AVG GER DAC P M TR P COS VI P P. Bust, laureate, draped, cuirassed, r.
Rev. S P Q R OPTIMO PRINCIPI, in ex., VIA TRAIANA. Woman reclining l. against rocks, holding wheel in r. hand, and branch in l. N, 7.28 gm. ↓.

The road from Beneventum to Brundisium was constructed by Trajan at his own expense.

552 Denarius Rome, AD 113

Obv. As No. 551.
Rev. S P Q R OPTIMO PRINCIPI. Column of Trajan, surmounted by statue of the emperor, and with eagle standing to l. and r. of base. Æ, 3.20 gm. ↓.

The column recording Trajan's military exploits was dedicated in 113.

553 Aureus AD 113

Obv. As No. 551.
Rev. In ex., FORVM TRAIANI. View of the forum showing six columns enclosing central doorway and four shrines with statues; above, facing quadriga flanked by trophies and Victories. N, 7.32 gm. ↓.

Trajan's forum was dedicated in 113.

554 Aureus AD 113

Obv. As No. 551.
Rev. In ex., BASILICA VLPIA. View of the basilica showing eight columns; above, facing quadriga in centre, flanked by warriors, facing bigae, and standards. N, 7.08 gm. ↓.

The basilica occupied the north-west side of Trajan's forum.

555 Sestertius Rome, AD 112

Obv. As No. 540, but COS VI.
Rev. DACIA AVGVST; in ex., PROVINCIA S C. Dacia seated l. on rock, holding legionary eagle in l. hand; in front, on second rock, child holding bunch of grapes; behind knee, child holding corn-ears. Æ, 25.80 gm. ↓.

A record of the creation of a new province from the recently captured territory.

556 Sestertius Rome, AD 112–113

Obv. As No. 555.
Rev. S P Q R OPTIMO PRINCIPI, in ex., ARAB ADQ. Arabia standing front, head l., holding branch and bundle of canes; to l., behind her, camel. Æ, 28.33 gm. ↓.

The annexation of Arabia Petrea in AD 106 continued to be commemorated in later coin issues.

557 Denarius Rome, c.AD 112–115

Obv. PLOTINA AVG IMP TRAIANI. Bust, draped, and wearing stephane, r.
Rev. CAES AVG GERMA DAC COS VI P P. Vesta seated l., holding palladium and sceptre. Æ, 2.95 gm. ↓.

The only coinage for Trajan's empress is late in the reign.

558 Aureus Rome, *c*.AD 113

Obv. DIVA AVGVSTA MARCIANA. Bust, draped, and
with stephane, r.
Rev. CONSECRATIO. Eagle, standing front, head r.
N, 7.24 gm. ↓.
Coinage commemorating the consecration of the
emperor's sister who died in AD 112.

559 Aureus Rome, *c*.AD 115–117

Obv. MATIDIA AVG DIVAE MARCIANAE F. Bust,
draped, and with stephane, r.
Rev. PIETAS AVGVST. Matidia, standing front, head
l., holding hands over two small figures to l.
and r. N, 7.09 gm. ↓.
Coinage for the emperor's niece is also late in the
reign, certainly later than the death in 112 of her
mother Marciana, described on the coin as Diva.

560 Aureus Rome, AD 112–114

Obv. IMP TRAIANVS AVG GER DAC P M TR P COS VI P P.
Bust, laureate, draped, cuirassed, r.
Rev. DIVVS PATER TRAIANVS. Bust, draped, head
bare, r. N, 7.21 gm. ↓.
· The inclusion at this time of the emperor's deified
father in the coinage honouring members of the
imperial family may partly be due to a recollection
of his military success against the Parthian enemy
against whom Trajan was about to take the field.

561 Aureus Rome, *c*.AD 116

Obv. IMP CAES NER TRAIAN OPTIM AVG GER DAC
PARTHICO. Bust, laureate, draped, cuirassed, r.
Rev. P M TR P COS VI P P S P Q R; in ex., PARTHIA
CAPTA. Trophy between two captives seated
l. and r. on shield; in front of each, bow-
case. N, 7.04 gm. ↓.
Commemoration of Trajan's defeat of the Parthians
and the capture of Ctesiphon.

562 Aureus Rome, *c*.AD 116

Obv. As No. 561.
Rev. REGNA ADSIGNATA. Trajan, extending r.
hand, and holding parazonium in l., seated l.
on platform between two standing officers;
below, three robed kings standing r., the
foremost holding out r. hand.
N, 7.19 gm. ↓.
Trajan's military success enabled him to make
political settlements confirming the rulers of local
kingdoms.

563 Sestertius Rome, AD 116–117

Obv. IMP CAES NER TRAIANO OPTIMO AVG GER DAC
PARTHICO P M TR P COS VI P P. Bust, laureate,
draped, r.
Rev. ARMENIA ET MESOPOTAMIA IN POTESTATEM P R
REDACTAE S C. Trajan, in military dress,
standing r., holding spear and parazonium;
to l. and r., the river gods Euphrates and

51

Tigris, recline facing one another; between them, Armenia, seated l. Æ, 25.09 gm. ↓.

With the creation of the two provinces of Armenia and Mesopotamia the empire's greatest territorial expansion was reached.

Hadrian, AD 117–138

564 Aureus Rome, AD 117

Obv. IMP CAES TRAIAN HADRIANO OPT AVG GER DAC. Bust, laureate, draped, cuirassed, r.
Rev. PARTHIC DIVI TRAIAN AVG F P M TR P COS P P, in ex., ADOPTIO. Trajan and Hadrian, laureate and togate, standing r. and l., facing one another, clasping r. hands, and holding roll. N, 6.91 gm. ↓.

The first coinage issue makes a point of recording Trajan's adoption of Hadrian as his successor.

565 Aureus Rome, AD 117–118

Obv. IMP CAES TRAIAN HADRIAN OPT AVG G D PART. Bust, laureate, draped, cuirassed, r.
Rev. DIVO TRAIANO PATRI AVG. Bust, laureate, draped, cuirassed, r. N, 7.35 gm. ↓.

The recording of Trajan's deification on a reverse of Hadrian again emphasises Hadrian's succession.

566 Aureus Rome, AD 117–118

Obv. DIVO TRAIANO PARTH AVG PATRI. Bust, laureate, draped, r.
Rev. TRIVMPHVS PARTHICVS. Trajan, holding branch and eagle-tipped sceptre, standing r. in triumphal quadriga. N, 7.24 gm. ↓.

The triumph for the Parthian victory which Trajan did not live to celebrate in Rome is accorded posthumous record.

567 Aureus Rome, AD 117–118

Obv. As No. 566.
Rev. PLOTINAE AVG. Bust, draped, and with stephane r. N, 7.20 gm. ↓.

Hadrian's succession is said to have been owed in part to the favour of Trajan's empress, Plotina.

568 Denarius Rome, AD 118

Obv. IMP CAESAR TRAIAN HADRIANVS AVG. Bust, laureate, r., with drapery on l. shoulder.
Rev. P M TR P COS II; in field, AET AVG. Aeternitas standing front, head l., holding head of Sun in r. hand, and Moon in l. R, 3.78 gm. ↓.

This type is probably to be associated with Hadrian's accession vows in early 118.

569 Dupondius Rome, AD 118

Obv. As No. 568, but bust, radiate, drapery on l. shoulder, r. shoulder and chest bare.
Rev. PONT MAX TR POT COS II; in ex., ADVENTVS AVG S C. Roma, helmeted, seated r. on cuirass and shield, holding spear in l. hand, and

clasping r. hands with Hadrian standing l.
Æ, 11.73 gm. ↓.

Coinage recording the emperor's arrival in Rome in July, 118.

570 Sestertius Rome, AD 119

Obv. As No. 568.
Rev. PONT MAX TR POT COS III; in ex., LIBERALITAS AVG S C. Hadrian seated l. on platform, extending r. hand; in front, attendant seated l., making distribution to citizen mounting steps; in background, Liberalitas standing l., holding account board. Æ, 26.19 gm. ↓.

The largesse pictured here was the second of Hadrian's reign.

571 Denarius Eastern mint, AD 119–122

Obv. As No. 568.
Rev. P M TR P COS III; in field, FELIC AVG. Felicitas standing l., holding caduceus and cornucopiae. Æ, 2.59 gm. ↓.

A series of denarii and rare aurei is attributed, by comparison with local styles, to a Syrian mint, perhaps Antioch.

572 Aureus Rome, AD 119–122

Obv. As No. 568, but bust, laureate, draped, cuirassed, r.
Rev. P M TR P COS III; in field, HERC GADIT. Hercules, standing r., holding club and apple; to l., prow l.; to r., river-god reclining l. Ν, 7.27 gm. ↓.

The choice of type of Hercules of Gades may be connected with Hadrian's visit to Spain in 121.

573 Silver medallion Rome, AD 119–122

Obv. IMP CAESAR TRAIANVS HADRIANVS AVG. Bust laureate l., showing chest and shoulders bare.
Rev. PONT MAX TR POT COS III. Jupiter seated l., holding Victory on r. hand, and sceptre in l. ÆR, 25.62 gm. ↓.

By weight this medallion represents an 8 denarius piece.

574 Silver medallion Rome, AD 119–122

Obv. As No. 573, but bust, laureate, draped, cuirassed l.
Rev. PONT MAX TR POT COS II. Felicitas standing l., holding caduceus and cornucopiae. ÆR, 21.44 gm. ↓.

This medallion is by weight a 7 denarius piece.

575 Aureus Rome, AD 125–128

Obv. HADRIANVS AVGVSTVS. Bust, laureate r., with drapery on l. shoulder.
Rev. COS, in ex., III. She-wolf and twins, l.
N, 7.27 gm. ↓.
This type with its reference to the legendary founders of Rome may have formed part of the coinage of Hadrian's decennalian year, AD 127–128.

576 Denarius Rome, AD 135–136

Obv. HADRIANVS AVG COS III P P. Head, bare, r.
Rev. TELLVS STABIL. Tellus standing l., holding plough-handle and rake; in ground r., two ears of corn. Æ, 3.84 gm. ↓.
The unusual reverse type is probably to be associated with Hadrian's *vicennalia*, but AD 133, the 400th anniversary of the foundation of this temple of Tellus, has also been suggested as its occasion.

577 Aureus Rome, c.AD 136

Obv. HADRIANVS AVG COS III P P. Bust, head bare, l., with drapery at back and front of neck.
Rev. ADVENTVI AVG AFRICAE. Hadrian togate, standing r., raising r. hand and holding roll in l., facing Africa standing l., wearing elephant-skin head-dress, sacrificing out of patera in r. hand over tripod, and holding corn-ears in l. hand; to r. of tripod, calf.
N, 7.44 gm. ↓.
Representative of a small series of 'province' types in gold and silver. Hadrian's visit to Africa took place in 128.

578 Sestertius Rome, c.AD 136

Obv. HADRIANVS AVG COS III P P. Bust, head bare, draped, r.
Rev. ADVENTVI AVG IVDAEAE; in ex., S C. Hadrian standing r., as on No. 577, facing Judaea standing l., sacrificing out of patera in r. hand over tripod, and holding bowl in l.; in front of Judaea, child standing l., holding palm; behind her second child holding palm. Æ, 23.96 gm. ↓.
Hadrian visited Judaea in 130, and founded Aelia Capitolina on the site of Jerusalem.

579 Aureus Rome, c.AD 136

Obv. As No. 578, but bust l.
Rev. NILVS. Nilus, naked to waist, reclining l., holding cornucopiae in r. hand, and reed in l., resting l. arm on sphinx; in front, hippopotamus; below, crocodile.
N, 7.17 gm. ↓.
Nilus, though not strictly a 'province' type can be taken as a synonym for Egypt. It was on the occasion of Hadrian's voyage on the river in 130 that his favourite, Antinous, was drowned.

580 Sestertius Rome, c.AD 136

Obv. As No. 578, but head, laureate, r.
Rev. BRITANNIA; in ex., S C. Britannia, draped,
seated l., supporting head on r. hand, and
holding spear in l., r. foot resting on rocks;
at side, shield. Æ, 25.48 gm. ↓.

The type records Hadrian's visit to Britain in 122,
and the stones under Britannia's foot may stand for
the Tyne-Solway wall begun at that time.

581   Sestertius Rome, *c.*AD 137

Obv. As No. 578 but laureate.
Rev. EXERCITVS, in ex., SYRIACVS S C. Hadrian on
horseback l., raising r. hand, and holding
sceptre in l., addressing three soldiers
holding standards. Æ, 26.87 gm. ↓.

A representative of the series of bronzes honouring
various armies of the empire. This army furnished
part of the force used to crush the second Jewish
revolt in 132.

582   Aureus Rome, *c.*AD 136

Obv. As No. 574.
Rev. RESTITVTORI ACHAIAE. Hadrian standing l.,
holding roll in l. hand, and with r. hand
raising Achaea, kneeling r.; in centre, vase
with palm. N, 7.21 gm. ↓.

The series which records the provinces which
obtained benefit from the emperor's care, not
surprisingly in view of Hadrian's phil-Hellenism,
includes Achaea.

583   Tetradrachm Asia, *c.*AD 136–138

Obv. As No. 578.
Rev. DIANA EPHESIA. Cult figure of Ephesian
Diana facing. Æ, 11.01 gm. ↓.

The tetradrachm (= 3 denarii) coinage from eastern
mints is markedly more extensive under Hadrian
than in preceding or subsequent reigns.

584   Denarius Rome, *c.*AD 137

Obv. HADRIANVS AVG COS III P P. Head, laureate, r.
Rev. ROMVLO CONDITORI. Romulus in military
dress, advancing r., holding transverse spear
and trophy over l. shoulder. Æ, 3.45 gm. ↓.

This first appearance of Rome's founder as a coin
type is connected with the issue celebrating
Hadrian's dedication of the temple of Roma and
Venus.

585   Aureus Rome, *c.*AD 136

Obv. SABINA AVGVSTA. Bust draped r., with
stephane, and hair in plait down neck.
Rev. IVNONI REGINAE. Juno draped, and wearing
stephane, standing l., holding patera and
sceptre; to l., peacock. N, 7.36 gm. ↓.

Juno Regina is queen of Heaven as the empress
Sabina is of earth.

586 Aureus Rome, AD 137

Obv. L AELIVS CAESAR. Bust, bare-headed, l., with drapery on l. shoulder.

Rev. TR POT COS II; in ex., CONCORD. Concordia seated l., holding patera in r. hand, and resting l. arm on cornucopiae set on ground. AV, 7.22 gm. ↓.

Lucius Aelius was designated as Hadrian's Caesar and successor in 136, but died on 1 January 138.

587 Aureus Rome, AD 138

Obv. IMP T AEL CAES ANTONINVS. Head, bare, r.

Rev. TRIB POT PIETAS. Pietas standing r., holding up r. hand, and holding incense box in l.; to r., altar. AV, 7.34 gm. ↓.

Following the death of Aelius Hadrian adopted Antoninus as his Caesar and heir.

5 The Antoninines
AD138–192

The traditional term, the Antonine emperors, has been retained here but in fact three of the emperors were adopted and were not dynastic heirs. Hadrian at the end of his reign adopted as his heir Antoninus Pius who in turn adopted Marcus Aurelius, and he, on succeeding, adopted Lucius Verus not as his heir but as his co-emperor. It was only following the death of Verus that Marcus Aurelius abandoned the principle of adoption, and appointed his son, Commodus, first as his Caesar and then as his co-emperor. A feature of the coinage of the Antonine period is the significant representation of other members of the imperial family. Pius coined extensively for his wife Faustina I, both in her lifetime and after her deification, as well as for his heir, Marcus Aurelius, and his wife, Faustina II. In the joint reign of Marcus and Verus also there were coinage issues for Faustina II and Lucilla, wife of Verus. For the whole of this period the only imperial mint remained that at Rome.

No serious change is to be recorded in the monetary system under the Antonines. The weight of the denarius remained fairly constant, but its fineness fell under Marcus to 70% and slipped further to 65% under Commodus whose denarii also declined in weight to just under 3 gm. In bronze the quadrans was issued under Pius but then ceased to be struck.

Antoninus Pius, AD138–161

588 Aureus Rome, AD 138

Obv. IMP CAES AEL ANTONINVS AVG. Head, laureate, r.
Rev. PONT MAX TR POT COS. Pietas standing r. by altar, raising r. hand, and holding box in l. N, 6.79 gm. ↓.

The earliest coinage of Antoninus shows him as COS DES II, and the reversion here to simple COS reflects senatorial reluctance to ratify Hadrian's acts, including Antoninus' designation to a second consulship.

589 Aureus Rome, AD 138

Obv. IMP T AEL CAES HADRI ANTONINVS. Head, laureate, r.
Rev. AVG PIVS P M TR P COS DES II. Pietas standing l. by altar, raising r. hand, and holding box in l. N, 7.27 gm. ↓.

That the Senate yielded to Antoninus' insistence on the ratification of Hadrian's acts is implicit in the resumption of the title COS DES II, and the addition of Pius to the emperor's name.

590 Aureus Rome, AD 139

Obv. DIVVS HADRIANVS AVG. Head, laureate, r.
Rev. CONSECRATIO. Eagle soaring r., bearing Divus Hadrianus, with robe in circle round head, and holding sceptre. N, 7.19 gm. ↓.

Antoninus secured not only the ratification of Hadrian's acts but also his official consecration.

591 Aureus Rome, AD 139

Obv. FAVSTINA AVG ANTONINI AVG P P. Bust, draped, r.

Rev. IVNONI REGINAE. Ornamented throne against which leans a sceptre; to l., peacock standing l.; to r., basket of fruit. N, 7.13 gm. ↓.

Types referring to Juno, the queen of the gods, are commonly used as reverses of coins of the empress.

592 Quadrans Rome, AD 139

Obv. ANTONINVS AVG PIVS P P. Head, laureate, r.

Rev. TR POT COS II. Eagle standing l. on branch. s c l. and r. in field. Æ, 3.41 gm. ↓.

An example of the smallest bronze denomination still being struck, though only rarely, under Antoninus. Thereafter it is absent from the coinage.

593 Sestertius Rome, AD 139

Obv. ANTONINVS AVG PIVS P P. Head, laureate, r.

Rev. CAPPADOCIA; in ex., COS II. Cappadocia standing l., wearing tunic and cloak, holding crown in r. hand, and vexillum in l.; at feet l., Mons Argaeus. Æ, 27.29 gm. ↓.

The *aurum coronarium*, the tax levied on the emperor's accession, was remitted by Antoninus in whole to Italy and half to the provinces. The provinces which so benefited were recorded on a series of bronze coins, with a personification of each province with a distinctive attribute, as Cappadocia here with Mons Argaeus.

594 Aureus Rome, AD 139

Obv. ANTONINVS AVG PIVS P P. Head, laureate, r.

Rev. AVRELIVS CAES AVG PII F COS DES. Head, bare, r. N, 7.05 gm. ↑.

Coinage in gold and silver in this year publicised the adoption of Marcus Aurelius by Antoninus as heir, and his designation as consul for 140.

595 Sestertius Rome, AD 140

Obv. ANTONINVS AVG PIVS P P TR P COS III. Head, laureate, r.

Rev. AVRELIVS CAESAR AVG PII F COS; below bust, s C. Bust, bare-headed, draped, cuirassed, r. Æ. 28.22 gm. ↑.

A similar series with the portraits of the emperor and his heir, as on No. 594, was produced in 140.

596 Aureus Rome, *c.*AD 140

Obv. ANTONINVS AVG PIVS P P. Bust, bare-headed, draped, r.

Rev. TR POT COS III. Aeneas advancing r., carrying Anchises on l. shoulder and leading Ascanius in r. hand. Anchises, veiled, holds a *cista* and Ascanius, wearing Phrygian cap, holds *pedum*. N, 7.18 gm. ↓.

This reverse, one of a number in this issue recalling Rome's legendary past, pictures the flight from Troy. The reverse figures may additionally have been intended to represent Antoninus, pious both to his father, Hadrian, and to his son, Marcus.

597 Aureus Rome, *c.*AD 140

Obv. As No. 596.

Rev. TR POT COS III. Romulus, bare-headed, advancing r., carrying spear and trophy. N, 7.30 gm. ↓.

Another reverse in the issue shows Romulus, the founder of Rome.

598   Denarius Rome, *c.*AD 140

Obv. As No. 596, but bust with only drapery on l. shoulder.

Rev. TR POT COS III. She-wolf and twins r. under cave. AR, 3.27 gm. ↓.

Another part of Rome's legend, the fostering of Romulus and Remus by the she-wolf, is here illustrated.

599   Sestertius Rome, *c.*AD 140

Obv. ANTONINVS AVG PIVS P P TR P COS III. Head, laureate, r.

Rev. In ex., S C. The Great Sow standing r. under tree, suckling her young. Æ, 23.96 gm. ↑.

The bronze coins also illustrate Roman legend with here, the Great Sow, which marked for Aeneas the site of his new Troy.

600   As Rome, *c.*AD 140

Obv. ANTONINVS AVG PIVS P P. Head, laureate, r.

Rev. TR POT COS III S C. Mars helmeted, holding spear and shield, descending r. to Rhea Silvia, asleep on the ground l. Æ, 12.14 gm. ↑.

The reference here is to the legendary descent of Romulus and Remus from Mars and Rhea Silvia.

601   Sestertius Rome, *c.*AD 140

Obv. ANTONINVS AVG PIVS P P TR P COS III. Head, laureate, r.

Rev. TIBERIS; in ex., S C. Tiberis, crowned with reeds, reclining l., resting l. elbow on urn from which water flows, placing r. hand on stem of boat to l., and holding reed in l. hand. Æ, 23.27 gm. ↑.

The identification of the river Tiber with Rome's origins probably accounts for the inclusion of the type in this series of legends.

602   Sestertius Rome, *c.*AD 140

Obv. As No. 601.

Rev. ROMAE AETERNAE; in ex., S C. Temple of ten columns on podium of three steps; in pediment, standing figure flanked by standing and recumbent figures; on roof, in centre, Roma, facing, enthroned, and, at angles, Victory holding diadem in both hands. Æ, 25.30 gm. ↓.

The reverse probably marks the completion of the temple of Venus and Roma dedicated by Hadrian in 135.

603 Sestertius Rome, *c*.AD 143

Obv. As No. 601.
Rev. REX ARMENIS DATVS; in ex., S C. Antoninus, togate, standing l., holding roll in l. hand, and with r. hand placing tiara on head of king of Armenia, standing l., raising r. hand. Æ, 28.75 gm. ↑.

Because of Parthian weakness at this time Rome was able to impose a king of her choice on the buffer kingdom of Armenia.

604 Aureus Rome, *c*.AD 140

Obv. ANTONINVS AVG PIVS P P. Bust, bare-headed, draped, r.
Rev. COS III; in ex., TR POT. Antoninus, holding sceptre in r. hand, standing l. with Marcus Aurelius and Lucius Verus in quadriga drawn l. N, 7.26 gm. ↓.

Antoninus and Marcus, joint consuls in 140, are depicted in the consular procession. Lucius Verus, also adopted by Antoninus, shares in the honour.

605 Aureus Rome, *c*.AD 142

Obv. AVRELIVS CAESAR AVG PII F COS. Head, bare, r.
Rev. PIETAS AVG. Emblems of priesthood: knife, sprinkler, jug, lituus, and simpulum. N, 7.65 gm. ↓.

In the second and third centuries this became one of the reverse types regularly used on the coinage of the Caesar.

606 Aureus Rome, *c*.AD 144

Obv. As No. 605.
Rev. HONOS. Honos, togate, standing l., holding branch in r. hand, and cornucopiae in l. N, 7.28 gm. ↓.

In earlier coinage Honos is associated with Virtus, but here the togate personification of Honos may represent Marcus himself.

607 Sestertius Rome, AD 141

Obv. DIVA AVGVSTA FAVSTINA. Bust, draped, veiled, r.
Rev. CONSECRATIO S C. Eagle flying l., carrying Faustina with star-adorned mantle in circle round head, and holding sceptre in r. hand. Æ, 24.31 gm. ↓.

The death of the empress in 141 was followed by her consecration.

608 Aureus Rome, *c*.AD 141

Obv. DIVA AVG FAVSTINA. Bust, draped, r.
Rev. PVELLAE FAVSTINAE. Two storey building: on top floor, Antoninus standing r., extending r. hand, and holding roll in l.; before him, man seated l. at table, and woman leaning forward l., pointing to document on table; on ground floor, group of six figures, most holding child. N, 7.15 gm. ↑.

The granting of a charter to a guild of poor orphan girls founded in honour of Faustina.

609 Aureus Rome, *c.*AD 142

Obv. As No. 607.
Rev. EX SENATVS CONSVLTO. Faustina, draped, holding corn-ears and sceptre, seated l. on chair set on biga drawn l. by two elephants ridden by two mahouts. *N*, 7.32 gm. ↓.

The reverse depicts one of the funeral honours accorded to Faustina by decree of the Senate.

610 Sestertius Rome, *c.*AD 142

Obv. DIVA FAVSTINA. Bust, draped, veiled, r.
Rev. AETERNITAS S C. Aeternitas, draped, standing l., holding nimbate phoenix on globe in r. hand, and with l. holding out fold of dress. Æ, 27.70 gm. ↓.

One series of the extensive coinage in honour of the deified Faustina is inscribed AETERNITAS. In the present instance the type is in fact Aeternitas but goddesses such as Ceres, Juno, and Vesta are also represented with the same inscription.

611 Sestertius Rome, *c.*AD 143

Obv. DIVA FAVSTINA. Bust, draped, r.
Rev. AVGVSTA S C. Ceres, draped, standing l., holding corn-ears in r. hand, and short torch in l. Æ, 25.54 gm. ↑.

A second great series inscribed AVGVSTA depicts the same range of deities as listed under No. 609.

612 Aureus quinarius Rome, *c.*AD 143

Obv. As No. 610.
Rev. CONSECRATIO. Peacock standing front with tail spread. *N*, 3.58 gm. ↓.

This somewhat rare denomination may form part of the coinage issued for the third largesse dispensed by Antoninus in 143.

613 Aureus Rome, AD 143

Obv. ANTONINVS AVG PIVS P P TR P COS III. Head, bare, l.
Rev. IMPERATOR II. Victory, winged and draped, r., holding trophy in both hands. *N*, 7.20 gm. ↓.

The victory marked by the emperor's second imperatorial salutation was the extension of the Roman province in Britain into South Scotland and the construction of a new *limes* between the Forth and the Clyde.

614 Sestertius Rome, AD 143

Obv. As No. 613, but head laureate.
Rev. BRITANNIA S C. Britannia, wearing tunic and breeches, seated l. on rock, holding a standard in r. hand, and resting l. elbow on shield, set on rock. Æ, 29.46 gm. ↑.

This type also records the creation of the new Antonine Wall. The representation of Britannia here differs in detail from that on No. 580.

615 Aureus Rome, AD 145

Obv. AVRELIVS CAESAR AVG PII F COS II. Head, bare, r.
Rev. HILARITAS. Hilaritas standing l., holding long palm and cornucopiae. N, 7.11 gm. ↓.
The type is appropriate on coinage issued at the time of the marriage of Marcus Aurelius with the emperor's daughter, Faustina.

616 Aureus Rome, AD 148

Obv. ANTONINVS AVG PIVS P P. Head, laureate, r.
Rev. LIBERALITAS AVG COS III. Liberalitas standing l., holding *abacus* and cornucopiae. N, 7.25 gm. ↓.
The occasion of the distribution of Antoninus' fifth largesse is not certain, but it may have been connected with the recent grant of the tribunician power to Marcus.

617 Aureus Rome, AD 149

Obv. ANTONINVS AVG PIVS P P TR P XII. Head, laureate, r.
Rev. TEMPORVM FELICITAS COS IIII. Crossed cornucopiae, each surmounted by bust of child. N, 7.33 gm. ↑.
This coin celebrates the birth of twins to Faustina and Marcus.

618 Aureus Rome, AD 149

Obv. FAVSTINAE AVG PII AVG FIL. Bust, draped, and wearing stephane, r.
Rev. LAETITIAE PVBLICAE. Laetitia standing l., holding wreath and baton. N, 7.32 gm. ↓.
The public rejoicing alluded to here was probably at the birth of the imperial grandchildren recorded by No. 617.

619 Aureus Rome, *c*.AD 150

Obv. FAVSTINA AVG ANTONINI AVG PII FIL. Bust, draped, r., with band of pearls in hair.
Rev. VENERI FELICI. Dove standing r. N, 7.23 gm. ↓.
The dove, the symbol of Venus, may allude to the married bliss of Faustina and Marcus.

620 Sestertius Rome, AD 159

Obv. ANTONINVS AVG PIVS P P TR P XXII. Head, laureate, r.
Rev. TEMPLVM DIVI AVG REST COS IIII S C. Temple of eight columns on podium of two steps: in centre, two figures seated facing; in pediment, uncertain figures; on roof, facing quadriga at apex, and standing figure at each angle, in front of columns l. and r., a statue. Æ, 25.30 gm. ↑.
The coin celebrates the restoration by Antoninus of the temple of Divus Augustus and Livia.

621 **Aureus** Rome, AD 158–159

Obv. As No. 620, but bust, laureate, draped, r.
Rev. VOTA SVSCEPTA DEC III COS IIII. Antoninus, veiled, togate, standing l., sacrificing out of patera in r. hand over tripod, and holding roll in l. hand. N, 7.32 gm. ↓.

On the completion of twenty years of rule vows were taken for a third decennium.

622 **Bronze medallion** Rome, AD 159

Obv. AVRELIVS CAES ANTON AVG PII F. Bust, bare-headed, draped, cuirassed, r.
Rev. TR POT XIII COS II. Neptune standing l., r. foot on prow to l., extending r. hand towards gateway and walls of Troy, and holding sceptre in l.; by feet r., a dolphin. Æ, 48.56 gm. ↑.

This is one of a series of second-century medallions which seem to be based on famous statuary types, in this case the famous Lysippan Poseidon before the walls of Troy, which, legend said, he, together with Apollo, built for King Laomedon.

Marcus Aurelius, AD161-180

623 **Aureus** Rome, AD 161

Obv. IMP CAES M AVREL ANTONINVS AVG. Head, bare, r.
Rev. LIB AVGVSTOR TR P XV COS III. Marcus Aurelius and Lucius Verus seated l. on curule chairs on platform, extending r. hands; in front, attendant standing l., holding *abacus* and wand; by platform, citizen standing r., holding out fold of toga in both hands. N, 7.28 gm. ↑.

The two emperors are shown dispensing largesse at the outset of the joint reign.

624 **Aureus** Rome, AD 161

Obv. IMP CAES L AVREL VERVS AVG. Head, bare, r.
Rev. CONCORDIAE AVGVSTOR TR P COS II. Marcus, laureate, togate, standing l., and Verus, bare-headed, togate, standing r., clasping r. hands, and holding roll in l. N, 7.34 gm. ↓.

This is the first instance in the history of the principate of a joint reign of two Augusti whose intention, the type proclaims, is to rule in harmony.

625 Denarius Rome, AD 161

Obv. DIVVS ANTONINVS. Bust, bare-headed, r. with drapery on l. shoulder.
Rev. DIVO PIO. Column on low base, surrounded by trellis-work, and surmounted by statue of Divus Antoninus holding branch and sceptre. Æ, 3.19 gm. ↓.

The reverse depicts the still extant column erected in memory of the now deified Antoninus Pius.

626 Aureus Rome, AD 161–176

Obv. FAVSTINA AVGVSTA. Bust, draped, r.
Rev. MATRI MAGNAE. Cybele, towered, draped, seated r. on throne between two lions, and holding drum on knee with l. hand. Æ, 7.21 gm. ↑.

There is probably some identification of Faustina, the mother of the imperial family, with Cybele who appears here for the first time on Roman coins.

627 Sestertius Rome, AD 161

Obv. As No. 626.
Rev. TEMPOR FELIC S C. Felicitas, draped, standing front, head l., holding child on each arm; to l. and r., two children. Æ, 27.52 gm. ↑.

There is an obvious reference to the children with which the imperial family was blessed, and the specific occasion may be the birth of the twin sons, Commodus and Annius Verus in 161.

628 Aureus Rome, AD 162

Obv. IMP CAES L VERVS AVG. Bust, head bare, draped, r.
Rev. PROFECTIO AVG TR P II COS II. Verus, in military dress, holding spear in r. hand, on horse r. Æ, 7.34 gm. ↓.

Verus, appointed to supreme command in the war occasioned by the Parthian invasion of Armenia, left Rome for the East in 162.

629 Aureus Rome, AD 163

Obv. L VERVS AVG ARMENIACVS. Bust, head bare, draped, cuirassed, r.
Rev. TR P III IMP II COS II ARMEN. Armenia seated in dejection l., holding bow in r. hand, at foot of trophy. Æ, 7.22 gm. ↓.

The Roman army successfully invaded Armenia and captured the capital, Artataxta; Verus was accorded the title Armeniacus.

630 Sestertius Rome, AD 164

Obv. L AVREL VERVS AVG ARMENIACVS. Bust, laureate, cuirassed, r., seen from back.
Rev. REX ARMENIIS DATVS IMP II TR P IIII COS II S C. Verus seated l. on curule chair on platform, accompanied by three officers, with r. hand placing diadem on head of king Sohaemus, standing l. raising r. hand. Æ, 24.85 gm. ↑.

The Armenian campaign was concluded in 164 with the coronation of Rome's protège, Sohaemus.

631 Aureus Rome, c.AD 164

Obv. LVCILLA AVGVSTA. Bust, draped, r.
Rev. PVDICITIA. Pudicitia, veiled, draped, standing
  front, head l., drawing back veil with r.
  hand. N, 7.31 gm. ↑.
The first coinage for Lucilla was probably issued
soon after the marriage of Lucilla and Verus in 164.
Pudicitia is one of the stock virtues chosen for the
reverse of coins of the imperial ladies.

632 Aureus Rome, AD 165

Obv. M ANTONINVS AVG ARMENIACVS. Bust,
  laureate, draped, cuirassed, r., seen from
  back.
Rev. P M TR P XIX IMP III COS III. Felicitas, draped,
  standing front, head l., r. foot on globe,
  holding caduceus and cornucopiae.
  N, 7.11 gm. ↑.
Felicitas expresses the happy outcome of the war
against Parthia.

633 Denarius Rome, AD 165

Obv. L VERVS AVG ARM PARTH MAX. Head, laureate, r.
Rev. TR P V IMP III COS II. Parthia, seated r. on
  ground, hands tied behind back; in front,
  quiver, bow and shield. R, 3.34 gm. ↓.
For the defeat of Parthia here shown Verus assumed
the title of Parthicus Maximus.

634 Bronze medallion Rome, AD 166

Obv. COMMODVS CAES VERVS CAES. Confronting
  busts, bare-headed, draped, of Commodus
  to r. and Annius Verus to l.
Rev. TEMPORVM FELICITAS. The four seasons
  represented by little boys: Spring, naked, r.,
  holds a basket of flowers on his shoulder;
  Summer, naked, r., holds falx and corn-ears;
  Autumn, naked, l., holds a fawn and patera;
  Winter, in short tunic, l., carries a hare and
  staff with brace of birds. Æ, 70.85 gm. ↑.
The occasion of this medallion was the appointment
of Commodus and Annius Verus as Caesars in 166.

635 Aureus Rome, AD 167

Obv. M ANTONINVS AVG ARM PARTH MAX. Bust,
  bare-headed, draped, cuirassed, r., seen from
  back.
Rev. TR P XX IMP IIII COS III. Victory, standing
  front, head r., holding palm and placing
  shield, inscribed VIC/PAR, on palm-tree.
  N, 7.28 gm. ↓.
This type was part of the coinage on the occasion of
the triumph celebrating the victory over Parthia.

636   Denarius Rome, *c.*AD 168

Obv. ANTONINVS AVGVR III VIR R P C. Galley l.
Rev. ANTONINVS ET VERVS AVG REST. Legionary
eagle between two standards; between,
LEG VI. Æ, 3.14 gm. ↓.
A convincing explanation for the 'restitution' of
Mark Antony's legionary denarius, and specifically
the reference to the Sixth Legion, is hard to find. It
has, of course, been noted that the date of issue
probably coincided with the 200th anniversary of
the original issue.

637   Sestertius Rome, AD 169

Obv. DIVVS VERVS. Head, bare, r.
Rev. CONSECRATIO S C. Verus seated r. in shrine set
on car drawn r. by four elephants, each
ridden by mahout. Æ, 25.23 gm. ↓.
The coin illustrates the procession which formed
part of the consecration rites of Verus who died in
AD 169.

638   Sestertius Rome, AD 170

Obv. M ANTONINVS AVG TR P XXIIII. Head,
laureate, r.

Rev. COS III PROFECTIO AVG S C. Marcus, in
military dress, on horse r.; in front, a soldier
holding spear and shield; behind, two
soldiers, holding legionary eagles.
Æ, 26.33 gm. ↓.
The departure of Marcus to take command in the
war against the Marcomanni.

639   Aureus Rome, AD 172

Obv. M ANTONINVS AVG TR P XXVI. Bust, laureate,
draped, cuirassed, r.
Rev. IMP VI COS III. Victory standing front, head
r., with l. hand placing shield inscribed
VIC/GER on palm-tree. N, 7.29 gm. ↑.
The emperor records his sixth imperatorial
salutation for the victory won in the Danubian
campaign against the Marcomanni.

640   Denarius Rome, AD 173

Obv. As No. 639, but TR P XXVII and head,
laureate, r.
Rev. RELIG AVG IMP VI COS III. Mercury wearing
petasus and short cloak, standing front, head
l., holding patera and caduceus.
Æ, 3.25 gm. ↓.
The reverse is a reference to the story that in a battle
against the Quadi the Roman troops, exhausted by
thirst, were relieved by a rain shower sent by
Mercury, invoked as god of the air.

641 Aureus Rome, AD 175

Obv. COMMODO CAES AVG FIL GERM. Bust, head bare, draped, cuirassed, r.
Rev. PRINC IVVENT. Commodus, in military dress, standing front, head l., holding branch and sceptre; to r., trophy at foot of which shield, spear, and bow. *N*, 7.30 gm. ↓.

Commodus, made Caesar in 172, shared in the coinage for the first time in 175 with the traditional title of the heir-apparent, Princeps Iuventutis.

642 Aureus Rome, AD 176

Obv. M ANTONINVS AVG GERM SARM. Bust, laureate, draped, cuirassed, r.
Rev. TRP XXX IMP VIII COS III P P DE GERM. Pile of arms. *N*, 7.31 gm. ↓.

The coinage celebrates the successful conclusion of the campaigns which earned the emperor the titles of Germanicus and Sarmaticus.

643 Aureus Rome, *c.*AD 176

Obv. DIVAE FAVSTINAE PIAE. Bust, veiled, draped, r.
Rev. MATRI CASTRORVM. Diva Faustina seated l., holding phoenix on globe and sceptre; to l., three legionary eagles set on base. *N*, 7.18 gm. ↓.

Coinage commemorates the consecration of Faustina who died in 175. The reverse, describing her as 'Mater Castrorum', is an allusion to her loyal accompaniment of the emperor on his travels. Her death took place in Cappadocia during the visit of Marcus to the East.

644 Sestertius Rome, *c.*AD 176

Obv. DIVA FAVSTINA PIA. Bust, draped, r.
Rev. SIDERIRVS RECEPTA S C. Faustina, with veil floating behind her, standing r. in biga of horses r., and holding reins in r. hand. Æ, 25.57 gm. ↓.

The reverse is an unusual piece of imagery in the consecration series showing the deified Faustina in the guise of Diana Lucifera.

645 Aureus Rome, AD 177

Obv. IMP CAES L AVREL COMMODVS GERM SARM. Bust, laureate, draped, r.
Rev. TR POT COS II DE SARM. Pile of arms. *N*, 7.24 gm. ↑.

The coinage now shows Commodus sharing with his father in the celebration of the victories over Germans and Sarmatians.

646 Aureus Rome, AD 178

Obv. L AVREL COMMODVS AVG. Bust, laureate, draped, cuirassed, r.
Rev. Castor, wearing round cap, standing l. by horse l., holding bridle and spear. *N*, 7.29 gm. ↓.

Commodus, now Augustus along with Marcus, is shown as under the protection of Castor, patron of the knights.

Commodus, AD180-192

Obv. M COMMODVS ANTON AVG PIVS. Head, laureate, r.

Rev. MVNFICENTIA AVG TR P VIIII IMP VI; in ex., COS IIII P P S C. Elephant, cuirassed, walking r. Æ, 10.67 gm. ↑.

647 Denarius Rome, AD 180

Obv. M COMMODVS ANTONINVS AVG. Head, laureate, r.

Rev. TR P V IMP IIII COS II P P. Trophy at base of which are two captives seated back to back on shields. Æ, 2.94 gm. ↑.

The reverse type refers to the second defeat of the Marcomanni just before the death of Marcus. On his accession Commodus concluded a peace and returned to Rome.

651 Denarius Rome, AD 184

Obv. As No. 650.

Rev. P M TR P VIIII IMP VI COS IIII P P. Victory standing front, head r., inscribing shield set on palm-tree; captive seated r. Æ, 2.94 gm. ↓.

Commodus received his sixth imperatorial acclamation for the victory in Britain of Ulpius Marcellus in crushing the Caledonian invasion of the province.

648 Aureus Rome, AD 180

Obv. DIVVS M ANTONINVS PIVS. Head, bare, r.

Rev. CONSECRATIO. Funeral pyre of four tiers, surmounted by facing quadriga, in which stands Sol, raising r. hand. Ν, 7.30 gm. ↑.

The consecration of Marcus Aurelius was voted immediately on the day of his funeral.

652 Sestertius Rome, AD 184

Obv. M COMMODVS ANTONINVS AVG PIVS BRIT. Head, laureate, r.

Rev. P M TR P VIIII IMP VII COS IIII P P S C; in ex., VICT BRIT. Victory seated r. on shields and arms, inscribing shield set on knee. Æ, 21.14 gm. ↓.

A more explicit commemoration of the victory in Britain. Commodus now adds Britannicus to his titles.

649 Aureus Rome, *c.*AD 180

Obv. CRISPINA AVGVSTA. Bust, draped, r.

Rev. VENVS VICTRIX. Venus standing r., holding helmet and sceptre, and leaning l. elbow on column; at foot r., shield. Ν, 7.27 gm. ↑.

Coinage for Crispina is only of the early years of the reign before she fell into disgrace in 183.

653 Bronze medallion Rome, AD 185

Obv. As No. 652, but bust, laureate, draped, cuirassed, r.
Rev. BRITTANIA P M TR P X IMP VII COS IIII P P. Britannia seated l. on rock holding standard and spear, and resting l. arm on shield set on helmet. Æ, 66.08 gm. ↑.

The celebration of the British victory begun in 184 was continued into the following year.

654 Quinarius Rome, AD 185

Obv. As No. 652, but ANTON.
Rev. P M TR P X IMP VII COS IIII P P. Victory advancing l., holding wreath and palm. Æ, 1.37 gm. ↓.

An example of the quinarius, by this time an infrequent denomination.

655 Aureus Rome, AD 186

Obv. M COMM ANT P FEL AVG BRIT. Bust, laureate, draped, cuirassed, r.
Rev. P M TR P XI IMP VII COS V P P; in ex., CONC MIL. Commodus standing front, head l.; in front of him, four soldiers, two l., two r.; the two in centre clasp hands and hold legionary eagles; the two outside hold spears and shields. Æ, 7.11 gm. ↑.

The appeal for military concord may hark back to the fall in the previous year of the Praetorian Prefect, Perennis, suspected of planning a coup with the support of the rebellious army of Britain.

656 Aureus Rome, AD 187

Obv. As No. 655.
Rev. NOBILIT AVG P M TR P XII IMP VIII COS V P P. Nobilitas standing front, head r., holding sceptre and palladium. Æ, 7.26 gm. ↓.

Nobilitas as a personification makes its first appearance on Roman coins in this reign. The precise significance of the type is unclear, unless it be majesty, as the imperial attributes of sceptre and palladium suggest.

657 Denarius Rome, AD 187

Obv. As No. 655, but head laureate, r.
Rev. PATER SENAT P M TR P XII IMP VIII COS V P P. Commodus, togate, standing front, head l., holding branch and eagle-tipped sceptre. Æ, 3.37 gm. ↑.

A type acclaiming Commodus – of all emperors – as Pater Senatus seems inept in view of the relation between this emperor and the Senate.

658 Denarius Rome, c.AD 188

Obv. As No. 657.
Rev. FORTVNAE MANENTI C V P P. Fortuna seated l., holding in l. hand by bridle, horse standing l., head turned r., and in r. hand cornucopiae. Æ, 2.72 gm. ↑.

Fortuna here has the unusual epithet 'Manens' – abiding. Fortuna's guiding role in affairs, most commonly indicated by the attribute of a rudder, is here suggested by the hand holding a horse by the bridle.

659 Denarius Rome, AD 189

Obv. As No. 657.

Rev. IOVI IVVEN P M TR P XIIII COS V P P. Jupiter standing front, head l., holding thunderbolt and sceptre; at foot l., eagle to l.
Æ, 2.33 gm. ↓.

In Jupiter, described here as Iuvenis, is probably to be seen an identification with the youthful emperor, Commodus.

660 Denarius Rome, AD 190

Obv. M COMM ANT P FEL AVG BRIT P P. Head, laureate, r.

Rev. APOL MONET P M TR P XV COS VI. Apollo, naked, standing r., placing r. hand on head, and resting l. on column. Æ, 2.95 gm. ↑.

Apollo is one of the patron deities of the mint to whom a dedication by one of the mint officials is recorded in an inscription of Trajanic date.

661 Aureus Rome, AD 191

Obv. As No. 660, but bust, laureate, draped, cuirassed, r.

Rev. HERC COMM P M TR P XVI COS VI. Hercules standing l., sacrificing out of patera over altar, and holding cornucopiae; on altar rests a club; on tree to l. hang lion-skin and quiver. N, 7.30 gm. ↓.

The cult of Hercules, much favoured by Commodus, is widely reflected on coin types in the last years of the reign. The scene here is probably the sacrifice of Hercules at the Ara Maxima after slaying the robber Cacus.

662 Sestertius Rome, AD 190

Obv. M COMMOD ANT P FELIX AVG BRIT P P. Head, laureate, r.

Rev. COL L AN COM P M TR P XV IMP VIII COS VI S C. Commodus, veiled, togate, ploughing r. with a yoke of two oxen. Æ, 23.40. ↑.

The scene of the ritual ploughing of the furrow marking out a new foundation refers to Commodus' refounding of Rome as Colonia Lucia Annia Commodiana.

663 Denarius Rome, AD 191

Obv. L AEL AVREL COMM AVG P FEL. Head, in lion-skin, r.

Rev. HERCVL ROMAN AVGV. Club upright.
Æ, 2.97 gm. ↓.

From this date Commodus abandons his Antonine name in favour of Aelius marking his succession right back to Hadrian. The reverse continues to celebrate the cult of Hercules.

664 Sestertius Rome, AD 191

Obv. As No. 663.

Rev. HERCVLI ROMANO AVGV S C. Club, bow, and quiver. Æ, 22.71 gm. ↑.

A fuller version of the Herculian type on the previous coin.

665 Aureus Rome, AD 191

Obv. As No. 663, but head, laureate, l.
Rev. HERCVLI ROMANO AVG. Hercules standing
front, head r., placing r. hand on trophy,
and holding club and lion-skin in l.
𝒩, 7.20 gm. ↑.

The Roman Hercules here is probably to be seen as
Commodus himself.

666 Aureus Rome, AD 192

Obv. As No. 663, but bust, laureate, draped,
cuirassed, r.
Rev. COS VII P P. Commodus standing l., holding
roll in l. hand and crowned by Victory,
extends r. hand over lighted altar to Serapis
standing r. and Isis holding sistrum.
𝒩, 7.18 gm. ↑.

The type suggests an imperial acceptance of the
Egyptian cult not otherwise explicitly recorded.

667 Bronze medallion Rome, AD 192

Obv. L AELIVS AVRELIVS COMMODVS AVG PIVS FELIX.
Head, in lion-skin, r.
Rev. HERCVLI ROMANO AVG P M TR P XVIII COS VII P P.
Hercules, seen from back, standing l.,
holding with l. hand, by the strap, case
containing bow and arrows, and resting r.
on club; to l., on rock, boar-skin; to r., on
rock, lion-skin. Æ, 61.45 gm. ↑.

One of the finest and most elaborate medallic
expressions of the cult of Hercules. The inclusion of
TR P XVIII in the reverse inscription dates the piece to
the last weeks of December 192.

6 The Civil War and the Severans
AD192-235

The assassination of Commodus on 31 December 192 was followed by the short reigns of Pertinax and Didius Julianus in the early months of 193, and a period of civil war from which Septimius Severus emerged as victor over the other contenders, Pescennius Niger in the East, and Clodius Albinus in the West. Severus associated with himself his sons Caracalla and Geta, successively as Caesars and subsequently Augusti. The direct Severan dynasty ended with the assassination in 217 of Caracalla who was replaced by his praetorian prefect, Macrinus, the first equestrian to be proclaimed emperor. In 218 the army declared for Elagabalus, high-priest of the sun-god Ba'al at Emesa in Syria, and grandson of Julia Maesa, the sister of Julia Domna who was the wife of Septimius Severus. After only four years Elagabalus was assassinated in a palace revolution and replaced by his cousin, Severus Alexander.

The exigencies of the civil war called into being a number of mints in the provinces. Coinage was issued for Pescennius Niger at Antioch, and for Severus' eastern campaigns at two other eastern mints at least, probably at Emesa and Laodicea-ad-Mare; and coinage for Clodius Albinus as Augustus was struck at Lyons. The mint at Laodicea continued active down to about AD 202, but thereafter Rome was the sole mint for Severus and his sons. Coinage was issued again at Antioch for Elagabalus and for the first two years of the reign of Severus Alexander.

This period saw some major changes in the monetary system as well as some smaller modifications. The aureus was reduced to some 6.82 gm. by Didius Julianus but was soon restored by Severus to 7.39 gm., the weight maintained until Caracalla's major reform in AD 215 lowered it to 6.54 gm., a standard of fifty to the pound of gold. The double aureus, marked as such by the radiate-crowned portrait, was now introduced. The denarius was reduced to 2.94 gm. by Didius Julianus, but restored to just over 3 gm. by Severus. Its fineness, however, continued to fall to an average of 50%. As well as altering the standard of the aureus in 215 Caracalla introduced a new silver denomination, the piece termed an antoninianus after the reference to the *argenteus antoninianus* in the *Historia Augusta*. This coin, by weight about 5.11 gm., considerably less than twice the weight of the denarius, was pre-

sumably tariffed as a double-denarius, for it has a radiate-crowned portrait, as does the double aureus, and, in bronze, the dupondius, the double of the *as*. The denarius of the early empire was tariffed at twenty-five to the aureus, but as there is some evidence that about AD 225 the aureus was equivalent to 50 denarii, it is probable that at the time of Caracalla's innovation the denarius rate was already around this figure. Under Didius Julianus the sestertius was reduced to about 21.20 gm. but was soon restored again to its former weight under Severus. From the Severan period bronze denominations appear to have been struck in increasingly reduced quantity. At this time the dupondii issued for the imperial ladies began to be distinguished from the *asses* by placing the portrait bust on a crescent; this was also done on their antoniniani.

Pertinax, AD193

668   Aureus Rome, AD 193

Obv. IMP CAES P HELV PERTIN AVG. Head, laureate, r.
Rev. OPI DIVIN TR P COS II. Ops seated l., holding two corn-ears in l. hand. *N*, 7.31 gm. ↓.
The personification of Ops, specifically described as *divina*, was probably meant to suggest divine assistance for the new reign rather than simply wealth and riches.

669   Denarius Rome, AD 193

Obv. IMP CAES P HELV PERTIN AVG. Head, laureate, r.
Rev. IANO CONSERVAT. Two-headed Janus, standing front, holding sceptre in r. hand. Æ, 3 gm. ↓.

This rare appearance of Janus in the imperial coinage is a particularly apt type in the first coinage of Pertinax who acceded on 1 January.

670 Sestertius Rome, AD 193

Obv. As No. 668.
Rev. TR P COS II S C; in ex., LIB AVG. Pertinax seated l. on curule chair on platform, extending r. hand and holding roll in l.; behind, lictor standing l., holding vertical staff; in front, Libertas standing l., holding abacus and cornucopiae; at foot of platform, citizen standing l., about to mount platform, and holding out fold of toga. Æ, 26.30 gm. ↑.

An unusually fine illustration of the distribution of largesse customary at the beginning of a reign.

Didius Julianus, AD193

671 Aureus Rome, AD 193

Obv. IMP CAES M DID IVLIANVS AVG. Head, laureate, r.
Rev. CONCORD MILIT. Concordia standing l., holding legionary eagle in r. hand, and standard in l. Æ, 6.77 gm. ↓.

Didius was proclaimed by the Praetorians but to maintain his position he needed the wider support of the army for which the reverse type makes appeal.

672 Aureus Rome, AD 193

Obv. MANL SCANTILLA AVG. Bust, draped, r.
Rev. IVNO REGINA. Juno, draped, standing l., holding patera and sceptre; at foot l., peacock. Æ, 6.56 gm. ↓.

This queenly type had become standard for the empress from Sabina onwards.

673 Aureus Rome, AD 193

Obv. DIDIA CLARA AVG. Bust, draped, r.
Rev. HILAR TEMPOR. Hilaritas, draped, standing l., holding palm and cornucopiae. Æ, 6.73 gm. ↓.

The type had been used for princes such as Marcus Aurelius and Commodus and is here associated with the emperor's daughter, Didia Clara. The choice may have been influenced by the recent celebration of the *Hilaria*, the festival of Cybele, on 25 March, just before the accession of Didius Julianus on 28 March.

Pescennius Niger, AD193–194

674 Denarius Antioch, AD 193–194

Obv. IMP CAES C PESC NIGER IVST AV. Head, laureate, r.
Rev. BONI EVENTVS. Bonus Eventus, draped, standing r., holding corn-ears in r. hand, and bowl of fruit in l. Æ, 3.17 gm. ↓.

Bonus Eventus, the good luck of the emperor, is not a type found on coins from Rome but has more of a Greek flavour.

675 **Denarius** Antioch, AD 193–194

Obv. IMP CAES C PESC NIGER IVST AV. Head, laureate, r.
Rev. IOVI PRAE ORBIS. Jupiter seated l., holding Victory and sceptre. Æ, 3.08 gm. ↓.
An unusual description of Jupiter as 'guardian of the world'.

676 **Denarius** Antioch, AD 193–194

Obv. IMP CAES C PESCEN NIGER IVSTI AV. Head, laureate, r.
Rev. IVSTITIA AVG. Two capricorns l. and r., over shield, bearing globe with seven stars. Æ, 2.86 gm. ↑.
Justitia in the reverse inscription echoes the epithet *iustus* which Niger added to his titulature. The capricorn recalls the first princeps (Augustus) whose natal sign this was.

Septimius Severus, AD193–198

677 **Aureus** Rome, AD 193

Obv. IMP CAE L SEP SEV PERT AVG. Head, laureate, r.
Rev. LEG VIII AVG TR P COS. Legionary eagle on low perch between two standards. N, 7.16 gm. ↓.

The first coinage issued by Severus at Rome included a series honouring the legions which had supported him.

678 **Aureus** Rome, AD 193–196

Obv. IVLIA DOMNA AVG. Bust, draped, r.
Rev. VENERI VICTR. Venus, half-draped, standing r., resting l. elbow on column, and holding palm and apple. N, 7.91 gm. ↑.
Coinage was struck for the empress, Julia Domna, from the very outset of the reign.

679 **Aureus** Rome, AD 194

Obv. L SEPT SEV PERT AVG IMP II. Head, laureate, r.
Rev. DIS AVSPICIB TR P II COS II P P. Hercules, naked, on l., standing l., holding club on ground in r. hand, and lion-skin over l. arm; Liber, naked, on r., standing l., emptying cup for small panther, and holding thyrsus. N, 7.11 gm. ↓.
Hercules and Liber are the special gods of Lepcis Magna, the birthplace of Severus.

680 **Denarius** Emesa?, AD 194

Obv. IMP CAE L SEP SEV PERT AVG COS II. Head, laureate, r.
Rev. BONA SPEI. Spes advancing l., holding flower, and raising skirt. Æ, 3.11 gm. ↑.
The unusual style marks this as a coin of eastern rather than Roman mintage. The epithet *bona* is not found attached to Spes at Rome, and the lack of agreement between adjective and noun indicates a mint where Latin was not the familiar language.

681　Denarius Emesa?, AD 193–197

Obv.　IVLIA DOMNA AVG. Bust, draped, r.
Rev.　SAECVL FELICIT. Seven stars above crescent.
　　　　Æ, 2.22 gm. ↑.
From its style this coin is of eastern rather than
Roman mintage.

682　Aureus Rome, AD 194–195

Obv.　D CL SEPT ALBIN CAES. Head, bare, r.
Rev.　SAECVLO FRVGIFERO COS II. Saeculum
　　　　Frugiferum seated l., between two sphinxes,
　　　　raising r. hand, and holding corn-ears in l.
　　　　Ν, 7.22 gm. ↑.
An example of the coinage struck at Rome for
Clodius Albinus who, though proclaimed by his
own troops in Britain, accepted the position of
Caesar to Severus.

683　Sestertius Rome, AD 194–195

Obv.　D CL ALBIN CAES. Bust r., head bare, drapery
　　　　on l. shoulder.
Rev.　FELICITAS COS II S C. Felicitas standing l.,
　　　　holding caduceus in r. hand, and sceptre in l.
　　　　Æ, 24.55 gm. ↑.

684　Sestertius Rome, AD 195

Obv.　L SEPT SEV PERT AVG IMP V. Bust, laureate,
　　　　draped, cuirassed, r.
Rev.　PART ARAB PART ADIAB COS II P P S C. Trophy
　　　　of arms between two captives, seated l. and r.
　　　　Æ, 24.15 gm. ↑.
After the defeat of Pescennius Niger Severus
undertook successful campaigns against states to the
east which had profited by the civil war to
encroach, and in 195 took the titles *Parthicus
Arabicus*, and *Parthicus Adiabenus*.

685　Aureus Rome, AD 196

Obv.　L SEPT SEV PERT AVG IMP VIII. Bust, laureate,
　　　　r., with drapery on l. shoulder.
Rev.　ADVENTVI AVG FELICISSIMO. Severus on
　　　　horseback r., raising r. hand; to r., soldier
　　　　moving r., head l., holding bridle of horse
　　　　and vexillum. Ν, 7.13 gm. ↓.
The reverse records the visit of Severus to Rome,
possibly on his way to the confrontation with
Clodius Albinus in Gaul.

686　Sestertius Rome, AD 196–197

Obv.　M AVR ANTONINVS CAES. Bust, head bare,
　　　　draped, r.
Rev.　SEVERI AVG PII FIL S C. Priestly vessels.
　　　　Æ, 25.22 gm. ↑.

In AD 196 Severus adopted himself into the Antonine dynasty, appropriating the name Pius to himself and entitling his son Caracalla, now made Caesar, Marcus Aurelius Antoninus.

687   Denarius Lyons, AD 196–197

Obv. IMP CAES D CLO SEP ALB AVG. Head, laureate, r.
Rev. GEN LVG COS II. Genius, naked and turreted, standing l., holding sceptre and cornucopiae. Æ, 2.85 gm. ↓.

After the break with Severus, Albinus, proclaimed by his troops in Britain, adopted the title of Augustus, and established himself at Lyons where his coinage was struck, as this reverse confirms.

688   Denarius Lyons, AD 196–197

Obv. As No. 687.
Rev. FIDES LEGION COS II. Clasped hands holding legionary eagle. Æ, 3.17 gm. ↑.

The reverse type honours the British legions which formed Albinus' support.

689   As Lyons, AD 196–197

Obv. As No. 687.
Rev. FORTVNAE REDVCI COS II. Fortuna seated l., holding rudder on globe and cornucopiae. Æ, 14.06 gm. ↓.

The formula s c of the *aes* coinage of the mint of Rome is absent. The authenticity of this formerly unique coin was for long disputed, but a second example from the same dies was found in excavations at the Roman fort of Housesteads on Hadrian's Wall in 1962.

690   Aureus Rome, AD 197

Obv. L SEPT SEV PERT AVG IMP VIIII. Bust, laureate, draped, cuirassed, r.
Rev. PM TR P V; in ex., COS II P P. Sol, radiate, naked, mounting quadriga ascending r.; to r., Aurora holding torch in both hands; on ground r., Tellus reclining l., raising r. hand, and holding cornucopiae. Ν, 7.78 gm. ↑.

Severus' ninth imperatorial acclamation marked his victory over Clodius Albinus.

691   Denarius Laodicea-ad-Mare, AD 197

Obv. L SEPT SEV PERT AVG IMP VIIII. Head, laureate, r.
Rev. P M TR P V COS II P P. Sol, radiate, naked, standing l., raising r. hand, and holding whip in l. Æ, 3.11 gm. ↑.

Coins of this non-Roman style are attributed to an eastern mint, probably at Laodicea-ad-Mare in Syria.

692   Aureus Rome, AD 197–198

Obv. M AVR ANTON CAES PONTIF. Bust, head bare, draped, cuirassed, r.
Rev. PRINCIPI IVVENTVTIS. Caracalla, in military dress, standing l., holding baton and legionary eagle; to r., trophy of arms. Ν, 7.44 gm. ↑.

The further advancement of Caracalla is recorded with the titles of Pontifex and Princeps Iuventutis, the latter the traditional title of the heir-apparent.

693 Denarius Laodicea-ad-Mare, AD 197–198

Obv. As No. 692.
Rev. As No. 692. Æ, 2.98 gm. ↑.
Caracalla's new honours were also recorded on coinage marked by its style as of eastern mintage.

Septimius Severus and Caracalla, AD198–209

694 Denarius Rome, AD 198

Obv. IMP CAES M AVR ANTON AVG. Bust, laureate, draped, r.
Rev. IVVENTA IMPERII. Caracalla, in military dress, standing l., holding Victory in r. hand, and spear in l.; at foot l., captive seated l. Æ, 2.43 gm. ↓.
This type in the first coinage of Caracalla as Augustus when he was only ten, appropriately designates him *iuventa*, a rare synonym for *iuventus*.

695 Aureus Laodicea-ad-Mare, AD 198

Obv. L SEPT SEV AVG IMP XI PART MAX. Bust, laureate, draped, cuirassed, r.
Rev. VICTORIA AVGG. Victory advancing l., holding wreath and palm. N, 7.06 gm. ↑.
On the successful conclusion of the second Parthian war with the capture of Ctesiphon Severus was accorded the title of Parthicus Maximus.

696 Aureus Rome, AD 199

Obv. P SEPT GETA CAES PONT. Bust, head bare, draped, cuirassed, r.
Rev. SEVERI INVICTI AVG PII FIL. Bust of young Sol (Geta), radiate, cuirassed, with aegis, l., raising r. hand. N, 7.09 gm. ↑.
On the appointment of Caracalla as Augustus, Severus' younger son, Geta, was appointed Caesar.

697 Aureus Rome, AD 201

Obv. SEVERVS AVG PART MAX. Head, laureate, r.
Rev. AETERNIT IMPERI. Confronted busts of Caracalla, laureate, draped, cuirassed, r., and Geta, head bare, draped, cuirassed, l. N, 7.13 gm. ↓.
One of a number of types emphasising the permanence of the dynasty now that Geta had been appointed Caesar.

698 Aureus Rome, AD 201

Obv. SEVERVS PIVS AVG P M TR P VIIII. Head, laureate, r.
Rev. FELICITAS SAECVLI. Bust of Julia Domna, draped, facing, between busts of Caracalla, laureate, draped, cuirassed, r., and Geta, head bare, draped, l. N, 7.55 gm. ↓.
Another part of the dynastic issue showing the whole imperial family.

699 **Aureus** Rome, AD 201

Obv. IMP INVICTI PII AVGG. Busts, jugate r., of Severus and Caracalla, both laureate, draped, and cuirassed.
Rev. VICTORIA PARTHICA MAXIMA. Victory running l., holding wreath and palm. *N*, 7.22 gm. ↑.

This coin is both part of the dynastic issue, and a commemoration of Severus' Parthian victory.

700 **Aureus** Laodicea-ad-Mare, AD 201

Obv. ANTONINVS AVG PONT TR P IIII. Bust, laureate, draped, cuirassed, with aegis, r.
Rev. VICTORIAE AVGG. Victory running l., holding wreath and palm. *N*, 7.18 gm. ↑.

The coin appears by style to be of eastern mintage. The Parthian victory is celebrated on this issue also.

701 **Aureus** Rome, AD 202

Obv. PLAVTILLA AVGVSTA. Bust, draped, r.
Rev. CONCORDIA AVGG. Concordia, draped, seated r., holding patera and double cornucopiae; her feet rest on stool. *N*, 7.65 gm. ↑.

Coinage was issued in honour of Plautilla, daughter of the Praetorian prefect, Plautianus, to whom Caracalla was married after the return of the emperors from the eastern war.

702 **Aureus** Rome, AD 203

Obv. SEVERVS PIVS AVG. Bust, laureate, draped, cuirassed, r.
Rev. INDVLGENTIA AVGG IN CARTH. Dea Caelestis with high head-dress, draped, seated facing on lion, running r.; to l., water gushing from rocks; she sets r. hand on drum, and holds sceptre in l. *N*, 7.06 gm. ↑.

The type records some imperial benefit conferred on Carthage, the capital of Africa, the emperor's native province. The details suggest improvement of the water supply but there is no specific record of this.

703 **Aureus** Rome, *c.*AD 205

Obv. IVLIA AVGVSTA. Bust, draped, r.
Rev. MATER AVGG. Cybele seated on throne set on car, drawn l. by four lions, holding branch in r. hand, and resting l. on drum. *N*, 7.06 gm. ↑.

The empress, Julia Domna, the mother of two imperial sons, is identified here with Cybele, Magna Mater.

704 **Sestertius** Rome, AD 204

Obv. ANTONINVS PIVS AVG PONT TR P VII. Bust, laureate, draped, cuirassed, r.

Rev. COS LVD SAEC FEC S C. Caracalla, veiled, togate, standing r., sacrificing over lighted and garlanded altar; to r., Liber, standing l., pouring libation on altar from cup and holding thyrsus, accompanied by Hercules, standing l., resting r. hand on club, and holding lion-skin over l. arm; to r. front, *victimarius* and sow standing l.; to l., Tellus reclining l., holding reeds in l. hand, and resting r. arm on urn; behind altar, flute-player facing. Æ, 22.79 gm. ↑.

The reverse depicts one of the ceremonial sacrifices associated with the Saecular Games which were celebrated in this year.

705   Aureus Rome, *c.*AD 206

Obv. ANTONINVS PIVS AVG. Bust, laureate, draped, cuirassed, r.

Rev. LAETITIA TEMPORVM. Ship to l; in field above, two small quadrigae on l., two on r.; behind ship, cock, lion, panther, stag, bull and two bears. N, 7.35 gm. ↑.

The type clearly refers to a wild beast show in the arena. The obverse portrait of Caracalla suggests a date later than the festival celebrating the return of the emperors from the east in 202.

706   Aureus Rome, AD 206

Obv. SEVERVS PIVS AVG. Head, laureate, r.

Rev. P P COS III. View of building, possibly the Circus; on front, central archway flanked by complex of arches and a doorway; inside, groups of wrestlers and runners, with, at r., presiding figure, seated r. N, 7.40 gm. ↓.

This coin also may picture part of the celebrations for the return of Severus and Caracalla from the Parthian war, but seems to form part of a later issue.

707   Denarius Rome, AD 208

Obv. SEVERVS PIVS AVG. Head, laureate, r.

Rev. AFRICA. Africa, wearing elephant-skin head-dress, draped, r., r. hand at side and holding scorpion in l.; at feet r., lion standing r. Æ, 4.28 gm. ↑.

The type suggests a possible imperial visit to Africa, the native province of Severus.

708   Sestertius Rome, AD 208.

Obv. L SEPT SEVERVS PIVS AVG. Head, laureate, r.

Rev. P M TR P XVI PROF AVGG S C. Severus, holding spear sloping upwards, on horse pacing r.; in front, on r., soldier, holding spear and shield, standing r., head turned back l.; behind, to l., second soldier, standing r., holding transverse spear; head and shoulders of third soldier above rump of horse. Æ, 30.74 gm. ↑.

The reverse records the departure of Severus from Rome to take command of the war in Britain.

709 **As** Rome, AD 208

Obv. As No. 706.
Rev. P M TR P XVI COS III P P S C. Bridge, with five figures crossing, between two triumphal arches with three arches below and statuary on top; below, boat on river. Æ, 9.43 gm. ↑.

The coin is dated to the beginning of the war in Britain, but the bridge seems too elaborate to represent a campaign structure.

Septimius Severus, Caracalla and Geta, AD209–211

710 **Sestertius** Rome, AD 209

Obv. M AVREL ANTONINVS PIVS AVG. Head, laureate, r., with drapery on l. shoulder.
Rev. VICTORIAE BRITTANNICAE S C. Two Victories standing l. and r., placing round shield on palm-tree; at foot of palm, two captives seated l. and r., hands tied behind back. Æ, 22.67 gm. ↑.

The success of the Roman campaign into Scotland was celebrated by a variety of Victory types.

711 **Sestertius** Rome, AD 210

Obv. IMP CAES P SEPT GETA PIVS AVG. Head, laureate, r.
Rev. PONTIF TR P II COS II S C. Caracalla and Geta standing l., holding spears in l. hand; to r., two soldiers standing l., holding standards; between emperors, third soldier just visible; at foot l., captive with bound hands seated r. Æ, 28.35 gm. ↑.

Another military type connected with the war in Britain shows Geta also as an Augustus, the rank to which he had been advanced in 209.

712 **Aureus** Rome, AD 210

Obv. ANTONINVS PIVS AVG. Head, laureate, r.
Rev. PONTIF TR P XIII COS III. Caracalla advancing r., head l., holding spear and shield, and raising kneeling woman in turreted crown. N, 7.53 gm. ↓.

The reverse records the restoration of the province of Britain effected by the successful military campaigns, but the female figure with the turreted crown may refer to the city of Eboracum (York), the imperial military headquarters.

713 **Aureus** Rome, AD 210–211

Obv. SEVERVS PIVS AVG BRIT. Head, laureate, r.
Rev. VICTORIAE BRIT. Victory with wreath and palm, advancing l. N, 7.48 gm. ↓.

After victories in Britain the honorific Britannicus was added to the titulature of Severus and his two sons.

Caracalla and Geta, AD211–212

714 Aureus Rome, AD 211

Obv. DIVO SEVERO PIO. Head, bare, r.
Rev. CONSECRATIO. Funeral pyre of four tiers on base; on top, facing quadriga. N, 7.21 gm. ↑.
Part of the consecration coinage of Severus, deified after his death at York in 211.

715 Sestertius Rome, AD 211

Obv. M AVREL ANTONINVS PIVS AVG BRIT. Head, laureate, r.
Rev. FORT RED P M TR P XII COS III P P S C. Fortuna holding rudder and cornucopiae, seated l. on throne; below throne, wheel. Æ, 24.59 gm. ↑.
The type of Fortuna Redux relates to the return to Rome of Caracalla, together with Geta, immediately following the death of Severus in Britain.

716 Aureus Rome, AD 211

Obv. P SEPT GETA PIVS AVG BRIT. Bust, laureate, r., with drapery on l. shoulder.

Rev. TR P III COS II P P. Geta, in military dress, standing l., holding parazonium and spear, and setting r. foot on Britannia, reclining r. N, 7.32 gm. ↓.
One of the last of the types with reference to the successful conclusion of the war in Britain.

Caracalla, AD211–217

717 Aureus Rome, AD 213

Obv. ANTONINVS PIVS FEL AVG. Bust, laureate, draped, cuirassed, r.
Rev. VICTORIA GERMANICA. Victory running r., holding wreath and trophy. N, 7.15 gm. ↑.
The coin records Caracalla's success in war against the Germans, and probably in recognition of this Caracalla added *Felix* to his titulature in this year.

718 Sestertius Rome, AD 213

Obv. M AVREL ANTONINVS PIVS AVG BRIT. Head, laureate, r.
Rev. P M TR P XVI IMP II COS IIII P P S C. Circus Maximus; in front, arcade of arches; to l., quadriga r. on arch; at back, temple, colonnade, and arch surmounted by quadriga; to r., gallery with spectators; in centre, *spina* and three quadrigae driving l. Æ, 30.37 gm. ↑.
The reverse records rebuilding of parts of the Circus by Caracalla.

719 Sestertius Rome, AD 213

Obv. IVLIA PIA FELIX AVG. Bust, draped, r.
Rev. IVNO S C. Juno standing front, head l.,
holding patera and sceptre; to l., peacock l.
Æ, 21.91 gm. ↑.
The coinage of Julia Domna in this period has *Felix*
added to her titulature.

720 Antoninianus Rome, AD 215

Obv. ANTONINVS PIVS AVG GERM. Bust, radiate,
draped, cuirassed, r.
Rev. P M TR P XVIII COS IIII P P. Minos, seated l.,
extending r. hand, and holding sceptre in l.;
at foot l., Minotaur standing front.
Æ, 5.20 gm. ↑.
An example of the new silver denomination,
probably tariffed as a double denarius, but by
weight one-and-a-half denarii, introduced in this
year. The radiate crown distinguished this
denomination from the denarius. The reverse of
Minos makes its first appearance on the Roman
coinage.

721 Antoninianus Rome, AD 215

Obv. As No. 720.
Rev. P M TR P XVIII COS IIII P P. Sol, naked but for
cloak flying behind him, holding reins and
whip, mounting quadriga l. Æ, 5.17 gm. ↑.
This is one of the early appearances of Sol who was
to figure prominently on much of the third century
coinage.

722 Antoninianus Rome, AD 215

Obv. IVLIA PIA FELIX AVG. Bust, draped, r., on
crescent.
Rev. LVNA LVCIFERA. Luna, with drapery in circle
round head, standing l. in biga l., holding
reins. Æ, 5.06 gm. ↑.
In coinage for imperial ladies this denomination was
marked by placing the bust on a crescent. The
reverse type of Luna for Julia Domna parallels the
Sol type used by Caracalla.

723 Aureus Rome, AD 215

Obv. ANTONINVS PIVS AVG GERM. Bust, laureate,
draped, cuirassed, r.
Rev. P M TR P XVIII COS IIII P P. Caracalla standing
l., sacrificing out of patera over altar, and
accompanied by attendant standing l.,
holding roll; to l., Aesculapius standing r.,
placing r. hand on serpent-wreathed wand,
and accompanied by boy attendant standing
r., holding staff over shoulder; behind,
temple of four columns. N, 7.28 gm. ↑.
Herodian records that Caracalla, suffering ill-
health, visited Pergamum the great seat of
Aesculapius, the god of healing.

724 Aureus Rome, AD 215

Obv. As No. 723, but bust l.
Rev. P M TR P XVIII COS IIII P P. Sol, naked but for
cloak over l. arm, standing front, head l.,
raising r. hand, and holding globe in l.
N, 6.62 gm. ↓.
Another example of Sol imagery, on a gold coin.

725 Sestertius Rome, AD 215

Obv. M AVREL ANTONINVS PIVS AVG GERM. Bust, laureate, draped, cuirassed, r.

Rev. P M TR P XVIII IMP III COS IIII P P S C. Caracalla standing l., r. foot on crocodile, l.; he holds vertical spear reversed in l. hand, and extends r. to Isis, advancing r.; she holds corn-ears and sistrum. Æ, 25.72 gm. ↑.

Isis greeting the emperor is a reference to Caracalla's visit to Egypt in this year. The crocodile under the emperor's foot is probably an allusion to riots in Alexandria suppressed with great ferocity.

726 Double aureus Rome, AD 216

Obv. ANTONINVS PIVS AVG GERM. Bust, radiate, draped, cuirassed, r.

Rev. P M TR P XVIIII COS IIII P P. Jupiter seated l., holding Victory and sceptre; at foot l., eagle standing l., head r. N, 13.02 gm. ↓.

The radiate crown used to distinguish the antoninianus (cf. No. 720) was now also used to mark the double aureus.

727 Aureus Rome, AD 217

Obv. As No. 726, but laureate.

Rev. P M TR P XX COS IIII P P VICT PART. Victory seated r. on cuirass, inscribing VOT / XX on shield set on knee; to r., trophy and two captives, wearing robes and peaked caps, seated l. and r. N, 6.40 gm. ↑.

By an act of deception Caracalla defeated the Parthians and sacked Ctesiphon in 217, in which year he entered his twentieth year as Augustus, marked here by the mention of his *vota vicennalia*.

Macrinus, AD217–218

728 Aureus Rome, AD 217

Obv. IMP C M OPEL SEV MACRINVS AVG. Bust, laureate, draped, cuirassed, r.

Rev. VOTA PVBL P M TR P. Securitas seated l., holding sceptre, and supporting head on l. hand, elbow set on top of throne; at foot l., altar. N, 6.47 gm. ↑.

The vows are those for the accession of the new emperor. Securitas is only one of a number of types shown accompanied by this reverse inscription.

729 Antoninianus Rome, AD 217

Obv. As No. 728, but radiate.

Rev. IOVI CONSERVATORI. Jupiter, naked but for cloak on shoulders, standing front, head l., holding thunderbolt and sceptre; at foot l., Macrinus standing l. Æ, 5.83 gm. ↑.

The antoninianus introduced by Caracalla was continued by Macrinus, but apparently only in the early coinage.

730 Aureus Rome, AD 217

Obv. As No. 728.
Rev. LIBERALITAS AVG. Macrinus and
Diadumenian seated l. on platform,
extending r. hands and holding rolls; on r.,
officer standing l.; on l., Liberalitas standing
l., holding abacus and cornucopiae; at foot
of steps, citizen standing r. N, 6.82 gm. ↓.

The coin records the largesse distributed at the
beginning of the reign. The portrait with longer
beard as here has been thought to mark the coinage
of a mint at Antioch, but more properly
distinguishes later coins of the Rome mint.

731 Aureus Rome, AD 217–218

Obv. M OPEL ANT DIADVMENIANVS CAES. Bust,
draped, head bare, r.
Rev. PRINC IVVENTVTIS. Diadumenian standing
front, head r., holding legionary eagle and
sceptre; to r., legionary eagle and standard.
N, 7.11 gm. ↑.

The reverse shows Diadumenian as *Princeps
Iuventutis*, the traditional title of the heir.

732 Denarius Rome, AD 218

Obv. IMP C M OPEL ANT DIADVMENIAN AVG. Bust,
laureate, draped, cuirassed, r.
Rev. FELICITAS TEMPORVM. Felicitas standing l.,
holding cornucopiae and long caduceus.
Æ, 3.33 gm. ↑.

The rarity of the coinage of Diadumenian as
Augustus suggests that he was advanced to this rank
only shortly before the overthrow of Macrinus.

Elagabalus, AD218–222

733 Antoninianus Rome, AD 218–219

Obv. IMP CAES M AVR ANTONINVS AVG. Bust,
radiate, draped, cuirassed, r.
Rev. FIDES EXERCITVS. Fides seated l., holding
eagle on r. hand and standard in l.; to l., a
standard. Æ, 5.37 gm. ↑.

This denomination was issued by Elagabalus but
was apparently discontinued in 219. The reverse
type reflects the fact that the elevation of Elagabalus
was owed to the army.

734 Aureus Rome, AD 218–219

Obv. IVLIA MAESA AVG. Bust, draped, head bare, r.
Rev. IVNO. Juno, wearing stephane, standing l.,
holding patera and sceptre. N, 6.38 gm. ↑.

Julia Maesa, the emperor's grandmother, is credited
with the organisation of his proclamation and the
conduct of policy. Coinage was struck for her
throughout the reign.

735 Antoninianus Rome, AD 218–219

Obv. IVLIA MAESA AVG. Bust, wearing stephane,
draped r., set on crescent.
Rev. PIETAS AVG. Pietas standing l., dropping
incense on altar and holding open box in l.
hand. Æ, 5.66 gm. ↓.

Julia Maesa is the only one of the imperial ladies to
appear on this denomination early in the reign.

736 Aureus Rome, AD 219

Obv. IMP ANTONINVS PIVS AVG. Bust, laureate,
    draped, cuirassed, r.
Rev. CONSERVATOR AVG. Car drawn l. by four
    horses, carrying conical stone, surmounted
    by eagle standing front, head l.; in field high
    l., star. N, 6.56 gm. ↑.
The coin depicts the triumphal entry to Rome of
the god Ba'al of Emesa in the form of a conical stone
(*baetyl*), on the occasion of Elagabalus' arrival in
Rome late in 219.

737 Aureus Rome, AD 220

Obv. IVLIA SOAEMIAS AVGVSTA. Bust, draped, head
    bare, r.
Rev. IVNO REGINA. Juno, veiled and wearing
    stephane, standing r., holding sceptre and
    palladium. N, 7.24 gm. ↑.
Coinage for Julia Soaemias, the emperor's mother,
on the evidence of the dated tetradrachms from
Alexandria, was issued only in the last two years of
the reign.

738 Sestertius Rome, AD 219

Obv. IVLIA PAVLA AVG. Bust, draped, head bare, r.
Rev. CONCORDIA S C. Concordia draped, seated l.,
    holding patera and double cornucopiae; in
    field high l., star. Æ, 25.07 gm. ↑.
A portrait of the first of Elagabalus' three wives,
whom he married in 219.

739 Sestertius Rome, AD 220

Obv. IVLIA AQVILIA SEVERA AVG. Bust draped,
    wearing stephane, r.
Rev. CONCORDIA S C. Concordia standing l.,
    sacrificing out of patera over altar, and
    holding double cornucopiae; in field r., star.
    Æ, 26.15 gm. ↑.
Elagabalus married Aquilia Severa, a Vestal Virgin
in 220. Though soon dismissed in favour of a new
bride she was taken back into favour the following
year.

740 Sestertius Rome, AD 221

Obv. ANNIA FAVSTINA AVGVSTA. Bust, draped,
    wearing stephane, r.
Rev. CONCORDIA S C. Elagabalus standing r. and
    Annia Faustina standing l., clasping hands;
    in centre field, star. Æ, 25.27 gm. ↑.
A portrait of the third of Elagabalus' wives, a
member of the house of Marcus Aurelius. The
marriage in 221 was soon annulled and Aquilia
Severa restored.

741 Denarius Rome, AD 221–222

Obv. IMP ANTONINVS PIVS AVG. Bust, laureate,
    draped, cuirassed r., with small horn above
    forehead.

Rev. SACER DEI SOLIS ELAGABAL. Elagabalus, veiled, standing r., sacrificing out of patera over altar, and holding horn; in field r., star. Æ, 3.16 gm. ↓.

The reverse shows the emperor in his role as priest of the cult of the sun god, Ba'al or Elagabalus. The horn of divine power placed just above the forehead is a feature of the portrait on the late coinage of Elagabalus.

742 **Aureus** Antioch, AD 218–219

Obv. IMP C M AVG ANTONINVS PIVS AVG. Bust, laureate, draped, cuirassed, r.

Rev. SANCT DEO SOLI ELAGABAL. Car, drawn r. by four horses, carrying conical stone surmounted by eagle; about it, four parasols. Æ, 7.34 gm. ↑.

Coinage in gold and silver with a portrait style unlike that of Rome is attributed to an eastern mint, most probably Antioch. The reverse (cf. No. 736) may show the departure of the cult-stone from Emesa to accompany the emperor to Rome.

743 **Denarius** Antioch, AD 219

Obv. IMP ANTONINVS AVG. Bust, laureate, draped, cuirassed, r.

Rev. LIBERALITAS AVG II. Liberalitas standing l., holding abacus in r. hand, and resting l. arm on cornucopiae set on globe. Æ, 2.91 gm. ↑.

The second largesse of the reign was probably dispensed on the occasion of the emperor's marriage to Julia Paula.

Severus Alexander, AD222–235

744 **Aureus** Rome, AD 222

Obv. IMP C M AVR SEV ALEXAND AVG. Bust, laureate, draped, cuirassed, r.

Rev. P M TR P COS P P. Severus Alexander, laureate and togate, standing in quadriga l., holding branch and reins in r. hand, and eagle-tipped sceptre in l. Æ, 6.25 gm. ↓.

On the reverse of this coin, part of the proclamation issue, the emperor is shown in the consular procession.

745 **Sestertius** Rome, AD 223

Ob. IMP CAES M AVR SEV ALEXANDER AVG. Bust, laureate, draped, cuirassed, r.

Rev. PONTIF MAX TR P II COS P P S C. View of the Colosseum; to l., Severus Alexander standing l., sacrificing out of patera over altar; behind him, another figure; to r., shrine in two storeys. Æ, 22.36 gm. ↑.

The Colosseum, damaged by lightning in the previous reign, was one of several buildings repaired under Severus Alexander.

746   Aureus Rome, AD 225

Obv. SALL BARBIA ORBIANA AVG. Bust, draped,
wearing stephane, r.
Rev. CONCORDIA AVGVSTORVM. Concordia seated
l., holding patera and double cornucopiae.
₦, 6.86 gm. ↓.

A rare and brief coinage in this year celebrated the
marriage of the emperor to Orbiana.

747   As Rome, AD 226

Obv. IMP CAES M AVR SEV ALEXANDER AVG. Bust,
laureate, draped, cuirassed, r.
Rev. P M TR P V COS II P P S C. View of the
Nymphaeum. Above, façade with three
arches containing statuary; on roof, facing
quadriga in centre, with pieces of statuary l.
and r.; below, building with arches and
projecting wings l. and r., surmounted by
statue; in front of building, semicircular
wall. Æ, 11.50 gm. ↓.

748   Aureus Rome, AD 226

Obv. IVLIA MAMAEA AVG. Bust, draped, wearing
stephane, r.
Rev. VESTA. Vesta, veiled, standing l., holding
palladium and sceptre. ₦, 6.31 gm. ↑.

Coinage for Julia Mamaea, the emperor's mother,
was issued throughout the reign. In each issue one of
the six officinae of the mint was allocated to her
coinage.

749   Denarius Rome, AD 228

Obv. IMP C M AVR SEV ALEXAND AVG. Bust,
laureate, draped, cuirassed, r.
Rev. PERPETVITATI AVG. Perpetuitas standing l.,
holding globe and sceptre, and resting l. arm
on column. Æ, 2.75 gm. ↓.

This is the first instance in the imperial coinage of
the personification of Perpetuitas who, with her
attributes of globe and sceptre, suggests the
permanency of imperial rule.

750   Medallion Rome, AD 228

Obv. IVLIA MAMAEA AVGVSTA. Bust, winged and
draped, seen to waist, r., wearing stephane
ornamented with ears of corn, and necklace;
behind neck, a crescent; on r. arm she holds
cornucopiae, and in l. hand torch with ears
of corn; cloak over l. arm.
Rev. FELICITAS PERPETVA. Julia Mamaea, wearing
stephane, seated l., feet on footstool, holding
sceptre in l. hand, and accepting in r., apple
presented by female figure, standing r.; to r.,
Felicitas standing l., holding caduceus; in
centre, female figure standing facing.
Æ, 47.40 gm. ↑.

This remarkable portrait is an unusual example of
syncretism showing Julia Mamaea with the
identifiable attributes of at least Victory and Ceres.

751 Dupondius Rome, AD 228

Obv. IMP SEV ALEXANDER AVG. Head, radiate, r.
Rev. RESTITVTOR MON S C. Severus Alexander
  standing l., extending r. hand, and holding
  spear in l. Æ, 12.86 gm. ↑.
Since there is no reform of the coinage to which the
reverse could allude, the reference probably is to
some rebuilding of the mint by Severus Alexander,
not otherwise recorded.

752 Denarius Rome, AD 230

Obv. IMP SEV ALEXAND AVG. Head, laureate, r.
Rev. ABVNDANTIA AVG. Abundantia standing r.,
  emptying fruits from cornucopiae held in
  both hands. Æ, 2.91 gm. ↓.
The somewhat unusual reverse type may refer to
the provision of some extra corn-dole.

753 Sestertius Rome, AD 230

Obv. As No. 752, but ALEXANDER.
Rev. P M TR P VIIII COS III P P S C. Sol, naked but for
  cloak over shoulders, standing front, head l.,
  raising r. hand, and holding globe in l.
  Æ, 30.57 gm. ↑.
This remarkably fine coin was struck on an unusually wide flan.

754 Sestertius Rome, AD 231

Obv. IMP SEV ALEXANDER AVG. Bust, laureate,
  draped, cuirassed, r., seen from front.
Rev. PROFECTIO AVGVSTI S C. Severus Alexander,
  holding spear in r. hand, on horseback r.,
  preceded by Victory holding wreath.
  Æ, 23.96 gm. ↑.
This semi-medallic sestertius records the emperor's
departure for the Persian War.

755 Denarius Antioch, AD 222

Obv. IMP SEV ALEXAND AVG. Bust, laureate,
  draped, cuirassed, r.
Rev. P M TR P COS. Fortuna standing l., holding
  rudder on globe and cornucopiae; star in
  field, high l. Æ, 3.17 gm. ↓.
Early denarii differing from those of the Rome mint
in portrait style, form of obverse inscription, and
presence of star in the reverse field, are attributed to
an eastern mint.

756 Denarius Antioch, AD 223

Obv. IMP C M AVR SEV ALEXAND AVG. Bust,
  laureate, draped, cuirassed, r.
Rev. NOBILITAS. Nobilitas standing r., holding
  sceptre and palladium. Æ, 3.31 gm. ↓.
Slightly later coins of the eastern mint conform to
the obverse titulature in use at Rome. The reverse,
Nobilitas, makes one of its rare appearances here.

7 The Military Emperors
AD235-270

The mid-third century was a period of crisis, politically, militarily and financially. It was marked by a succession of short-lived emperors and usurpers proclaimed and deposed by military groups, and the only reign of appreciable duration was that of Gallienus (AD 253–268). In the West a successful revolt under Postumus in 260 established a separate Gallic empire which controlled Spain and Britain as well, and lasted down to 274. In the East Valerian I was captured at Edessa by the invading Sassanians under Shapur in 260. The Sassanian invasion was repelled with the help of Odenathus of Palmyra, but subsequently much of the Roman East came under his control and later of his widow, Zenobia; Roman sovereignty was only re-established by Aurelian.

One consequence of these events was the establishment of mints at a number of provincial centres. In the East a mint at Antioch was active from the time of Gordian III, and a second eastern mint was set up by Valerian I, probably at Cyzicus. A second mint in the West was opened also by Valerian but its precise identification has not been settled. This mint was subsequently transferred by Gallienus about 257 to Gaul, probably to Trier, and part of its organisation was moved to establish a mint at Milan around 259. In the Balkans a new mint was established at Siscia by Gallienus in 262. On the coinage issued in connection with the celebration of Rome's millennium in 248 the reverses of the antoniniani were marked with the Roman numerals I–VI, or the Greek numerals A–ϛ, of the six officinae of the Rome mint. With increasing regularity from this time, both at Rome and at the other mints, the officina number became a feature of the reverse.

The coinage underwent considerable modification in this period, not so much as regards the formal system, but in respect of weight and fineness. The aureus of 6.54 gm. of the late Severan period was reduced by Balbinus and Pupienus to 5.75 gm., by Gordian III to some 4.86 gm., and by the reign of Trajan Decius to 4 gm. Under Trebonianus Gallus and Volusian the aureus declined to 3.60 gm. but was accompanied by a heavier aureus, averaging 5.75 gm. and distinguished by a radiate obverse. By the beginning of Gallienus' sole reign the radiate gold piece had fallen to about 4.50 gm.,

while his laureate gold declined from 2.50 gm. to around 1.10 gm. His late gold with reed-crowned obverse has two successive groups of about 6 gm. and 3.20 gm. Under Claudius II the aureus was re-established at an average of 5.20 gm. The antoninianus, re-introduced by Balbinus and Pupienus at a reduced weight of 4.75 gm., became the standard silver denomination, for the denarius after Gordian III became a rare denomination. The antoninianus underwent a continuous diminution in weight and fineness until under Trajan Decius antoniniani are commonly found overstruck on earlier, mostly Severan, denarii. Under Decius the fineness of the antoninianus was about 40%, but by 266 under Gallienus it had fallen to 5% and by the end of his reign to as low as 2.5%. The weight of bronze denominations also fell, the sestertius from about 23 gm. to 20 gm., and the dupondius and *as* from 11.50 gm. to 10 gm. The use of orichalcum for the sestertius and dupondius ceased, and all bronze denominations were struck in leaded bronze. A new denomination, the double sestertius, was issued by Trajan Decius and Etruscilla at a weight of 41 gm., and Decius also revived the semis at a weight of 4.50 gm. The series of bronzes with the traditional s c mark came to an end in the early years of Gallienus' sole reign.

Maximinus, AD235-238

757 Aureus Rome, AD 235

Obv. IMP MAXIMINVS PIVS AVG. Bust, laureate, draped, cuirassed, r.
Rev. PAX AVGVSTI. Pax standing l., holding branch and transverse sceptre. N, 656 gm. ↑.
The portrait on the first coinage of Maximinus is little more than a somewhat more bearded portrait of his predecessor, Severus Alexander.

758 **Sestertius** Rome, AD 236

Obv. As No. 757.
Rev. FIDES MILITVM S C. Fides standing l., holding
standard in each hand. Æ, 19.35 gm. ↑.
The portrait on the second issue is somewhat more
virile but still not completely realistic.

759 **Denarius** Rome, AD 236

Obv. IVL VERVS MAXIMVS CAES. Bust, draped, head
bare, r.
Rev. PIETAS AVG. Jug between lituus and knife to
l., and simpulum and sprinkler to r.
Æ, 3.10 gm. ↑.
The second issue included coinage for the emperor's
son, Maximus, as Caesar. This reverse is a standard
type for the coinage of the Caesar in the third
century.

760 **Denarius** Rome, AD 235–238

Obv. DIVA PAVLINA. Bust, veiled, draped, r.
Rev. CONSECRATIO. Paulina, raising r. hand, and
holding sceptre in l., seated l., on peacock
flying r. Æ, 3.08 gm. ↑.
The date of the consecration and this coinage of
Paulina, wife of Maximinus, is uncertain.

761 **Sestertius** Rome, AD 236–237

Obv. MAXIMINVS PIVS AVG GERM. Bust, laureate,
draped, cuirassed, r.
Rev. VICTORIA AVGVSTORVM S C. Maximinus
standing l., holding short sceptre in l. hand,
and Maximus, standing r., holding between
them small Victory; between them, two
captives seated facing each other; behind, on
either side, helmeted soldier, one to l.
holding spear, one to r. holding shield and
short sword. Æ, 18.04 gm. ↑.
The later coinage incorporates the title Germanicus
and is marked by a realistic portrait with jutting
chin.

762 **Sestertius** Rome, AD 236–238

Obv. MAXIMVS CAES GERM. Bust, draped, head
bare, r.
Rev. PRINCIPI IVVENTVTIS S C. Maximus standing
l., holding baton and spear; to r., two
standards. Æ, 22.49 gm. ↑.
Maximus is also accorded the honorific,
Germanicus. The reverse shows him as *Princeps
Iuventutis*, the standard title of the heir apparent.

Gordian I and Gordian II, AD238

763 Denarius Rome, AD 238

Obv. IMP M ANT GORDIANVS AFR AVG. Bust,
laureate, draped, cuirassed, r.
Rev. P M TR P COS P P. Gordian I standing l.,
holding branch and short sceptre.
AR, 2.77 gm. ↓.

The two Gordians, both father and son, have the
epithet Africanus in their obverse titulature. The
revolt which proclaimed them took place in Africa.
The portrait of the elder Gordian is distinguished by
thin features and low forehead.

764 Sestertius Rome, AD 238

Obv. As No. 763, but also CAES.
Rev. SECVRITAS AVGG S C. Securitas seated l.,
holding short sceptre. Æ, 18.37 gm. ↑.

765 Denarius Rome, AD 238

Obv. As No. 763, but Gordian II.
Rev. PROVIDENTIA AVGG. Providentia standing l.,
holding wand over globe in r. hand, and
resting l. arm on low column.
AR, 3.55 gm. ↓.

The portrait of the younger Gordian is distinguished by plumper features and a high forehead.

766 Sestertius Rome, AD 238

Obv. As No. 765, but also CAES.
Rev. ROMAE AETERNAE S C. Rome seated l.,
holding Victory on r. hand, and sceptre in
l.; oval shield in front of throne.
Æ, 23.98 gm. ↑.

Balbinus and Pupienus, AD238

767 Denarius Rome, AD 238

Obv. IMP C D CAEL BALBINVS AVG. Bust, laureate,
draped, cuirassed, r.
Rev. LIBERALITAS AVGVSTORVM. Liberalitas
standing l., holding abacus and cornucopiae.
AR, 2.39 gm. ↓.

Part of the proclamation coinage commemorates
the largesse distributed on the emperors' accession.

768   Medallion Rome, AD 238

Obv.   IMP CAES M CLOD PVPIENVS AVG. Bust,
laureate, mantled, l., holding Victory on
globe and parazonium.
Rev.   LIBERALITAS AVGVSTORVM. Balbinus,
Pupienus, and Gordian III seated l. on
platform, extending r. hands; behind them,
officer standing l., holding spear; in front,
Liberalitas, standing l., holding abacus and
cornucopiae; to l., citizen mounting steps of
platform. Æ, 50.15 gm. ↑.

A more elaborately designed component of the
same coinage as No. 767.

769   Sestertius Rome, AD 238

Obv.   As No. 767, but also CAES.
Rev.   PROVIDENTIA DEORUM S C. Providentia
standing l., holding wand over globe, and
cornucopiae. Æ, 20.79 gm. ↑.

770   Denarius Rome, AD 238

Obv.   IMP C M CLOD PVPIENVS AVG. Bust, laureate,
draped, cuirassed, r.

Rev.   CONCORDIA AVGG. Concordia seated l.,
holding patera and double cornucopiae.
Æ, 2.70 gm. ↓.

In the first coinage of the reign the only silver
denomination was the denarius.

771   Antoninianus Rome, AD 238

Obv.   IMP CAES D CAEL BALBINVS AVG. Bust, radiate,
draped, cuirassed, r.
Rev.   FIDES MVTVA AVGG. Clasped hands.
Æ, 5.02 gm. ↑.

In the second coinage of the reign the antoninianus
was re-introduced. The only type for both
emperors is that of clasped hands, accompanied for
each emperor by three varieties of inscription all,
with one exception (No. 773), expressing the theme
of harmony and concord.

772   Antoninianus Rome, AD 238

Obv.   IMP CAES M CLOD PVPIENVS AVG. Bust,
radiate, draped, cuirassed, r.
Rev.   AMOR MVTVA AVG. Clasped hands.
Æ, 4.42 gm. ↑.

773   Antoninianus Rome, AD 238

Obv.   IMP CAES PVPIEN MAXIMVS AVG. Bust, radiate,
draped, cuirassed, r.
Rev.   PATRES SENATVS. Clasped hands.
Æ, 4.80 gm. ↑.

Of the two emperors Pupienus uses a new form of
obverse inscription on his latest coinage. The
reverse inscription underlines the fact that the two
emperors were for once chosen by the Senate from
its own members.

774 Sestertius Rome, AD 238

Obv. As No. 773.
Rev. PAX PVBLICA S C. Pax seated l., holding
branch and sceptre. Æ, 21.33 gm. ↑.

775 Sestertius Rome, AD 238

Obv. M CAES GORDIANVS CAES. Bust, draped, head
bare, r.
Rev. PIETAS AVGG S C. Jug between lituus and
knife to l., and simpulum and sprinkler to r.
Æ, 16.81 gm. ↑.
The young Gordian, grandson of Gordian I, was
associated with the emperors as Caesar and heir
designate.

Gordian III, AD238–244

776 Antoninianus Rome, AD 238

Obv. IMP CAES M ANT GORDIANVS AVG. Bust,
radiate, draped, cuirassed, r.
Rev. FIDES MILITVM. Fides standing l., holding
standard and sceptre. Æ, 4.44 gm. ↑.
The antoninianus, re-introduced by his prede-
cessors, became from the time of Gordian III
onwards, the principal silver denomination.

777 Aureus Rome, AD 240

Obv. IMP GORDIANVS PIVS FEL AVG. Bust, laureate,
draped, cuirassed, r.
Rev. P M TR P III COS P P. Gordian on horseback r.,
raising r. hand and holding spear.
N, 5.24 gm. ↓.
The addition of *Felix* to the obverse titulature seems
to be connected with the suppression of a rising in
Africa in early 240.

778 Denarius Rome, AD 241

Obv. As No. 777.
Rev. VENVS VICTRIX. Venus stg. l., holding helmet
and sceptre and leaning on shield.
Æ, 3.03 gm. ↑.
The denarius in this reign tended to be struck
mainly as the silver denomination in issues
commemorating a special event, in this instance the
marriage of Gordian to Sabinia Tranquillina, the
daughter of the Praetorian Prefect Timistheus.

779 Denarius Rome, AD 241

Obv. SABINIA TRANQVILLINA AVG. Bust, draped and
wearing stephane, r.
Rev. CONCORDIA AVGG. Concordia seated l.,
holding patera and cornucopiae.
Æ, 2.51 gm. ↓.
The coinage of Tranquillina struck at Rome is quite
rare, though issues from provincial mints are more
plentiful. The types at Rome refer, as here, to her
marriage to Gordian.

780   Medallion Rome, AD 241–243

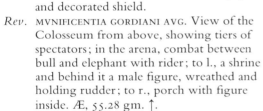

Obv. IMP GORDIANVS PIVS FELIX AVG. Bust, laureate, draped, cuirassed l., holding spear and decorated shield.

Rev. MVNIFICENTIA GORDIANI AVG. View of the Colosseum from above, showing tiers of spectators; in the arena, combat between bull and elephant with rider; to l., a shrine and behind it a male figure, wreathed and holding rudder; to r., porch with figure inside. Æ, 55.28 gm. ↑.

The type refers either to the emperor's generosity in presenting games or, possibly, in repairing the Colosseum.

781   Sestertius Rome, AD 243

Obv. As No. 780, but no spear and shield.

Rev. P M TR P VI COS II PP S C. Gordian, standing r., holding globe and spear. Æ, 27.61 gm. ↑.

782   As Rome, AD 243

Obv. As No. 781, but bust r.

Rev. VIRTVS AVGVSTI S C. Gordian seated l. on cuirass, holding spear and crowned by Victory, holding palm; to l., Virtus standing r., presenting branch; in centre, two standards. Æ, 9.36 gm. ↑.

The emperor left Rome in 242 for the Persian War. Only a few types such as this are connected with the campaign.

783   Antoninianus Rome, AD 243

Obv. IMP GORDIANVS PIVS FEL AVG. Bust, radiate, draped, cuirassed, r.

Rev. MARTEM PROPVGNATOREM. Mars advancing r., holding spear and shield. Æ, 4.49 gm. ↓.

Another of the few types which make reference to the Persian War. The reverse inscription is, unusually, in the accusative case, but the understood verb to be supplied is not obvious.

784   Antoninianus Antioch, AD 242–244

Obv. As No. 783.

Rev. ORIENS AVG. Sol standing l., raising r. hand, and holding globe. Æ, 4.11 gm. ↓.

An eastern mint, most probably Antioch, last active for Severus Alexander in 224, struck antoniniani for Gordian, distinguished by a distinctive stylistic treatment of the portrait, and a number of types not used at the Rome mint.

Philip I, AD244-249

785 Antoninianus Rome, AD 244

Obv. IMP M IVL PHILIPPVS AVG. Bust, radiate, draped, cuirassed, r.

Rev. LAET FVNDATA. Laetitia standing l., holding wreath and rudder. Æ, 4.58 gm. ↑.

As Philip was proclaimed in the East, the portrait on his first coinage from the Rome mint is more an older version of Gordian III than a realistic portrait. The epithet *fundata* is attached here for the first time to Laetitia to suggest the widespread joy at the acclamation of the new emperor.

786 Sestertius Rome, AD 245

Obv. M IVL PHILIPPVS CAES. Bust, draped, head bare, l.

Rev. PRINCIPI IVVENTVTIS S C. Philip II standing l., holding standard and reversed spear. Æ, 25.09 gm. ↑.

Philip II, appointed as Caesar by his father, has a reverse with the *princeps iuventutis* title of the heir-apparent.

787 Sestertius Rome, AD 245

Obv. MARCIA OTACIL SEVERA AVG. Bust, draped, and wearing stephane, r.

Rev. PVDICITIA AVG S C. Pudicitia veiled, seated l., holding out veil in r. hand, and sceptre in l. Æ, 22.91 gm. ↑.

Coinage for the empress, Otacilia Severa, formed a consistent part of each issue throughout the reign.

788 Medallion Rome, AD 245–247

Obv. IMP CAES M IVL PHILIPPVS AVG. Bust, laureate, draped, cuirassed, r.

Rev. AEQVITAS AVGG. The three Monetae standing facing, heads l., holding scales and cornucopiae; at foot l. by each, coin-dies (?). Æ, 20.38 gm. ↑.

The significance of this type on silver or billon medallions, struck with considerable consistency by third-century emperors, may have been to mark the authority of the emperor to strike in all three metals.

789 Antoninianus Rome, AD 247

Obv. IMP M IVL PHILIPPVS AVG. Bust of Philip II, radiate, draped, cuirassed, r.

Rev. AVG PATRI AVG MATRI. Bust of Philip I, laureate, draped, cuirassed r., facing bust of Otacilia, draped, and wearing stephane, l. Æ, 2.85 gm. ↓.

Part of a special 'family' coinage, probably on the occasion of the appointment of Philip II as Augustus.

790　Denarius Rome, AD 247

Obv. IMP PHILIPPVS AVG. Bust, laureate, draped, cuirassed, r.
Rev. AEQVITAS AVGG. Aequitas standing l., holding scales and cornucopiae. Æ, 3.04 gm. ↑.

To judge from its rarity, the denarius was now struck only infrequently. The shortened form of obverse inscription was used by Philip I from 247.

791　Medallion Rome, AD 247

Obv. CONCORDIA AVGVSTORVM. Jugate busts of Philip I, laureate, draped, cuirassed, r., and Otacilia, draped, and wearing stephane r., facing bust of Philip II, draped, head bare, l.
Rev. PONTIFEX MAX TR P IIII COS II P P. The two emperors in facing quadriga, Philip I holding laurel branch and crowned by Victory, holding palm, and Philip II extending r. hand; the two horses to l. are led by Roma, holding spear and palm; those to r. led by Mars, carrying palm, spear and shield. Æ, 89.50 gm. ↑.

The occasion of the medallion was the triumph celebrated by Philip I on his return to Rome in 247 after his victory over the Carpi.

792　Antoninianus Rome, AD 247

Obv. As No. 790, but radiate.

Rev. VICTORIA CARPICA. Victory advancing l., holding wreath and palm. Æ, 4.36 gm. ↓.

A specific reference to the victory over the Carpi.

793　Aureus Rome, AD 248

Obv. IMP PHILIPPVS AVG. Bust of Philip I, laureate, draped, cuirassed, r.
Rev. SAECVLARES AVGG. Column, inscribed COS III. Ν, 4.69 gm. ↑.

This, and the following four coins, form part of a special coinage issued in connection with the celebration of the Saecular Games in 248 to mark the thousandth anniversary of the foundation of Rome.

794　Aureus Rome, AD 248

Obv. OTACIL SEVERA AVG. Bust, draped, and wearing stephane, r.
Rev. SAECVLVM NOVVM. Hexastyle temple in which is statue of Roma. Ν, 4.51 gm. ↑.

See No. 793.

795　Antoninianus Rome, AD 248

Obv. As No. 792.
Rev. SAECVLARES AVGG. Lion r.; in exergue, I. Æ, 3.88 gm. ↑.

Coins of the several members of the imperial family have representations of the animals which featured in the games in the arena. The numeral in the exergue marks the coin as the product of the first officina. This series provides the first overt evidence that the mint of Rome at this period was organised in a system of six officinae.

796   Antoninianus Rome, AD 248

Obv. As No. 794, but Philip II.
Rev. As No. 794, but goat l., and in exergue, III.
    Æ, 3.79 gm. ↓.
See No. 795.

797   Antoninianus Rome, AD 248

Obv. As No. 793, but bust set on crescent.
Rev. As No. 794, but hippopotamus r., and in
    exergue, IIII. Æ, 4.23 gm. ↓.
See No. 795.

798   Antoninianus Rome, AD 248

Obv. As No. 794.
Rev. NOBILITAS AVGG. Nobilitas standing r.,
    holding sceptre and globe; in field l., ς.
    Æ, 4.22 gm. ↑.
In this issue the officinae are marked by Greek
numerals, here sigma for 6.

799   Antoninianus Rome, AD 248

Obv. As No. 795.
Rev. VIRTVS AVGG. Mars advancing l., holding
    trophy and spear; in field l., Γ.
    Æ, 4.15 gm. ↑.

800   Sestertius Rome, AD 248–249

Obv. IMP M IVL PHILIPPVS AVG. Bust of Philip I,
    laureate, draped, cuirassed, r.
Rev. AETERNITAS AVGG S C. Elephant ridden l. by
    mahout with goad and wand.
    Æ, 17.94 gm. ↑.
The idea of permanency is expressed here by the
type of the elephant, famous for its longevity.

801   Antoninianus Antioch, AD 248

Obv. IMP C M IVL PHILIPPVS AVG P M. Bust, radiate,
    draped, cuirassed, r.
Rev. PAX FVNDATA CVM PERSIS. Pax standing l.,
    holding branch and sceptre. Æ, 4.65 gm. ↑.
The coinage of antoniniani of the eastern mint is
distinguished from that of Rome by portrait style,
and the use of a longer form of obverse titulature,
including P M which here stands not for *pontifex
maximus* but *Persicus Maximus*, referring to the
recent Roman victory over the Persians, also
alluded to by the reverse.

Pacatian, AD248-249

802 **Antoninianus** Moesia, AD 248–249

Obv. IMP TI CL MAR PACATIANVS AVG. Bust, radiate, draped, cuirassed, r.
Rev. FORTVNA REDVX. Fortuna seated l., holding rudder and cornucopiae; to r., by seat, wheel. Æ, 4.65 gm. ↑.

The revolt of Pacatian in Moesia in 248 was suppressed by Trajan Decius the following year. The coinage is usually attributed to a mint at Viminacium, but it should be noted that this mint did not strike its usual provincial bronze coinage for Pacatian.

Jotapian, AD248-249

803 **Antoninianus** Syria, AD 248–249

Obv. IMP C M F RV IOTAPIANVS. Bust, radiate, draped, cuirassed, r.
Rev. VICTORIA AVG. Victory advancing l., holding wreath and palm. Æ, 3.88 gm. ↓.

A short-lived revolt in Syria against the extortionate government of Priscus, brother of the emperor Philip, was headed by Jotapian towards the end of Philip's reign.

Trajan Decius, AD249-251

804 **Aureus** Rome, AD 249

Obv. IMP TRAIANVS DECIVS AVG. Bust, laureate, draped, cuirassed, r.
Rev. GENIVS EXERCITVS ILLVRICANI. Genius standing l., holding patera and cornucopiae; to l., standard. Aʋ, 4.38 gm. ↑.

The simple form of obverse titulature was used on the coinage of the first issue. The reverse honours the Illyrian army which had proclaimed Decius emperor.

805 **Antoninianus** Rome, AD 249–251

Obv. IMP C M Q TRAIANVS DECIVS AVG. Bust, radiate, draped, cuirassed, r.
Rev. PANNONIAE. The two Pannoniae veiled, standing front, heads l. and r., respectively; Pannonia on l. holds standard in r. hand, Pannonia on r. holds standard in l. hand, and raises r. hand. Æ, 4.09 gm. ↑.

This reverse also pictures provinces in the area to which Decius owed his proclamation.

806 **Double sestertius** Rome, AD 249–251

Obv. As No. 805.
Rev. FELICITAS SAECVLI S C. Felicitas standing l.,
holding caduceus and cornucopiae.
Æ, 42.57 gm. ↑.
This novel large bronze denomination was
introduced in the coinage of Decius.

807   Semis Rome, AD 249–251

Obv. As No. 805, but laureate.
Rev. S C. Mars standing l., resting r. hand on
shield, and holding spear. Æ, 3.53 gm. ↑.
A very late instance of this small bronze
denomination.

808   Antoninianus Rome, AD 251

Obv. IMP CAE TRA DEC AVG. Bust, radiate, draped,
cuirassed, r.
Rev. DACIA FELIX. Dacia standing l., holding staff
surmounted by ass's head. Æ, 4.19 gm. ↑.
Coins with this obverse inscription, once attributed
to a second mint in the West, have now been
demonstrated to be only a late issue from Rome.

809   Aureus Rome, AD 249–251

Obv. HER ETRVSCILLA AVG. Bust, draped, and
wearing stephane, r.
Rev. PVDICITIA AVG. Pudicitia veiled, standing l.,
holding up veil in r. hand, and holding
sceptre in l. N, 3.90 gm. ↓.
Coinage for the empress, Etruscilla, formed a
regular part of the issues of this reign.

810   Double sestertius Rome, AD 249–251

Obv. HERENNIA ETRVSCILLA AVG. Bust draped, and
wearing stephane, r., set on crescent.
Rev. PVDICITIA AVG S C. As No. 809, but Pudicitia
seated l. Æ, 43.75 gm. ↓.
The double sestertius for the empress was
distinguished by the crescent on obverse in the same
manner as on the antoninianus.

811   Aureus Rome, AD 250–251

Obv. Q HER ETR MES DECIVS NOB C. Bust draped,
head bare, r.
Rev. PRINCIPI IVVENTVTIS. Herennius Etruscus
standing l., holding standard and spear.
N, 4.05 gm. ↓.
Decius appointed his elder son Caesar probably in
250.

812   Antoninianus Rome, AD 251

Obv. IMP C Q HER ETR MES DECIVS AVG. Bust,
radiate, draped, cuirassed, r.
Rev. VICTORIA GERMANICA. Victory advancing r.,
holding wreath and palm. Æ, 3.61 gm. ↓.
Shortly before the end of the reign Herennius was
promoted to the rank of Augustus.

813   Aureus Rome, AD 251

Obv. C VALENS HOSTIL MES QUINTVS N C. Bust,
draped, head bare, r.
Rev. MARTI PROPVGNATORI. Mars advancing r.,
holding spear and shield. *N*, 3.99 gm. ↓.
The emperor's younger son, Hostilian, was
appointed Caesar, possibly on the promotion of
Herennius to Augustus.

814   Antoninianus Antioch, AD 249–251

Obv. IMP C M Q TRAIANVS DECIVS AVG. Bust,
radiate, draped, cuirassed, r.; below, • •.
Rev. AEQVITAS AVG. Aequitas standing l., holding
scales and cornucopiae. *R*, 3.47 gm. ↑.
The antoniniani produced by the eastern mint are
distinguished by dots or numerals under the bust
and sometimes in the exergue of the reverse indi-
cating the officina responsible.

815   Antoninianus Antioch, AD 249–251

Obv. HER ETRVSCILLA AVG. Bust, draped, and
wearing stephane, r., below, IIV.
Rev. SAECVLVM NOVVM. Hexastyle temple, within,
figure of Roma. *R*, 4.22 gm.
The officina numeral here is more likely to be a
reversed VII rather than an unorthodox form of the
numeral three.

816   Antoninianus Antioch, AD 250–251

Obv. HEREN ETRV MES Q V DECIVS CAESAR. Bust,
radiate, draped, cuirassed, r.; below, •.
Rev. PANNONIAE. Pannonia, veiled, standing
front, hand r., holding helmet and standard.
R, 4.20 gm. ↑.

817   Antoninianus Antioch, AD 251

Obv. C VAL HOST MES QVINTVS CAESAR. Bust,
radiate, draped, cuirassed, r.; below, IV.
Rev. PVDICITIA AVG. Pudicitia, veiled, seated l.,
holding out veil in r. hand, and sceptre in l.
R, 2.83 gm. ↓.

818   Antoninianus Rome, AD 251

Obv. DIVO AVGVSTO. Head of Augustus, radiate, r.
Rev. CONSECRATIO. Eagle standing facing, head l.
R, 5 gm. ↓.
The most likely date for this series of antoniniani of
deified emperors is towards the end of the reign of
Decius. Rome, the only mint in the West in this
reign, must have been the mint of this series also.

819   Antoninianus Rome, AD 251

Obv. DIVO PIO. Head of Antoninus Pius, radiate, r.
Rev. CONSECRATIO. Altar. *R*, 3.79 gm. ↑.
This coin illustrates the other variety of reverse type
appearing on the deified emperor's coinage.

Trebonianus Gallus and Volusian, AD251-253

820   Antoninianus Rome, AD 251

Obv. IMP CAE C VAL HOS MES QVINTVS AVG. Bust, radiate, draped, cuirassed, r.

Rev. SECVRITAS AVGG. Securitas standing front, head l., placing r. hand on head, and leaning l. elbow on column. Æ, 3.76 gm. ↑.

After the death of Decius and Herennius in battle in 251, and the accession of Trebonianus Gallus, Hostilian, the younger son of Decius, became a co-Augustus, but died within the year.

821   Aureus Rome, AD 251–253

Obv. IMP CAE C VIB TREB GALLVS AVG. Bust, radiate, draped, cuirassed, r.

Rev. FELICITAS PVBLICA. Felicitas standing r., holding caduceus and cornucopiae. N, 5.99 gm. ↑.

The radiate crown is the usual convention to mark a double piece, but, as the weight is considerably less than twice that of the aureus with laureate portrait (see No. 822), it is probably more correct to regard it as marking simply gold coinage of a heavy weight standard.

822   Aureus Rome, AD 251–253

Obv. As No. 821, but laureate.

Rev. APOLL SALVTARI. Apollo standing l., holding branch and lyre set on rock. N, 3.84 gm. ↑.

The laureate portrait is used on coins of a lighter weight standard. The epithet *salutaris* may contain a reference to the plague which was rife in Italy and the provinces at this time.

823   Sestertius Rome, AD 251

Obv. C VIB VOLVSIANO CAES. Bust draped, head bare, r.

Rev. PRINCIPI IVVENTVTIS S C. Volusian standing l., holding baton and reversed spear. Æ, 20.62 gm. ↑.

In the first coinage Volusian, the son of Gallus, appears as Caesar alongside his father and Hostilian as Augusti.

824   Aureus Rome, AD 252

Obv. IMP CAE C VIB VOLVSIANO AVG. Bust, radiate, draped, cuirassed, r.

Rev. CONCORDIA AVGG. Concordia seated l., holding patera and cornucopiae; in field r., star. N, 5.65 gm. ↓.

On the death of Hostilian, Volusian was advanced to the rank of Augustus.

825 Aureus Rome, AD 253

Obv. As No. 824, but laureate.
Rev. P M TR P IIII COS II. Volusian standing l., sacrificing out of patera, and holding short sceptre. *N*, 3.25 gm. ↓.

The use of this tribunician date may be explicable on the assumption that Gallus regarded himself as adopted into the family of Decius, and simply continued the tribunician reckoning of Decius for himself and Volusian.

826 Medallion Rome, AD 255–257

Obv. IMP CAE C VIBIVS TREBONIANVS GALLVS AVG. Bust, laureate, draped, cuirassed, r.
Rev. IVVONI MARTIALI. Circular temple with domed and ribbed roof and with four columns visible; within, Juno seated facing, holding corn-ears in r. hand; to l. of throne, peacock; between columns uncertain object on pedestal. Æ, 56.26 gm. ↑.

Juno designated as *martialis* appears only in the coinage of this reign, and nothing is known of a cult of Juno with this aspect.

827 Antoninianus Rome, AD 253

Obv. IMP C C VIB TREB GALLVS AVG. Bust, radiate, draped, cuirassed, r.

Rev. PAX AETERNA. Pax standing l., holding branch and sceptre. Æ, 2.96 gm. ↑.

Antoniniani with this form of obverse inscription have been attributed to a second mint in the West, either Milan or Viminacium, but they seem only to represent the last phase of coinage at Rome.

828 Antoninianus Rome, AD 253

Obv. As No. 827, but VOLVSIANVS.
Rev. VIRTVS AVGG. Virtus standing r., holding spear, and resting r. hand on shield. Æ, 3.95 gm. ↓.

For the mint of this series, see No. 827.

829 Antoninianus Antioch, AD 251–253

Obv. IMP C C VIB TREB GALLVS P F AVG. Bust, radiate, draped, cuirassed, r.; below, •.
Rev. ROMAE AETERNAE. Roma seated l., holding Victory on r. hand, and spear in l.; by seat l., shield; in ex., •. Æ, 4.92 gm. ↑.

The coinage of this eastern mint has the same form of marking for the officinae as on its coinage for Decius.

830 Antoninianus Antioch, AD 251–253

Obv. IMP C AF GAL VEND VOLVSIANO AVG. Bust, radiate, draped, cuirassed, r.; below, • • • •.
Rev. AEQVITAS AVGG. Aequitas standing l., holding scales and cornucopiae; in ex., • • • •. Æ, 4 gm. ↑.

The eastern mint is unique in representing these elements of Volusian's full name – Afinius Gallus Vendumnianus.

Aemilian, AD253

831   Aureus Rome, AD 253

Obv. IMP AEMILIANVS PIVS FEL AVG. Bust, laureate,
     draped, cuirassed, r.
Rev. ERCVL VICTORI. Hercules standing r., resting
     r. hand on club and holding bow in l.;
     lionskin on l. arm. *N*, 3.14 gm. ↓.
The reverse inscription is unusual in dropping the
aspirate at the beginning of the name, Hercules.

832   Antoninianus Rome, AD 253

Obv. IMP CAES AEMILIANVS P F AVG. Bust, laureate,
     draped, cuirassed, r.
Rev. IOVI CONSERVAT. Jupiter standing l., holding
     thunderbolt in r. hand over small figure of
     Aemilian, and sceptre in l. *R*, 5.05 gm. ↑.
A second group of coinage in which no gold is
recorded uses the different form of obverse
titulature.

833   Antoninianus Rome, AD 253

Obv. C CORNEL SVPERA AVG. Bust, draped, and
     wearing stephane, r.
Rev. VESTA. Vesta veiled, standing l., holding
     patera and sceptre. *R*, 3.22 gm. ↑.
The very rare coins of Cornelia Supera are
attributed to this reign.

Uranius Antoninus, AD253-254

834   Aureus Emesa, AD 253–254

Obv. L IVL AVR SVLP VRA ANTONINVS. Bust,
     laureate, draped, cuirassed, r.
Rev. CONSERVATOR AVG. Conical stone, draped
     and ornamented; to l. and r., a parasol.
     N, 5.80 gm. ↑.
A coinage in gold only was issued by Uranius
Antoninus, high priest of the cult of Sol Elagabalus
whose cult stone is shown on the reverse. Uranius
held out in Emesa during the invasion of Syria by
the Sassanians under Sapor I.

Valerian and Gallienus, AD253-260

835   Aureus Rome, AD 253–254

Obv. IMP C P LIC VALERIANVS AVG. Bust, laureate,
     draped, cuirassed, r.
Rev. LAETITIA AVGG. Laetitia standing l., holding
     wreath and rudder. *N*, 4.07 gm. ↓.
The earliest coinage at Rome uses the form of
obverse inscription without P F. The reverse type
suggests rejoicing at the beginning of the new reign.

836 Denarius Rome, AD 253–254

Obv. As No. 835.
Rev. IOVI CONSERVATORI. Jupiter standing l.,
        holding thunderbolt and sceptre.
        Æ, 2.08 gm. ↑.
The reverse of this and of the next coin invoke the
protection of the gods, presumably for the
campaign in the East on which Valerian was about
to embark. By the mid-third century the denarius
had become a rare denomination.

837 Antoninianus Rome, AD 253–254

Obv. As No. 835, but radiate.
Rev. APOLLINI PROPVG. Apollo standing r.,
        drawing bow. Æ, 2.80 gm. ↑.

838 Medallion Rome, AD 254

Obv. IMP CAES P LIC VALERIANVS AVG. Bust,
        laureate, draped, cuirassed, l.
Rev. LIBERALITAS AVGG I. Valerian and Gallienus
        seated l. on platform, each holding scroll in
        l. hand, and accompanied by attendant; to l.,
        Liberalitas standing l., holding abacus and
        cornucopiae; citizen standing r. on steps of
        platform, holding up fold of cloak.
        Æ, 52.01 gm. ↑.
The first largesse was distributed at the beginning of
254 in connection with the assumption of the

consulship by both emperors. The mention of the
first largesse is usually not numbered, but the
numeral I appears to be integral with the reverse
inscription.

839 Aureus Rome, AD 254

Obv. DIVAE MARINIANAE. Bust, veiled and wearing
        stephane, draped, r.
Rev. CONSECRATIO. Peacock standing front, head
        l., with tail spread. Ǽ, 3.33 gm. ↑.
The only coinage for Mariniana, the wife of
Valerian, is for her as a deified empress.

840 Antoninianus Rome, AD 253–254

Obv. IMP C P LIC GALLIENVS AVG. Bust, radiate,
        draped, cuirassed, r.
Rev. VIRTVS AVGG. Virtus standing l., resting r.
        hand on shield, and holding inverted spear
        in l. Æ, 3.71 gm. ↑.
The earliest coinage of Gallienus also omits P F from
the obverse titulature.

841 Antoninianus Rome, AD 252–254

Obv. SALONINA AVG. Bust, draped and wearing
        stephane r., set on crescent.
Rev. IVNO REGINA. Juno standing l., holding
        patera and cornucopiae. Æ, 3.20 gm. ↓.
Coinage for Salonina, the wife of Gallienus, forms
part of the issues from early in the reign. Juno, the
queen of the gods, is a stock type on the coinage of
the empress.

842 Aureus Rome, AD 256

Obv. IMP C P LIC GALLIENVS AVG. Bust, laureate, draped, cuirassed, r.

Rev. LIBERALITAS AVGG III. Valerian and Gallienus seated l., extending r. hand; between them, citizen or attendant standing l.
Ν, 2.45 gm. ↑.

The third largesse was most probably distributed on the occasion of the nomination of Valerian II as Caesar.

843 Sestertius Rome, AD 256–257

Obv. IMP GALLIENVS P F AVG GM. Bust, laureate, draped, cuirassed, r.

Rev. RESTITVTOR ORBIS S C. Gallienus standing l., raising kneeling figure, and holding sceptre in l. hand. Æ, 21.16 gm. ↓.

The reverse type, coupled with the epithet *Germanicus* on the obverse, refers to Gallienus' success against the German tribes invading Gaul.

844 Antoninianus Rome, AD 256

Obv. P LIC VALERIANVS CAES. Bust, radiate, draped, r.

Rev. IOVI CRESCENTI. Child Jupiter riding r. on goat. Æ, 2.77 gm. ↑.

This novel type of the infant who became Jupiter, king of the gods, is an apt type for the young Caesar who might become emperor.

845 Medallion Rome, AD 256

Obv. PIETAS AVGVSTORVM. Bust of Valerian II, draped, head bare, r., facing bust of Valerian I, laureate, draped, cuirassed, l.

Rev. CONCORDIA AVGVSTORVM. Bust of Salonina, draped, and wearing stephane r., facing bust of Gallienus, laureate, draped, cuirassed, l.
Æ, 27.43 gm. ↑.

The most likely occasion for this medallion with portraits of all the members of the imperial family is the nomination of Valerian II as Caesar.

846 Antoninianus 'Western' mint, AD 253

Obv. IMP VALERIANVS P AVG. Bust, radiate, draped, cuirassed, r.

Rev. FIDES MILITVM. Fides standing l., holding vertical standard and transverse ensign.
Æ, 3.09 gm. ↓.

Coinage distinguished by this form of obverse titulature struck by a mint in the West other than Rome has been attributed either to Milan or Viminacium. The present state of knowledge precludes any certain mint attribution.

847 Antoninianus 'Western' mint, AD 254.

Obv. DIVAE MARINIANAE. Bust, veiled and draped, r., set on crescent.

Rev. CONSECRATIO. Peacock flying r., bearing empress holding sceptre in l. hand.
Æ, 2.98 gm. ↑.

848 Antoninianus 'Western' mint, AD 254

Obv. IMP GALLIENVS P AVG. Bust, radiate, draped, cuirassed, r.
Rev. SALVS AVGG. Salus standing l., feeding snake, rising from altar, out of patera in r. hand, and holding sceptre in l. Æ, 4.04 gm. ↓.

After a short first issue for Valerian alone, Gallienus shares in the coinage, using a form of titulature similar to that of his father.

849 Antoninianus Trier, AD 257

Obv. VALERIANVS CAES. Bust, radiate, draped, r.
Rev. PIETAS AVGG. Jug between lituus and knife to l., and simpulum and sprinkler to r. Æ, 4.94 gm. ↓.

The second mint in the West (see Nos. 846–8) was transferred to Gaul in 257. The mint has been identified as Cologne. While some coinage later was struck for Postumus at Cologne (see No. 921), it is not yet certain that the Gallic mint was from the beginning established there.

850 Antoninianus Trier, AD 258

Obv. IMP GALLIENVS AVG. Bust, radiate, cuirassed, r.
Rev. IOVI VICTORI. Jupiter holding Victory and spear, standing facing on base inscribed IMP C E S. Æ, 4.27 gm. ↓.

The inscription on the base is to be expanded as *Imperator cum exercitu suo*, and the whole type refers to the successes of Gallienus against the German invaders of Gaul.

851 Antoninianus Trier, AD 259

Obv. VALERIANVS P F AVG. Bust, radiate, draped, cuirassed, r.
Rev. DEO VOLKANO. Vulcan standing l. on tetrastyle temple, holding hammer and pincers; at foot l., anvil. Æ, 3.16 gm. ↑.

A series of antoniniani of this mint feature the shrines of deities as the reverse type for the different imperial personages.

852 Antoninianus Trier, AD 259

Obv. SALONINA AVG. Bust, draped and wearing stephane, r., set on crescent.
Rev. DEAE SEGETIAE. Segetia veiled, standing facing, in tetrastyle temple, and holding up apple in each hand. Æ, 3.60 gm. ↓.

Segetia was a goddess of the crops.

853 Antoninianus Trier, AD 259

Obv. DIVO VALERIANO CAES. Bust, radiate, draped, r.
Rev. CONSACRATIO. Eagle, flying r., bearing Valerian II holding sceptre in l. hand. Æ, 490 gm. ↓.

Coinage for the deification of Valerian II who died probably in 257. The reverse inscription is consistently mis-spelled thus at this mint.

854 Aureus Trier, AD 260

Obv. IMP SALON VALERIANVS AVG. Bust, laureate, draped, cuirassed, r.
Rev. FELICITAS AVGG. Felicitas standing l., holding caduceus and cornucopiae. N, 2.38 gm. ↑.

On the basis of portrait style and form of obverse titulature this unique coin is attributed to the Gallic mint. Rare antoniniani of Saloninus as Augustus from this mint include this reverse type. The proclamation of Saloninus as Augustus appears to have been a response to the usurpation of Postumus for the short period before Saloninus' death at the hands of the rebels.

855 Antoninianus Antioch, AD 255

Obv. IMP C P LIC VALERIANVS AVG. Bust, radiate, draped, cuirassed, r.
Rev. FELICITAS SAECVLI. Diana advancing r., holding torch. Æ, 3.34 gm. ↓.

The mint at Antioch, which had been over-run by the Sassanians under Sapor in the reign of Trebonianus Gallus, began to coin again for Valerian and his family in 254.

856 Antoninianus Antioch, AD 255

Obv. IMP C P LIC GALLIENVS AVG. Bust, radiate, draped, cuirassed, r.
Rev. RESTITVT GENER HVMANI. Gallienus advancing r., raising r. hand, and holding globe in l. Æ, 3.93 gm. ↓.

The reverse inscription provides a novel description of the emperor's rôle.

857 Antoninianus Antioch, AD 256–257

Obv. SALONINA AVG. Bust, draped and wearing stephane, r., set on crescent.
Rev. CONCORDIA AVGG. Concordia seated l., holding patera and cornucopiae. Æ, 2.66 gm. ↑.

858 Antoninianus Antioch, AD 256–257

Obv. P LIC COR VALERIANVS CAES. Bust, radiate, draped, r.
Rev. VICTORIA PART. Victory standing r., holding palm and presenting wreath to Valerian II standing l., holding globe and spear. Æ, 4.65 gm. ↓.

859 Antoninianus Antioch, AD 257

Obv. P COR SAL VALERIANVS CAES. Bust, radiate, draped, cuirassed, r.
Rev. DII NVTRITORES. Jupiter standing l., holding sceptre, presenting Victory to Saloninus standing r. Æ, 3.47 gm. ↓.

860 Antoninianus Cyzicus ?, AD 255

Obv. IMP C P LIC VALERIANVS AVG. Bust, radiate, draped, cuirassed, r.
Rev. VOTA ORBIS. Two Victories standing l. and r., placing shield inscribed S C on palm-tree. Æ, 3.87 gm. ↑.
Coinage distinguished by small neat portrait busts and a marked preference for two-figure reverse types was produced by a second mint in the East, tentatively identified as Cyzicus.

861 Antoninianus Cyzicus ?, AD 256–257

Obv. IMP C P LIC GALLIENVS P F AVG. Bust, radiate, draped, cuirassed, r.
Rev. RESTITVT ORIENTIS. Turreted female figure standing r., presenting wreath to Gallienus standing l., holding globe and sceptre. Æ, 3.98 gm. ↑.

862 Antoninianus Cyzicus ?, AD 256–257

Obv. VALERIANVS NOBIL CAES. Bust, radiate, draped, cuirassed, r.
Rev. PRINC IVVENTVTIS. Valerian II standing l., holding spear and shield in l. hand, and with r. placing wreath on trophy. Æ, 3.52 gm. ↓.

863 Antoninianus Cyzicus ?, AD 258–259

Obv. SALON VALERIANVS NOB CAES. Bust, radiate, draped, cuirassed, r.
Rev. SPES PVBLICA. Spes standing l., raising skirt and presenting flower to Saloninus standing r., holding sceptre; above, wreath with central dot. Æ, 3.34 gm. ↓.

864 Antoninianus Cyzicus ?, AD 259–260

Obv. SALONINA AVG. Bust, draped and wearing stephane, r. set on crescent.
Rev. ROMAE AETERNAE. Rome seated l., holding spear and presenting Victory to the emperor standing r.; to r. by seat, a shield; in centre field, star. Æ, 4.36 gm. ↑.

Gallienus, AD260-268

865 Medallion Rome, AD 260

Obv. IMP GALLIENVS AVG. Bust, helmeted, cuirassed, l., holding spear and shield.
Rev. VIRTVS AVG. Hercules standing facing, head r., holding club in r. hand, and bow and lion-skin in l. N, 13.22 gm. ↓.
An example of a four-aureus piece or quaternio.

866 Sestertius Rome, AD 260

Obv. IMP GALLIENVS AVG. Bust, laureate, cuirassed, r.
Rev. VICTORIA AVG S C. Victory advancing l.,
holding wreath and palm. Æ, 15.84 gm. ↑.
This was the last coinage from the mint of Rome of
which the bronze sestertius was a constituent part.

867 Quinarius Rome, AD 260

Obv. As No. 866.
Rev. As No. 866 but no S C. Æ, 1.47 gm. ↓.
An instance of the quinarius which still continued to
be struck, but only rarely.

868 Aureus Rome, AD 262–263

Obv. GALLIENVS AVG. Bust with lion-skin head-
dress, r.
Rev. FIDES MILITVM. Fides standing l., holding
standard in either hand. Ν, 5.72 gm. ↑.
A number of reverses with military reference
probably form part of a special issue in gold in
honour of Gallienus' decennalia.

869 Aureus Rome, AD 262–263

Obv. GALLIENVS AVG. Bust bare, head radiate, r.
Rev. FIDES PRAET. Legionary eagle between two
standards. Ν, 5.30 gm. ↑.
Another type in the same special issue as No. 868.

870 Aureus Rome, AD 262–263

Obv. GALLIENVM AVG P R. Bust, laureate,
cuirassed, r.
Rev. OB CONSERVAT SALVT. Salus standing r.,
feeding out of patera snake held in arms.
Ν, 3.33 gm. ↓.
The same event may have been the occasion of an
unusual issue of gold coinage and silver medallions
employing unusual formulae. In the obverse
inscription the subject is *P(opulus) R(omanus)*, the
object *Gallienum Aug(ustum)*, with a verb such as
honorat understood, while the sense is concluded by
the reverse inscription.

871 Medallion Rome, AD 262–263

Obv. GALLIENVM AVG SENATVS. Bust, laureate,
draped, l.
Rev. OB LIBERTATEM RECEPTAM. Libertas
standing l., holding pileus and sceptre.
Æ, 11.83 gm. ↑.
Another type in the same series as No. 870:

872 Aureus Rome, *c*.AD 265

Obv. IMP GALLIENVS AVG. Bust, helmeted, draped,
cuirassed, r.
Rev. VBERITAS AVG. Uberitas standing l., holding
purse and cornucopiae. Ν, 1.53 gm. ↓.
The weight of the aureus fell steadily throughout
the reign.

873 Denarius Rome, *c.*AD 265

Obv. IMP GALLIENVS AVG. Head, laureate, r.
Rev. ABVNDANTIA AVG. Abundantia standing r.,
emptying cornucopiae. Æ, 2.06 gm. ↑.
The denarius was still struck on occasions as part of
the coinage but not with regularity and probably as
part of special issues.

874 Sestertius Rome, AD 266

Obv. GENIVS P R. Bust, radiate, crowned with
modius, r.
Rev. INT VRB S C. Three line inscription enclosed
in laurel-wreath. Æ, 18.59 gm. ↑.
As the coin appears by weight to be a sestertius, the
radiate crown must be part of the iconography and
not a denominational indication. The obverse
portrait appears to have the features of Gallienus and
a possible expansion of the reverse inscription is
Int(roitus) Urb(is); this can be regarded as a special
issue for Gallienus' entry into Rome on his return
from Athens.

875 Aureus Rome, AD 266–267

Obv. GALLIENAE AVGVSTAE. Head with crown of
reeds, l.
Rev. VBIQVE PAX. Victory in biga r.
Ν, 5.97 gm. ↓.
The obverse inscription, seemingly a dative
feminine singular, is more likely to be a masculine
vocative with the unusual spelling *Gallienae*
replacing the normal *Galliene*. Other instances

110

occur in third century inscriptions and coins of the
letters *ae* being used for a long *e*.

876 Antoninianus Rome, AD 267–268

Obv. GALLIENVS AVG. Head, radiate, r.
Rev. LIBERO P CONS AVG. Panther l.; in ex. B.
Æ, 4.11 gm. ↑.
A late series of antoniniani of Gallienus features
reverses with inscriptions of various deities in the
dedicatory dative and described as *conservator
Augusti*, preserver of the emperor, and with type,
the animal associated with the deity, in this case the
panther of Liber or Bacchus.

877 Antoninianus Milan, AD 261–262

Obv. GALLIENVS AVG. Bust, radiate, cuirassed, r.,
with spear over shoulder.
Rev. LEG I I ADI VI P VI F. Pegasus r.
Æ, 4.34 gm. ↑.
The establishment of the mint at Milan is connected
with the creation by Gallienus of a mobile field
army, and this issue honours the legions which
contributed vexillations to it. The additional
formula, e.g. here *vi Pia vi Fidelis*, refers to the count
of Gallienus' victories.

878 Antoninianus Milan, AD 265–266

Obv. SALONINA AVG. Bust, draped and with
stephane, r., set on crescent.
Rev. AVGVSTA IN PACE. Salonina seated l., holding
branch and sceptre; in ex. P. Æ, 2.54 gm. ↓.
The empress Salonina is believed to have been a
Christian, and this reverse has been regarded as
having a certain Christian flavour.

879 **Antoninianus** Milan, AD 265–266

Obv. GALLIENVS AVG. Head, radiate, r.
Rev. CONCOR AVG. Concordia seated l., holding patera and cornucopiae; in ex. MT.
AR, 4.06 gm. ↑.
In the coinage of Gallienus the reverse of the antoninianus comes increasingly to be marked with the ordinal initial or numeral of the producing officina. Occasionally, this mark is preceded by the initial of the issuing mint, here M for Mediolanum.

880 **Antoninianus** Siscia, AD 262–264

Obv. As No. 878.
Rev. IO CANTAB. Jupiter standing l., holding thunderbolt and sceptre. AR, 3.95 gm. ↑.
The significance of this unusual type of *Io(vis) Cantab(rorum)* is not immediately obvious. The skill of the Cantabri as horsemen is mentioned in the phrase *impetus Cantabricus*, so that the type here may contain a reference to the cavalry of Gallienus' field army which had been so successful in campaigns against usurpers in the Balkans.

881 **Antoninianus** Sirmium, AD 265

Obv. As No. 878.
Rev. VICTORIA AET. Victory standing l., holding wreath and palm; in field l. and r., s and P. AR, 4.16 gm. ↑.
The letters S P are explained as abbreviations of *S(ecunda) P(annonia)* of which Sirmium was the principal city.

882 **Antoninianus** Antioch, AD 266

Obv. GALLIENVS AVG. Bust, radiate, draped, cuirassed, r.
Rev. SOLI INVICTO. Sol standing facing, head l., raising r. hand, and holding globe; in ex., PXV. AR, 3.83 gm. ↑.
The tribunician power XV is placed in the exergue here as a kind of issue mark.

Macrian and Quietus, AD260–261

883 **Aureus** Cyzicus, AD 260

Obv. IMP C FVL MACRIANVS P F AVG. Bust, laureate, draped, cuirassed, r.
Rev. CONSERVATRICI AVGG. Diana standing r., with r. hand drawing arrow from quiver on back and holding bow in l.; at foot r., stag; in field l., star. AV, 5.11 gm. ↓.
Antioch had been over-run by the Sassanians under Sapor, and the coinage for the two young usurpers was struck at the second eastern mint active under Valerian and Gallienus.

884 **Antoninianus** Cyzicus, AD 260

Obv. As No. 883, but radiate.
Rev. ROMAE AETERNAE. Roma seated l., holding victory and spear; by seat, shield; in field l., star. AR, 4.45 gm. ↑.

885 Antoninianus Cyzicus, AD 260

Obv. IMP C FVL QVIETVS P F AVG. Bust, radiate, draped, cuirassed, r.
Rev. SOLI INVICTO. Sol standing l., raising r. hand, and holding globe in l. Æ, 4.15 gm. ↑.

886 As Cyzicus, AD 260

Obv. As No. 885, but laureate.
Rev. AEQVTAS AVG. Aequitas standing l., holding scales and cornucopiae. Æ, 8 gm. ↑.
In bronze only the *as* with this type was struck, and for Quietus only. It lacks the s c mark of the bronze coinage of Rome.

Regalian, AD260–261

887 Antoninianus Carnuntum, AD 260–261

Obv. IMP C P C REGALIANVS AVG. Bust, radiate, draped, cuirassed, r.
Rev. ORIENS AVG. Sol standing facing, head l., raising r. hand and holding whip in l. Æ, 3.22 gm. ↑.
When the revolt in Pannonia under Ingenuus was suppressed, a new usurper, Regalian, was proclaimed and issued coins from his headquarters at Carnuntum. Most examples are overstruck on earlier coins.

888 Antoninianus Carnuntum, AD 260–261

Obv. SVLP DRYANTILLA AVG. Bust, draped and with stephane, r., set on crescent.
Rev. AEQVITAS AVGG. Aequitas standing l., holding scales and cornucopiae. Æ, 2.25 gm. ↓.
On this example of the coinage of Regalian's wife traces of the original undertypes are readily visible.

Claudius II, AD268–270

889 Aureus Rome, AD 268

Obv. IMP CLAVDIVS AVG. Head laureate l.
Rev. VICTORIA AVG. Victory standing r., head l., holding wreath and palm; at foot l. and r., seated captive. N, 5.50 gm. ↓.

890 Antoninianus Rome, AD 269–270

Obv. IMP CLAVDIVS AVG. Bust, radiate, cuirassed, r.
Rev. AETERNIT AVG. Sol standing l., raising r. hand and holding globe in l.; in field r., N.
Æ, 3.25 gm. ↓.
The mint of Rome at this period produced coinage from twelve officinae. Officinae 1–8 were marked by Greek numerals *A–H*, 10 to 12 by Roman numerals X–XII, and officina 9 by the initial of the ordinal *nona*. It is said that the Greek numeral for 9, the letter Θ was avoided as it was the initial letter of Θάνατος, death.

891 As Rome, AD 268–270

Obv. IMP CLAVDIVS P F AVG. Head laureate l.
Rev. MARTI PACIFERO. Mars standing l., holding
  branch and spear. Æ, 12.41 gm. ↑.
The traditional bronze denominations marked with
S C cease with Gallienus. Bronzes of the later third
century lack this mark.

892 Antoninianus Milan, AD 268–270

Obv. IMP CLAVDIVS P F AVG. Bust, radiate, draped,
  cuirassed, r.
Rev. FIDES MILIT. Fides standing l., holding
  standard in either hand; in ex., S.
  Æ, 3.61 gm. ↑.

893 Antoninianus Siscia, AD 268–270

Obv. IMP CLAVDIVS AVG. Bust, radiate, cuirassed, r.
Rev. VBERITAS AVG. Uberitas standing l., holding
  purse and cornucopiae; in field r., Q.
  Æ, 2.84 gm. ↓.
The organisation of the mint of Siscia was increased
by the addition of a fourth officina in this reign.

894 Antoninianus Cyzicus, AD 269–270

Obv. IMP CLAVDIVS P F AVG. Bust, radiate, draped,
  cuirassed, r.; below, ● ●.
Rev. VICTORIAE GOTHIC. Trophy between two
  seated captives. Æ, 2.47 gm. ↓.
A specific commemoration of the defeat of the
Goths by Claudius in battle near Nish.

895 Antoninianus Antioch, AD 268–269

Obv. IMP CLAVDIVS AVG. Bust, radiate, draped,
  cuirassed, r.
Rev. REGI ARTIS. Vulcan standing r., holding
  hammer and tongs; in ex., Z. Æ, 3.46 gm. ↑.
Vulcan features rarely in the Roman coinage, and
only in the coinage of Claudius II is he accorded this
unusual title. Antioch ceased to coin for Claudius
when it was seized by Zenobia, Queen of Palmyra,
in AD 269.

896 Antoninianus Rome, AD 270

Obv. DIVO CLAVDIO. Head, radiate, r.
Rev. CONSECRATIO. Eagle standing l., head turned
  r. Æ, 3.59 gm. ↓.
Claudius died of the plague shortly after his
resounding defeat of the Goths in a battle near Nish.
His consecration, decreed by the Senate, was
recorded on coins issued by his brother, Quintillus,
and his successor, Aurelian.

897 Antoninianus Milan, AD 270

Obv. DIVO CLAVDIO GOTHICO. Head, radiate, r.
Rev. CONSECRATIO. Altar. Æ, 2.09 gm. ↑.
The epithet *Gothicus* is added to Claudius' titles here
in honour of his successful battle against the Goths.

898   Antoninianus Cyzicus, AD 270

Obv.   DIVO CLAVDIO. Head, radiate, r.;
    below, • • • •.
Rev.   CONSECRATIO. Funeral pyre. Æ, 3.79 gm. ↓.

Quintillus, AD270

899   Antoninianus Rome, AD 270

Obv.   IMP C M AVR CL QVINTILLVS AVG. Bust,
    radiate, draped, cuirassed, r.
Rev.   FIDES MILITVM. Fides standing l., holding
    standard and spear; in field r., ε.
    Æ, 2.92 gm. ↑.
This coinage of Quintillus repeats the exact types
and allocation to officinae of the last coinage of
Claudius.

900   Antoninianus Milan, AD 270

Obv.   IMP QVINTILLVS AVG. Bust, radiate, draped,
    cuirassed, r.
Rev.   CONCO EXER. Concordia standing l., holding
    standard and cornucopiae; in ex., T.
    Æ, 4.08 gm. ↑.

901   Antoninianus Siscia, AD 270

Obv.   IMP C M AVR QVINTILLVS AVG. Bust, radiate,
    draped, cuirassed, r.
Rev.   VBERITAS AVG. Uberitas standing l., holding
    purse and cornucopiae; in field r., Q.
    Æ, 4.28 gm. ↑.
Some types at Siscia, as at Rome, are direct con-
tinuations of the coinage of Claudius.

8 The Gallic Empire
AD260-274

The revolt of Postumus in Gaul in 260, whether as a concomitant to or as a consequence of the capture of Valerian I in the East, resulted in the establishment of a separate Gallic empire which exerted control over Spain and Britain as well as Gaul itself, and which lasted until its reconquest by Aurelian in 274. The mints of the Gallic empire remain controversial. The only certain mint is Cologne whose signature, appearing only on issues of Postumus late in the reign, was given prominence to record the transfer of the mint at that time from some other place which, on the evidence of a pre-tetrarchic inscription, appears to have been Trier. On stylistic evidence Cologne continued as a mint for Marius, Victorinus, and the Tetrici. The mint which struck for the usurper Laelian and for the subsequent Gallic emperors may well have been Lyons, whose signature appears on coins issued by Aurelian after the reconquest.

The coinage system of the Gallic empire closely paralleled that of the central empire, and in the case of the antoninianus the decline in silver fineness followed a comparable course until under the Tetrici it also had fallen to some 2.5%. In the early coinage of Postumus bronzes in the traditional denominations were issued in some quantity, with the addition of a double sestertius, but, as in the central empire, the series appears to end in the early 260s.

Postumus, AD260-268

902   Antoninianus Trier, AD 260

Obv. IMP C POSTVMVS P F AVG. Bust, radiate, draped, cuirassed, r.
Rev. SALVS PROVINCIARVM. The Rhine reclining l., resting l. arm on urn, and placing r. hand on prow of boat. Æ, 4.20 gm. ↓.

The portrait of Postumus on early issues is reminiscent of that on coins of Gallienus from this mint. The reverse alludes to the role of the Rhine in the defence of the province of Gaul.

903   Aureus Trier, AD 260

Obv. As No. 902, but laureate.
Rev. AETERNITAS AVG. Three busts of Sol, radiate, draped, facing r., facing front, and facing l., respectively. Æ, 6.32 gm. ↓.

It is not unusual for *Aeternitas* to be represented by a personification of Sol, but the significance of the triple portrait here is unclear. The suggestion that these are the portraits of Postumus' wife and two sons carries little conviction.

904   Double sestertius Trier, AD 260

Obv. IMP C M CASS LAT POSTVMVS P F AVG. Bust, radiate, draped, cuirassed, r.
Rev. P M T R P COS II PP. SC. Postumus, helmeted, standing r., holding spear, and resting l. hand on shield. Æ, 21.80 gm. ↓.

In the first years of the coinage Postumus produced substantial issues of bronze, including a double sestertius after the manner of Trajan Decius (cf. No. 806).

905 Double sestertius Trier, AD 260

Obv. As No. 904.
Rev. RESTITVTOR GALLIAR S C. Postumus standing
l., holding spear, and raising woman
kneeling r., holding branch. Æ, 31.92 gm. ↓.
The reverse copies quite closely the 'Restitutor'
series of Hadrian more than a century earlier.

906 Double sestertius Trier, AD 260

Obv. As No. 904 (overstruck, with traces of
undertype).
Rev. [VICTORIA AVG]. Victory advancing l.,
holding wreath and palm; at foot l., captive,
(overstruck, with traces of undertype).
Æ, 25.43 gm. ↑.
This coin has been overstruck, obverse on reverse,
on an earlier sestertius. The obverse portrait and
part of the titles of Marcus Aurelius are visible as
well as the inscription RELIG AVG and part of the
reverse type of a sestertius of Marcus Aurelius
(*BMC* 1441–8).

907 Sestertius Trier, AD 261

Obv. IMP C POSTVMVS PIVS · F · AVG. Bust, laureate,
draped, cuirassed, r.
Rev. VICTORIA AVG. Victory advancing l., holding
wreath and palm; at foot l., seated captive.
Æ, 26.79 gm. ↓.
This, and the following three bronzes, are without
S C.

908 Sestertius Trier, AD 261

Obv. As No. 907.
Rev. FIDES MILITVM. Fides standing l., holding two
standards. Æ, 19.76 gm. ↓.

909 Sestertius Trier, AD 261

Obv. IMP C POSTVMVS P F AVG. Bust, laureate,
draped, cuirassed, l., r. hand raised.
Rev. LAETITIA AVG. Galley r. Æ, 13.92 gm. ↓.

910 Sestertius Trier, AD 261

Obv. VIRTVS POSTVMI AVG. Bust, helmeted,
   cuirassed, l., with spear and shield.
Rev. HERC DEVSONIENSI. Hercules standing l.,
   holding club in r. hand, and bow in l., with
   lion-skin over l. arm. Æ, 16.63 gm. ↓.
Hercules is a frequent type on coins of Postumus,
often, as here, with the epithet *Deusoniensis*, of
Deuso, the modern Deutz on the Rhine.

911 Antoninianus Trier, AD 262

Obv. IMP C POSTVMVS · P · F · AVG. Bust, radiate,
   draped, cuirassed, r.
Rev. HERC DEVSONIENSI. Hercules standing r.,
   holding club and lion-skin in tetrastyle
   temple. Æ, 3.08 gm. ↑.
A representation of the shrine of Hercules at Deutz.

912 Antoninianus Trier, AD 262

Obv. As No. 911.
Rev. MONETA AVG. Moneta standing l., holding
   scales and cornucopiae. Æ, 3.58 gm. ↓.

913 Aureus quinarius Trier, AD 263

Obv. POSTVMVS AVG. Bust, helmeted, cuirassed, l.

Rev. PROVIDENTIA AVG. Providentia standing l.,
   holding globe and sceptre. A, 2.15 gm. ↑.
A rare example of the half-piece in gold.

914 Aureus Trier, AD 263

Obv. POSTVMVS AVG. Bust, three-quarter facing,
   head bare, cuirassed.
Rev. INDVLG PIA POSTVMI AVG. Postumus seated l.
   on curule chair, extending r. hand to
   suppliant kneeling r. A, 6.68 gm. ↓.
This unusual presentation of the portrait produces
one of the most arresting obverses in the whole of
the Roman imperial coinage.

915 Antoninianus Trier, AD 265

Obv. IMP C POSTVMVS P F AVG. Bust, radiate,
   draped, cuirassed, r.
Rev. INTERNVNTIVS DEORVM. Mercury standing l.,
   holding purse and cornucopiae.
   Æ, 2.91 gm. ↓.
The gods, between whom Mercury is here
described as the messenger, are presumably the
emperors Postumus and Gallienus. The occasion is
probably the termination of hostilities in this year.

916 Aureus Trier, AD 265

Obv. POSTVMVS PIVS FELIX AVG. Jugate busts r. of
   Postumus, laureate, with drapery on l.
   shoulder, and of Hercules, laureate.
Rev. FELICITAS AVG. Jugate busts r. of Victory,
   laureate, draped, holding wreath and palm,
   and Felicitas, laureate, holding branch.
   A, 6.02 gm. ↓.

917   **Aureus** Trier, AD 265

Obv. As No. 916.
Rev. CONSERVATORES AVG. Jugate busts r. of Mars, helmeted and cuirassed, and of Victory laureate, holding wreath and palm. *N*, 5.75 gm. ↓.

The elaborate types on this and the previous coin distinguish the gold coins of a special issue honouring the emperor's quinquennalia.

918   **Denarius** Trier, AD 266

Obv. As No. 916.
Rev. HERCVLI ARGIVO. Hercules standing l., attacking hydra with club in r. hand, and holding lion-skin in l. *R*, 2.59 gm. ↑.

A series of denarii portray the labours of Hercules.

919   **Antoninianus** Trier, AD 266

Obv. IMP C POSTVMVS P F AVG. Bust, radiate, draped, cuirassed, r.
Rev. SAECVLO FRVGIFERO. Winged caduceus. *R*, 3.38 gm. ↓.

920   **Antoninianus** Trier, AD 266

Obv. POSTVMVS AVG. Bust, radiate, bare, l., holding club over shoulder in r. hand; on l. shoulder, lion-scalp.
Rev. HERCVLI ROMANO AVG. Bow, club, and quiver. *R*, 3.54 gm. ↑.

921   **Antoninianus** Cologne, AD 267

Obv. As No. 919.
Rev. COL CL AGRIP COS IIII. Moneta standing l., holding scales and cornucopiae. *R*, 3.01 gm. ↓.

The specific reference to Cologne (*Colonia Claudia Agrippinensium*), combined with the type of Moneta and the consulship date, provides strong evidence that it was in this year that Postumus moved his mint organisation to Cologne from Trier.

922   **Antoninianus** Milan, AD 268

Obv. IMP POSTVMVS AVG. Bust, radiate, draped, cuirassed, r.
Rev. FIDES EQVIT. Fides seated l., holding patera and standard; in ex., P. *R*, 4.13 gm. ↑.

Representatives of a group of antoniniani which on the basis of portrait style, use of officina letters, and reference to *equites*, has been attributed to Milan, the headquarters of the cavalry of the field army. In 268 Aureolus, the cavalry commander, revolted against Gallienus and declared for Postumus.

Laelian, AD268

923 Aureus Lyons, AD 268

Obv. IMP C LAELIANVS P F AVG. Bust, laureate,
draped, cuirassed, r.

Rev. TEMPORVM FELICITAS. Female figure reclining
l., holding branch in r. hand; to r., a rabbit.
N, 6.64 gm. ↑.

As Postumus controlled the mint at Cologne when
Laelian revolted, the latter's coinage will have been
struck elsewhere, most probably at the traditional
Gallic mint at Lyons which continued to strike for
subsequent emperors in Gaul and survived as the
only mint for Aurelian.

924 Antoninianus Lyons, AD 268

Obv. As No. 923, but radiate.

Rev. VICTORIA AVG. Victory advancing r., holding
wreath and palm. Æ, 3.87 gm. ↓.

Marius, AD268

925 Aureus Cologne, AD 268

Obv. IMP C MARIVS P F AVG. Bust, laureate, draped,
cuirassed, r.

Rev. CONCORDIA MILITVM. Clasped hands.
N, 6.28 gm. ↓.

926 Antoninianus Cologne, AD 268

Obv. As No. 925, but radiate.

Rev. SAEC FELICITAS. Felicitas standing l., holding
caduceus and cornucopiae. Æ, 2.72 gm. ↑.

927 Antoninianus Lyons, AD 268

Obv. IMP C MARIVS AVG. Bust, radiate, draped,
cuirassed, r.

Rev. VICTORIA AVG. Victory advancing r., holding
wreath and palm. Æ, 3.43 gm. ↓.

A very similar reverse type and similar obverse
portrait style to that of Laelian, No. 924 above.

Victorinus, AD268–270

928 Antoninianus Cologne, AD 268

Obv. IMP C PIAVONIVS VICTORINVS P F AVG. Bust,
radiate, draped, cuirassed, r.

Rev. FIDES MILITVM. Fides standing l., holding two
standards. Æ, 3.74 gm. ↓.

929   Antoninianus Cologne, AD 269

Obv.   IMP C PIAV VICTORINVS P F AVG. Bust, radiate,
draped, cuirassed, r.
Rev.   INVICTVS. Sol advancing l., raising r. hand,
and holding whip in l.; in field l., star.
Æ, 3.27 gm. ↑.

930   Aureus Cologne, AD 269

Obv.   IMP VICTORINVS AVG. Half-length bust r.,
laureate, cuirassed, and holding spear and
shield.
Rev.   VICTORIA AVG. Bust of Victory r., laureate,
holding palm and wreath. N, 4.08 gm. ↑.

931   Aureus Cologne, AD 269

Obv.   IMP VICTORINVS P F AVG. Bust, laureate,
cuirassed, l., holding spear and shield.
Rev.   VOTA AVGVSTI. Bust of Apollo, laureate,
draped, r., with quiver on back, and of
Diana, laureate, l., with bow on shoulder.
N, 5.65 gm. ↓.

932   Aureus Cologne, AD 269

Obv.   IMP C VICTORINVS P F AVG. Bust, laureate,
draped, cuirassed, r.
Rev.   INVICTVS. Bust of Sol, radiate, draped, r.
N, 4.72 gm. ↓.

933   Antoninianus Cologne, AD 270

Obv.   As No. 932, but radiate.
Rev.   PAX AVG. Pax standing l., holding branch
and sceptre; in field l., V, and in r., star.
Æ, 2.47 gm. ↑.

934   Antoninianus Lyons, AD 268

Obv.   IMP C PI VICTORINVS AVG. Bust, radiate,
draped, cuirassed, r.
Rev.   AEQVITAS AVG. Aequitas standing l., holding
scales and cornucopiae. Æ, 2.90 gm. ↑.

935   Aureus Lyons, AD 269

Obv.   IMP VICTORINVS P F AVG. Bust, laureate, r.,
with drapery on l. shoulder.
Rev.   LEG XXX VLP VICT P R. Jupiter standing r.,
head l., holding sceptre and thunderbolt; to
l., capricorn r. N, 5.06 gm. ↑.
A series of aurei honours various legions of which at
least vexillations were serving with the Gallic army.

936 Antoninianus Lyons, AD 270

Obv. IMP C VICTORINVS P F AVG. Bust, radiate,
       draped, cuirassed, r.
Rev. PIETAS AVG. Pietas standing l., dropping
       incense on altar from r. hand, and holding
       box in l. Æ, 3.09 gm. ↓.

Tetricus I and Tetricus II, AD270–274

937 Antoninianus Cologne, AD 270

Obv. IMP C G P ESVVIVS TETRICVS AVG. Bust,
       radiate, draped, cuirassed, r.
Rev. VICTORIA AVG. Victory advancing l., holding
       wreath and palm. Æ, 2.72 gm. ↑.
The portrait of Tetricus I on his first coinage closely
resembles that of Victorinus.

938 Aureus Cologne, AD 270

Obv. IMP C G P ESV TETRICVS AVG. Bust, laureate,
       draped, cuirassed, l.
Rev. VICTORIA AVG. Victory advancing l., holding
       wreath and palm. N, 3.46 gm. ↓.

939 Antoninianus Cologne, AD 270

Obv. As No. 938, but radiate r.
Rev. SPES PVBLICA. Spes advancing l., holding
       flower in r. hand; and raising skirt with l.
       Æ, 1.72 gm. ↑.

940 Aureus Cologne, AD 270

Obv. IMP C TETRICVS P F AVG. Bust, laureate,
       draped, cuirassed, r.
Rev. P M TR P COS P P. Tetricus standing l.,
       holding branch and short sceptre.
       N, 3.66 gm. ↓.

941 Aureus Cologne, AD 270

Obv. IMP TETRICVS AVG. Bust, laureate, cuirassed,
       r., with spear and shield.
Rev. As No. 939. N, 3.84 gm. ↑.

942 Antoninianus Cologne, AD 272

Obv. IMP C TETRICVS P F AVG. Bust, radiate,
       draped, cuirassed, r.
Rev. COMES AVG. Victory advancing l., holding
       wreath and palm. Æ, 2 gm. ↑.

943 Antoninianus Cologne, AD 273

Obv. C P E TETRICVS CAES. Bust, radiate, draped, r.
Rev. PIETAS AVGVSTOR. Jug between lituus and
    knife to l., and simpulum and sprinkler to r.
    Æ, 2.66 gm. ↑.

944 Antoninianus Cologne, AD 274

Obv. As No. 942.
Rev. SALVS AVGG. Salus standing l., sacrificing out
    of patera over altar round which snake is
    twined, and holding rudder in l. hand.
    Æ, 2.35 gm. ↓.

945 Antoninianus Lyons, AD 270

Obv. DIVO VICTORINO PIO. Head, radiate, r.
Rev. CONSACRATIO. Eagle standing r. on globe,
    with head turned l. holding wreath.
    Æ, 2 gm. ↓.

946 Antoninianus Lyons, AD 270

Obv. IMP C P ESV TETRICVS AVG. Bust, radiate,
    draped, cuirassed, r.
Rev. FIDES MILITVM. Fides standing l., holding two
    standards. Æ, 2.21 gm. ↑.

947 Antoninianus Lyons, AD 271

Obv. IMP TETRICVS AVG. Bust, radiate, draped,
    cuirassed, r.
Rev. As No. 946. Æ, 2.80 gm. ↑.

948 Aureus Lyons, AD 272

Obv. IMP C TETRICVS P F AVG. Bust, laureate,
    draped, cuirassed, r.
Rev. AEQVITAS AVG. Aequitas standing l., holding
    scales and cornucopiae. N, 4.08 gm. ↓.

949 Antoninianus Lyons, AD 272

Obv. IMP TETRICVS P F AVG. Bust, radiate, draped,
    cuirassed, r.
Rev. LAETITIA AVG N. Laetitia standing l., holding
    wreath and rudder. Æ, 3.65 gm. ↑.

950 Antoninianus Lyons, AD 273–274

Obv. IMP C TETRICVS P F AVG. Bust, radiate,
    draped, cuirassed, r.
Rev. MARS VICTOR. Mars advancing r., holding
    spear and trophy. Æ, 3 gm. ↓.

951 Aureus Lyons, AD 273–274

Obv. IMP TETRICVS P F AVG. Bust, laureate, draped, cuirassed, r.

Rev. SALVS AVGG. Salus standing l., sacrificing out of patera over altar, and holding sceptre in l. hand. N, 3.97 gm. ↑.

952 Aureus Lyons, AD 274

Obv. C P ESV TETRICVS CAES. Bust, draped, head bare, r.

Rev. SPEI PERPETVAE. Spes advancing l., holding flower and raising skirt. N, 4.66 gm. ↓.

953 Antoninianus Lyons, AD 274

Obv. As No. 952, but radiate.

Rev. SPES AVGG. Spes as No. 952. R, 2.61 gm. ↓.

954 Aureus Lyons, AD 274

Obv. IMPP TETRICI AVGG. Bust of Tetricus II, draped, head bare, r., facing bust of Tetricus I, laureate, draped, l.

Rev. P M TR P COS III P P. Tetricus I, veiled, togate, standing l., holding, in r. hand, patera over altar and, in l., short sceptre, facing Tetricus II, veiled and togate, standing r., holding short sceptre in l. hand and, in r., patera over altar; in ex., VOT X. N, 5.12 gm. ↓.

The reverse commemorates the celebration of the quinquennalia of Tetricus I, and records the taking of vows for the decennalia.

9 The Recovery of the Empire
AD270-294

The empire weathered the crisis of the mid-third century, and under a succession of strong emperors in the latter half of the century some progress was made towards recovery. The unity of the empire was re-established by Aurelian by his regaining control of the eastern province with the defeat of Zenobia of Palmyra, and of the western provinces by the defeat of Tetricus in Gaul. The continuing barbarian incursions were kept in check notably by Aurelian and Probus. A serious obstacle to recovery was the continuing power of the armies to make and unmake emperors, and in an effort to prevent this Diocletian, after his succession, first adopted Maximian as a co-emperor and subsequently appointed Galerius and Constantius as Caesars to himself and Maximian respectively, thus creating the first Tetrarchy. A partial reform of the monetary system was undertaken by Aurelian in 274, and in 294 by Diocletian who also instituted more wide ranging political and administrative reforms.

The mints established in the provinces for the production of Roman coinage in the previous period were maintained and added to. In Italy Rome retained its pre-eminence as a mint, though a revolt of the moneyers at the beginning of Aurelian's reign seems to have caused its temporary closure. Under Aurelian also the mint organisation at Milan was moved to nearby Ticinum, and in the Balkans a second mint in addition to Siscia was set up at Serdica. In the East the mints at Cyzicus and Antioch continued to be active, while in the West Lyons, taken over from the Gallic empire, was retained and very shortly before Diocletian's monetary reform of 294 a second mint was created at Trier. In this period the reverse of the antoninianus was marked by the number of the officina which produced it, and with increasing frequency by at least the initial letter of the issuing mint. On gold also, the mint-signature began to be recorded on the reverse.

Aurelian's early gold continued to be struck on the standard of 60 to the pound of metal, a weight of 5.54 gm., together with a heavier piece at 8.50 gm. marked with a radiate obverse. As part of the coinage reform of 274 the aureus was struck at 50 to the pound, rare pieces being marked I · L, at a weight of 6.54 gm., the standard maintained except briefly at the beginning of the reign of Carus when the aureus was struck at 4.68 gm., 70 to the pound. Early gold of Diocletian reverted to this standard, some pieces being marked with the Greek numeral O = 70, but the standard was again raised to 60 to the pound, sometimes marked with a form of the Greek numeral $\gtrless$ = 60. Between 271–273 Aurelian somewhat improved the weight and fineness of the antoninianus, and in the reform of 274 introduced a new antoninianus at a weight around 3.90 gm., an improved silver fineness of 4.5%, and marked with the formula XXI or its Greek counterpart KA. Controversy continues to rage over the interpretation of this formula. The most favoured solutions are that it expresses the fact that the new unit contains 20 units of another kind, or that it is a statement of silver-bronze relationship of the constituent metal, or that it is simply a restatement of the fact that the antoninianus is the equivalent of two denarii. Some exceptional variants of the formula are found: XI and IA on coins of Tacitus (see Nos. 1001 and 1003 below), and X ET I on coins of Carus (see No. 1037 below). Alongside the new antoninianus Aurelian also struck a smaller coin with laureate obverse, presumably a denarius, occasionally marked with the enigmatic formula VSV. In bronze a new series without S C, instituted by Aurelian, of radiate dupondii and laureate *asses* continued down to Diocletian's reform.

Aurelian,
AD270-275

955 **Antoninianus** Lyons, AD 275

Obv. IMP C AVRELIANVS AVG. Bust, radiate, draped, cuirassed, r.
Rev. PACATOR ORBIS. Sol advancing l., raising r. hand, and holding whip in l.; in ex., ·A·L·. Æ, 4.22 gm. ↑.

The defeat of Tetricus and the re-incorporation into the empire of the western provinces took place in 274, but to judge from the rarity of coinage for Aurelian from the Gallic mint, now definitely marked with the initial L for Lugdunum, this class of coinage for Aurelian began only shortly before his death in August 275.

956   Antoninianus Lyons, AD 275

Obv. SEVERINA AVG. Bust, draped and with
      stephane r., set on crescent.
Rev. CONCORD MILIT. Concordia seated l., holding
      patera and cornucopiae; in ex., D L.
      Æ, 3.98 gm. ↓.
The four officinae of this mint were shared – A and C for Aurelian, B and D for Severina.

957   Antoninianus Rome, AD 270

Obv. IMP C L DOM AVRELIANVS AVG. Bust, radiate,
      draped, cuirassed, r.
Rev. MARTI PACIF. Mars advancing l., holding
      branch, spear and shield; in field l., X.
      Æ, 3.05 gm. ↑.
The first coinage at Rome is marked by the use of the full obverse titulature, a portrait almost identical with that of Quintillus and Claudius II, and a range of reverse types with officina letters repeated exactly from the coinages of these two previous emperors.

958   Aureus Rome, AD 272–273

Obv. IMP C L DOM AVRELIANVS P F AVG. Bust,
      laureate, draped, cuirassed r.
Rev. VIRTVS AVG. Mars advancing r., holding
      spear and trophy; at foot r., seated captive.
      N, 5.25 gm. ↑.
Despite the long obverse legend the more realistic portrait of Aurelian suggests that the date of this coin is somewhat later than the first year of the reign.

959   Antoninianus Rome, AD 274

Obv. IMP AVRELIANVS AVG. Bust, radiate, draped,
      cuirassed, r.
Rev. ORIENS AVG. Sol r., holding branch and bow,
      and trampling on barbarian r.; mint-mark,
$$\frac{\Delta\mid}{\text{XXIR}}$$
      Æ, 4.40 gm. ↑.
Aurelian's antoninianus, reformed in 274, carries the mark of value XXI in the exergue together with the initial R of the mint. As Severina is absent from this issue, but shared in the coinage only from August, it must be dated to the earlier part of the year.

960   Antoninianus Rome, AD 275

Obv. SEVERINA AVG. Bust draped and with
      stephane r., set on crescent.
Rev. CONCORDIAE MILITVM. Concordia standing l.,
      holding two standards; mint-mark, $\dfrac{\mid\epsilon}{\text{XXIR}}$
      Æ, 3.70 gm. ↓.
As all six officinae strike coinage for Severina only, this issue must have been struck after Aurelian's death and before the proclamation of Tacitus.

961 Denarius Rome, AD 274

Obv. IMP AVRELIANVS AVG. Bust, laureate, draped, cuirassed, r.
Rev. VICTORIA AVG. Victory advancing l., holding wreath and palm; mint-mark, $\dfrac{\text{B}\,|}{\text{VSV}}$.

    Æ, 2.84 gm. ↓.

The letters in the exergue constitute a value-mark rather than a mint-mark. It has been suggested that the letters stand for *usu(alis)*, the coin of common account, but explanation remains a matter of controversy.

962 Denarius Rome, AD 274

Obv. As No. 961.
Rev. As No. 961, but at foot of Victory l., a captive; in ex., ϵ. Æ, 2.36 gm. ↓.

963 Denarius Rome, AD 274

Obv. SEVERINA AVG. Bust, draped and with stephane, r.
Rev. VENVS FELIX. Venus standing l., holding small cupid on r. hand, and sceptre in l., in ex., A. Æ, 2.35 gm. ↑.

964 Dupondius Rome, AD 274

Obv. IMP AVRELIANVS AVG. Bust, draped, cuirassed, r.
Rev. SEVERINA AVG. Bust draped and with stephane, r., set on crescent. Æ, 13.17 gm. ↓.

Aurelian's crown on the obverse, and the crescent on the reverse, suggest that the denomination is a dupondius.

965 As Rome, AD 274

Obv. As No. 964, but laureate.
Rev. CONCORDIA AVG. Aurelian and Severina standing l. and r. facing each other; above, radiate bust of Sol, r.; in ex., Δ. Æ, 8.69 gm. ↑.

966 As Rome, AD 274

Obv. As No. 964 *Rev.*, but no crescent.
Rev. IVNO REGINA. Juno standing l., holding patera and sceptre; at foot l., peacock; in ex., S. Æ, 8.82 gm. ↑.

967   As Rome, AD 274

Obv.   SOL DOM IMP ROMANI. Radiate bust of Sol
facing; to l. and r., two horses.

Rev.   AVRELIANVS AVG CONS. Aurelian standing l.,
sacrificing out of patera in r. hand over altar,
and holding sceptre in l.; in ex., s.
Æ, 6.79 gm. ↑.

The cult of Sol furnishes the most common reverse
types of Aurelain's coinage but the prominence
given to Sol as an obverse type on this and the
following coin is without precedent.

968   As Rome, AD 224

Obv.   SOL DOMINVS IMPERI ROMANI. Bust of Sol,
draped, r.

Rev.   As No. 967. Æ, 8.38 gm. ↓.

969   Aureus Milan, AD 270

Obv.   IMP C DOM AVRELIANVS AVG. Bust, laureate,
draped, cuirassed, r.

Rev.   VICTORIA AVG. Victory advancing r., holding
wreath and palm. N, 6.23 gm. ↑.

In the absence of a mint-mark attribution is
dependent on portrait style similar to that of
antoniniani with reverses linked to this mint.

970   Antoninianus Milan, AD 270

Obv.   IMP AVRELIANVS AVG. Bust, radiate, draped,
cuirassed, r.

Rev.   GENIVS ILLV. Genius standing l., holding
patera and cornucopiae; to r., standard; in
ex., P. Æ, 4.09 gm. ↑.

The early coinage from Milan has no mint-
signature, but is produced by Milan's three officinae
organisation. The obverse portrait resembles that of
Quintillus and Claudius II.

971   Antoninianus Milan, AD 272–273

Obv.   As No. 970, but IMP C.

Rev.   ORIENS AVG. Sol advancing l., raising r. hand,
and holding globe in l.; l. and r., seated
captive; mint-mark, TM. Æ, 3.79 gm. ↑.

The final coinage from Milan before it was closed
and the mint organisation transferred to Ticinum is
marked by the mint's initial letter as well as by
officina letter.

972   Antoninianus Ticinum, AD 274

Obv.   As No. 971.

Rev.   As No. 971, but mint-mark, SXXT.
Æ, 4.17 gm. ↓.

The first issue from Ticinum coincides with the
introduction of the reformed antoninianus. In the
exergue the value mark is shown as XX and not as
XXI as at other mints. It is preceded by the officina
letter and followed by the mint initial.

973   Antoninianus Ticinum, AD 275

Obv.   SEVERINA AVG. Bust, draped and with
        stephane, r.; set on crescent.
Rev.   CONCORDIAE MILITVM. Concordia standing l.,
        holding two standards; mint-mark, IVXXT.
        Æ, 4.14 gm. ↑.
As at Rome, there was a final issue for Severina
alone after the death of Aurelian.

974   Antoninianus Siscia, AD 270–271

Obv.   IMP C AVRELIANVS AVG. Bust, radiate, draped,
        cuirassed r.
Rev.   CONCORDIA MILI. Concordia standing l.,
        holding two standards; in field r., Q.
        Æ, 2.88 gm. ↑.

975   Aureus Siscia, AD 271–272

Obv.   IMP AVRELIANVS AVG. Bust, laureate, draped,
        cuirassed, r.
Rev.   FORTVNA REDVX. Fortuna seated l., holding
        rudder and cornucopiae; by seat r., wheel;
        in ex., *P. Ν, 6.44 gm. ↓.
The diminution or perhaps even temporary
cessation of coining at Rome at this time was
compensated for by increased production of gold
and antoniniani at Siscia.

976   Antoninianus Siscia, AD 271–272

Obv.   As No. 975, but radiate.
Rev.   RESTITVT ORIENTIS. Aurelian standing l.,
        holding sceptre, receiving wreath from
        female figure standing r.; in ex., *T.
        Æ, 4.10 gm. ↓.
The type commemorates Aurelian's recovery of the
eastern provinces and the defeat of Zenobia of
Palmyra.

977   Antoninianus Siscia, AD 271–272

Obv.   As No. 976, but IMP C.
Rev.   CONCORDIA MILITVM. Aurelian standing r.,
        clasping hands with Concordia standing l.;
        in ex., P*. Æ, 4.01 gm. ↑.

978   Antoninianus Siscia, AD 274

Obv.   As No. 977.
Rev.   ORIENS AVG. Sol advancing l., raising r. hand
        and holding whip; to l. and r., a seated
        captive; mint-mark, $\frac{\text{S}\mid}{\text{XXIQ}}$.

        Æ, 3.67 gm. ↓.
In common with most other mints, this issue of the
new antoninianus carried on the reverse its initial
letter, s.

979 Antoninianus Serdica, AD 271–272

Obv. As No. 976.
Rev. CONSERVATOR AVG. Aesculapius standing r., holding staff entwined with serpent; mint-mark, SERD. Æ, 2.60 gm. ↑.

A new mint in the Balkans was opened shortly after the beginning of the reign at Serdica (modern Sofia).

980 Antoninianus Serdica, AD 271–272

Obv. As No. 979.
Rev. IOVI CONSER. Aurelian standing r., holding spear, receiving globe from Jupiter standing l., holding sceptre; in ex., P. Æ, 2.78 gm. ↓.

This issue now has a more individual portrait of Aurelian.

981 Antoninianus Serdica, AD 274

Obv. SEVERINA AVG. Bust, draped and with stephane, r., set on crescent.
Rev. CONCORDIA AVGG. Aurelian standing r., clasping hands with Severina, standing l.; mint-mark, $\frac{*\ |}{KA\Delta}$.
Æ, 3.70 gm. ↑.

On the new antoniniani at this mint the Latin formula of value XXI is replaced by the Greek numerals *KA*.

982 Antoninianus Cyzicus, AD 270–271

Obv. IMP C DOM AVRELIANVS AVG. Bust, radiate, draped, cuirassed, r.; below . . .
Rev. FELICIT TEMP. Felicitas standing l., holding caduceus and cornucopiae. Æ, 3.04 gm. ↓.

The early coinage from this mint marks the product of its three officinae by the appropriate number of dots under the obverse bust as had been its practice in earlier reigns.

983 Antoninianus Cyzicus, AD 271–272

Obv. As No. 981, but no DOM.
Rev. RESTITVTOR ORBIS. Aurelian standing l., holding sceptre, receiving wreath from female figure, standing r.; mint-mark, B C. Æ, 3.68 gm. ↓.

The mint signature in the form of its initial letter made its appearance in this issue.

984 Antoninianus Cyzicus, AD 274

Obv. As No. 981, but no C DOM.
Rev. RESTITVTOR EXERCITI. Aurelian standing l., holding sceptre, receiving globe from Mars, helmeted and holding spear, standing r.; mint-mark, $\frac{B}{XXI}$.
Æ, 5.07 gm. ↓.

The new antoninianus with value mark at Cyzicus dropped the initial letter of the mint.

985   Aureus Antioch, AD 272–273

Obv.   IMP C AVRELIANVS AVG. Bust, laureate,
        draped, cuirassed, r.
Rev.   RESTITVTOR ORIENTIS. Sol standing r., head l.,
        raising r. hand, and holding globe in l.
        Ν, 5.37 gm. ↑.
Antioch, when recaptured from the Palmyrenes,
resumed coinage for the emperor with a type
celebrating Aurelian's recovery of the East.

986   Antoninianus Antioch, AD 272–273

Obv.   As No. 984, but radiate.
Rev.   CONSERVAT AVG. Sol advancing l., raising r.
        hand and holding globe in l.; at foot l.,
        seated captive; in ex., ϵ. Ꞃ, 4.90 gm. ↑.

987   Antoninianus Antioch, AD 275

Obv.   SEVERINA P F AVG. Bust, draped and with
        stephane, r., set on crescent.
Rev.   CONCORDIA AVG. Aurelian standing r.,
        clasping hands with Severina, standing l.;
        mint-mark, v .
                   ——
                   XXI
        Ꞃ, 3.21 gm. ↑.
At this mint Severina's titulature includes *P(ia)
F(elix)*, epithets usually reserved for the emperor.

Vabalathus,
AD270–271

988   Antoninianus Antioch, AD 270

Obv.   VABALATHVS V C R IM D R. Bust, radiate,
        draped, cuirassed, r.
Rev.   IMP C AVRELIANVS AVG. Bust, radiate, draped,
        cuirassed, r.; below, ϵ, Ꞃ, 3.51 gm. ↓.
The mint of Antioch under the control of the
Palmyrenes struck coinage for Vabalathus and
Aurelian. Vabalathus' abbreviated titulature is
expanded as *Vir Consularis Romanorum Imperator
Dux Romanorum*. The presence of the officina letter
under the bust of Aurelian indicates that this is the
reverse of the coin.

989   Antoninianus Emesa ?, AD 271

Obv.   IMP C VHABALATHVS AVG. Bust, radiate,
        draped, cuirassed, r.
Rev.   IOVI STATORI. Jupiter standing l., holding
        globe and sceptre; at foot l., eagle; in field l.,
        star. Ꞃ, 3.41 gm. ↑.
A subsequent coinage for Vabalathus as Augustus
was struck at some other mint in Syria, probably
Emesa.

Tacitus, AD275-276

990   **Aureus** Lyons, AD 275–276

Obv. IMP CL TACITVS AVG. Bust, laureate, draped, cuirassed, r.

Rev. ROMAE AETERNAE. Roma, seated l., holding globe and spear; by seat, shield.
$\mathcal{N}$, 4.93 gm. ↑.

The coin is attributed to this mint from the similarity of the portrait to that on the antoninianus below.

991   **Antoninianus** Lyons, AD 275–276

Obv. As No. 990, but radiate,

Rev. SALVS PVBLICA. Salus standing r., feeding out of patera, snake held in arms; in field l. and r., C and star. $\mathcal{R}$, 3.81 gm. ↑.

Though the coinage carries no mint letter, the numbering of the officinae by the letters A to D marks this as a coinage of Lyons.

992   **Aureus** Rome, AD 275–276

Obv. IMP CM CL TACITVS AVG. Bust, laureate, draped, cuirassed, r.

Rev. ROMAE AETERNAE. Roma seated l., holding Victory on globe, and spear; by seat, shield; in ex., S C. $\mathcal{N}$, 4.36 gm. ↓.

The fact that Tacitus was, exceptionally, elected emperor by the Senate lends support to the attribution to Rome of gold marked with S C.

993   **Antoninianus** Rome, AD 275–276

Obv. As No. 992, but radiate.

Rev. CLEMENTIA TEMP. Mars standing l., holding branch and spear, and resting l. hand on shield; in ex., XXIZ. $\mathcal{R}$, 3.78 gm. ↓.

A mint organisation of seven officinae marks this series as from the mint of Rome.

994   **As** Rome, AD 275–276

Obv. As No. 992.

Rev. MARS VLTOR. Mars advancing r., holding spear and shield. Æ, 7.43 gm. ↓.

The new series of bronze coins without S C, begun by Aurelian, was continued in this reign.

995   **Antoninianus** Ticinum, AD 275–276

Obv. As No. 993.

Rev. VICTORIA GOTHI. Victory standing l., holding wreath and palm; in ex., P. $\mathcal{R}$, 3.71 gm. ↑.

The reverse records the defeat of the Goths who had invaded Asia Minor as far south as Cilicia.

996   Antoninianus Ticinum, AD 276

Obv. IMP CM CL TACITVS P AVG COS III. Half-length
bust l., radiate, mantled, and holding eagle-
tipped sceptre.
Rev. SALVS PVBLI. Salus standing r., feeding, out
of patera, snake held in arms; in ex., T.
Æ, 3.50 gm. ↓.

Tacitus had been consul in 273 before becoming
emperor. Coins and an inscription appear to date his
second consulship to 276, and his third consulship
recorded here must, unusually, have also been held
in the same year.

997   Aureus Siscia, AD 275–276

Obv. IMP CM CL TACITVS AVG. Bust, radiate,
cuirassed, l. with spear and decorated shield.
Rev. ROMAE AETERNAE. Roma seated l., holding
Victory on globe, and sceptre; by seat,
shield. Ν, 6.93 gm. ↑.

998   Antoninianus Siscia, AD 275–276

Obv. IMP CM CL TACITVS AVG. Bust, radiate,
draped, cuirassed, r.
Rev. FELICITAS SAECVLI. Felicitas standing l.,
sacrificing out of patera over altar, and
holding caduceus; in ex., V. Æ, 3.29 gm. ↓.

999   Antoninianus Serdica, AD 275–276

Obv. As No. 998.
Rev. PROVIDEN DEOR. Providentia standing l.,
holding two standards, facing Sol standing
l., raising r. hand, and holding globe in l.; in
ex., καΓ. Æ, 4.49 gm. ↓.

1000   Antoninianus Cyzicus, AD 275–276

Obv. As No. 998.
Rev. CLEMENTIA TEMP. Tacitus standing r., holding
spear, and receiving globe from Jupiter.
standing l., holding sceptre; in ex., V.
Æ, 4.46 gm. ↑.

1001   Antoninianus Antioch, AD 275–276

Obv. As No. 998.
Rev. As No. 1000, but Tacitus holds eagle-tipped
sceptre; in field T; in ex., XI.
Æ, 4.26 gm. ↗.

The doubling of value suggested by the use of the
formula XI instead of the usual XXI is difficult to
explain. The rarity of such pieces has so far
precluded destructive analysis which might reveal a
higher silver percentage in the alloy, but from visual
inspection the fabric appears to be the same as in XXI
pieces.

1002 Antoninianus Antioch, AD 275–276

Obv. As No. 998, but IMP C TACITVS AVG.
Rev. As No. 1001, but PROVIDENT DEOR; in field z, and in ex., XXI. Æ, 4.89 gm. ↓.

1003 Antoninianus Tripolis, AD 275–276

Obv. As No. 998.
Rev. CLEMENTIA TEMP. Mars standing l., holding branch and spear, and resting l. hand on shield; in field l., star; in ex., IA. Æ, 4.53 gm. ↓.

In place of the usual value formula in Greek numerals (κα), this piece is marked IA (cf. No. 1001). The attribution to Tripolis in Syria depends on manner of officina marking and on style repeated on later coins with mint abbreviation TR.

Florian, AD276

1004 Antoninianus Lyons, AD 276

Obv. IMP C M AN FLORIANVS AVG. Bust, radiate, draped, cuirassed, r.
Rev. PACATOR ORBIS. Sol advancing l., raising r. hand, and holding whip in l., in ex., III. Æ, 3.14 gm. ↓.

The Roman numeral marking of this four officina mint organisation used on the last issue of Tacitus was continued for Florian.

1005 Aureus Rome, AD 276

Obv. VIRTVS FLORIANI AVG. Bust, laureate, cuirassed, with spear and shield, l.
Rev. VICTORIA PERPET. Victory standing r., inscribing XXX on shield. AV, 4.56 gm. ↑.

The recording of *vota vicennalia* on early coinage of a reign had become quite a convention in the third century, but if XXX on the shield here refers to tricennalia it is quite exceptional.

1006 Antoninianus Rome, AD 276

Obv. IMP FLORIANVS AVG. Bust, radiate, draped, cuirassed, r.
Rev. LAETITIA FVND. Laetitia standing l., holding wreath and anchor; in ex., XXIB. Æ, 3.60 gm. ↓.

1007 As Rome, AD 276

Obv. IMP C M ANN FLORIANVS AVG. Bust, laureate, draped, cuirassed, r.
Rev. VIRTVS AVG. Florian standing r., holding globe and spear. Æ, 6.88 gm. ↓.

1008 Antoninianus Ticinum, AD 276

Obv. As No. 1007, but radiate.
Rev. PERPETVITATE AVG. Perpetuitas standing l., holding globe and sceptre, and resting l. elbow on column; mint-mark, QTI. Æ, 4.11 gm. ↑.

The personification combines the attributes of globe and sceptre commonly associated with Providentia, and the column of Securitas. This issue is exceptional in the coinage of Florian in bearing the initial letters TI of its mint, Ticinum.

1009 Antoninianus Siscia, AD 276

Obv. IMP C M AN FLORIANVS PAAVG. Bust, radiate, draped, cuirassed, r.
Rev. REDITVS AVG. Florian standing l., holding sceptre, and receiving globe from Roma, seated l., holding sceptre; by seat, shield, in ex., XXIV. Æ, 3.30 gm. ↑.

The reverse expresses a wish rather than an accomplished event, as Florian was murdered in the East.

1010 Antoninianus Serdica, AD 276

Obv. As No. 1009, but IMP C M ANN FLORIANVS AVG.
Rev. VICTORIA PERPETVA AVG. Victory standing r., holding palm and presenting wreath to Florian standing l., extending r. hand, and holding sceptre in l.; in field, star; in ex., KAB. Æ, 3.84 gm. ↑.

1011 Antoninianus Cyzicus, AD 276

Obv. As No. 1009, but IMP FLORIANVS AVG.
Rev. CONCORDIA MILITVM. Type as No. 1010; in ex., S. Æ, 3.74 gm. ↓.

Probus, AD276–282

1012 Antoninianus Lyons, AD 277

Obv. VIRTVS PROBI AVG. Bust, radiate-helmeted, cuirassed, with spear and shield, l.
Rev. MARS VICTOR. Mars advancing r., holding trophy and spear; in ex., II. Æ, 3.93 gm. ↑.

The mint is identified by the form of its officina numbering.

1013 Aureus Lyons, AD 282

Obv. IMP C M AVR PROBVS AVG. Bust, laureate, cuirassed, l.
Rev. VICTORIA PROBI AVG. Victory advancing r., holding wreath and palm; to r., trophy at foot of which two seated captives. Ν, 6.67 gm. ↑.

The victory recorded here is the suppression of revolts in Gaul, notably that of the usurper Bonosus.

1014 Antoninianus Rome, AD 279

Obv. IMP PROBVS AVG. Bust, radiate and mantled
  l., holding eagle-tipped sceptre.
Rev. ROMAE AETER. Hexastyle temple with seated
  figure of Roma, mint-mark, R~B.
  Æ, 4.36 gm. ↓.

1015 Aureus Rome, AD 281

Obv. IMP PROBVS P F AVG. Bust, laureate, bare
  except for aegis, and holding spear, l.
Rev. VICT PROBI AVG. Roma seated l., holding
  sceptre and presenting Victory to Probus
  standing r.; behind him, soldier standing r.,
  holding standard; in background, another
  standard; in ex., wreath. N, 6.06 gm. ↑.
A special coinage in honour of the emperor's success
in suppressing the revolt in Gaul was struck at
Rome on the return of Probus in 281. The
following five coins form part of this special issue.

1016 Aureus Rome, AD 281

Obv. IMP PROBVS AVG. Bust, helmeted, cuirassed,
  with spear and decorated shield, l.
Rev. SOLI INVICTO COMITI AVG. Bust of Sol,
  radiate, draped, r. N, 6.18 gm. ↗.

1017 Aureus quinarius Rome, AD 281

Obv. PROBVS AVG. Bust, laureate, draped,
  cuirassed, r.
Rev. FIDES MILITVM. Fides standing l., holding
  standard in either hand. N, 2.66 gm. ↓.

1018 As Rome, AD 281

Obv. PROBVS P F AVG. Bust, as No. 1017.
Rev. As No. 1017. Æ, 8.18 gm. ↑.

1019 Denarius Rome, AD 281

Obv. IMP PROBVS AVG. Bust, as No. 1017.
Rev. P M TR P V COS IIII P P. Probus standing l.,
  raising r. hand and holding sceptre in l.; to l.
  and r., a standard. Æ, 2.33 gm. ↓.

1020 Quinarius Rome, AD 281

Obv. IMP C M AVR PROBVS AVG. Bust, laureate,
  mantled, l., holding eagle-tipped sceptre.
Rev. FELICIA TEMPORA. The Four Seasons
  represented by four little boys, two to r.,
  and two to l. Æ, 1.65 gm. ↑.

1021 Medallion Rome, AD 281

Obv. IMP C PROBVS INVIC P F AVG. Half length bust of Probus, laureate, draped, cuirassed, r., holding spear and shield; behind, head of Sol, radiate, r.

Rev. MONETA AVG. The three Monetae standing l., holding scales and cornucopiae; at foot of each to l., a die(?). Æ, 47.91 gm. ↑.

1022 Aureus Ticinum, AD 277

Obv. IMP C M AVR PROBVS AVG. Bust, laureate and mantled, r., holding eagle-tipped sceptre and globe.

Rev. CONSERVAT AVG. Sol standing r., head l., raising r. hand and holding globe in l. N, 6.45 gm. ↗.

Probus held his first consulship in 277 and the obverse shows him in consular dress. Ticinum lay on the route of the army's march from the East to Gaul.

1023 Antoninianus Ticinum, AD 277

Obv. VIRTVS PROBI AVG. Bust, radiate-helmeted, curassed, l., with spear and shield.

Rev. VOTIS X PROBI AVG ET XX within laurel-wreath. Æ, 3.74 gm. ↑.

The *vota decennalia* commonly feature on early coinage of a reign in the third century but here *vicennalia suscepta* are also mentioned.

1024 Antoninianus Ticinum, AD 277

Obv. VIRTVS PROBI AVG. Bust, radiate, cuirassed, l., with spear and shield inscribed VOTIS X ET XX.

Rev. CONCORD MILIT. Probus standing r., clasping hands with Concordia standing l.; mint-mark, PXXT. Æ, 3.43 gm. ↑.

The recording of the *vota* on the emperor's shield is an innovation.

1025 Aureus Siscia, AD 277

Obv. IMP C M AVR PROBVS AVG. Bust, laureate, draped, cuirassed, r.

Rev. ORIENS AVGVSTI. Sol standing r., head l., raising r. hand, and holding globe in l.; mint-mark, SIS. N, 6.44 gm. ↓.

Gold coinage was struck at Siscia, the mint city of Probus' native province, which he visited on his march from the East to Gaul.

1026 Antoninianus Siscia, AD 277

Obv. IMP C PROBVS P F AVG. Bust, radiate, draped, cuirassed, r.

Rev. ORIGINI AVG. She-wolf standing r., suckling the twins, Romulus and Remus; in ex., XXIT. Æ, 3.85 gm. ↑.

The reference of this novel reverse inscription is to Romulus and Remus as the founders of Rome.

1027 Antoninianus Siscia, AD 277

Obv. IMP C M AVR PROBVS P AVG. Bust, radiate, mantled, l., holding eagle-tipped sceptre.

Rev. SISCIA PROBI AVG. Siscia seated facing, head l., holding diadem in both hands, between the two river gods, Savus and Colopis; l. and r., respectively, pouring water from urn; in ex., XXIQ. Æ, 4.24 gm. ↑.

The coin illustrates the situation of Siscia at the confluence of these two rivers. The reverse repeats the types of a coin of Gallienus who opened the mint at Siscia.

1028 Aureus Siscia, AD 278

Obv. IMP C M AVR PROBVS P AVG. Bust, laureate, mantled l., holding branch and eagle-tipped sceptre.

Rev. HERCVLI ARCADIO. Hercules standing r., subduing the Arcadian stag. Ν, 5.94 gm. ↓.

Several reverses illustrating the labours of Hercules were included in a gold coinage struck when the emperor was once again in Siscia in this year.

1029 Antoninianus Serdica, AD 276

Obv. IMP M AVR PROBVS P AVG. Bust, radiate-helmeted, cuirassed, l., with spear and shield.

Rev. VIRTVS PROBI AVG. Probus galloping r., spearing enemy whose shield lies below horse; in ex., KAB. Æ, 3.76 gm. ↓.

1030 Aureus Serdica, AD 280

Obv. IMP C M AVR PROBVS AVG. Bust, laureate, draped, cuirassed, r.

Rev. SECVRITAS SAECVLI. Securitas seated l., holding sceptre in r. hand, and raising l. hand to head. Ν, 5.37 gm. ↓.

A coinage in gold is probably associated with the emperor's presence in Serdica on his way to the East.

1031 Antoninianus Cyzicus, AD 280

Obv. IMP C M AVR PROBVS P F AVG. Bust, radiate, mantled, l., holding eagle-tipped sceptre.

Rev. SOLI INVICTO. Sol in facing quadriga, with two horses to l., and two to r.; mint-mark,
$$\frac{\text{CM}\,.}{\text{XXI}}$$
Æ, 4.37 gm. ↑.

1032 Aureus Antioch, AD 280

Obv. IMP C M AVR PROBVS AVG. Bust, laureate, draped, cuirassed, r.

Rev. P M TR P V COS IIII P P. Probus in quadriga l., holding branch and sceptre; mint-mark, ANT. Ν, 6.23 gm. ↓.

The reverse shows the *processus consularis* on the occasion of Probus entering on his fourth consulship and provides one of the earliest instances of this mint's signature on the coinage.

1033 Antoninianus Antioch, AD 280

Obv. IMP C M AVR PROBVS P F AVG. Bust, radiate, draped, cuirassed, r.
Rev. RESTITVT ORBIS. Female figure standing r., presenting wreath to Probus standing l., holding globe and sceptre; in ex., ϵⲆ . Ⱥ, 4.01 gm. ↑. $\frac{}{XXI}$

Because of the superstitious avoidance of the Greek numeral for nine, the letter Θ, the ninth officina is marked by the numerals ϵⲆ (5+4).

1034 Antoninianus Tripolis, AD 276

Obv. As No. 1033.
Rev. CLEMENTIA TEMP. Probus standing r., holding eagle-tipped sceptre, receiving globe from Jupiter standing l., holding sceptre; mint-mark, $\frac{T}{KA}$.
Ⱥ, 3.59 gm. ↑.

The initial letter of this mint makes its earliest appearance here.

Carus and Family, AD282–285

1035 Aureus Lyons, AD 282–283

Obv. IMP CARVS·P·F·AVG. Bust, laureate, cuirassed, r., with spear and shield.
Rev. FORTVNA AVG. Fortuna standing l., holding rudder and cornucopiae. N, 4.22 gm. ↑.

The attribution to the Gallic mint is confirmed by the portrait style, reminiscent of Tetricus I, and the punctuation of the obverse legend, similar to that on coins of the Gallic emperors.

1036 Antoninianus Lyons, AD 282–283

Obv. CARVS ET CARINVS AVGG. Busts jugate, radiate, draped, cuirassed, r. of Carus and Carinus.
Rev. PAX AVG. Pax advancing l., holding branch and sceptre. Ⱥ, 3.36 gm. ↓.

The form AVGG in the obverse inscription places the coin after the advancement of Carinus to the rank of Augustus in the summer of 283 and soon after that event, for the reverse has simply AVG from a die carried on from Carus as sole Augustus.

1037 Double antoninianus Lyons, AD 282–283

Obv. IMP C M AVR CARVS P F AVG. Bust, with double radiate crown, draped, cuirassed, r.
Rev. ABVNDANTIA AVG. Galley l.: in ex., X ET I. Ⱥ, 4.70 gm. ↓.

Though the form of radiate crown suggests that this could be a double piece, the weight of this example is not twice the weight of the average antoninianus of the period; and no ready explanation of the formula X ET I suggests itself (cf. Nos. 1001 and 1063).

1038 Antoninianus Lyons, AD 283–284

Obv. IMP C NVMERIANVS AVG. Bust, radiate, draped, cuirassed, r.
Rev. PACATOR ORBIS. Numerian standing r., holding spear and shield, and attacking fallen enemy; in ex., c. Æ, 2.97 gm. ↓.

1039 Antoninianus Lyons, AD 283–284

Obv. IMP CARINVS P F AVG. Bust, radiate, cuirassed, l., with spear and shield.
Rev. SALVS AVGG. Salus standing r., feeding, out of patera, snake held in arms; mint-mark, $\frac{| D}{LVG}$.
Æ, 4.05 gm. ↓.
Only this last joint issue for Carinus and Numerian carries the signature of the mint.

1040 Aureus Rome, AD 282–283

Obv. IMP C M AVR CARVS P F AVG. Bust, laureate, draped, cuirassed r.
Rev. SPES PVBLICA. Spes standing l., holding flower and raising skirt. N, 4.50 gm. ↑.

1041 Aureus Rome, AD 282–283

Obv. M AVR CARINVS NOB CAES. Bust, laureate, draped, cuirassed, r.
Rev. PAX AETERNA. Pax advancing l., holding branch and sceptre. N, 4.04 gm. ↓.

1042 Denarius Rome, AD 282–283

Obv. CARINVS NOBIL CAES. Bust, laureate, draped, cuirassed, r.
Rev. PRINCIPI IVVENTVT. Carinus standing l., raising r. hand, and holding inverted spear; to l. and r., two standards. Æ, 4.48 gm. ↑.

1043 Antoninianus Rome, AD 282

Obv. M AVR CARINVS NOB CAES. Bust, radiate, draped, cuirassed, r.
Rev. PIETAS AVGG. Jug between sprinkler and simpulum to l., and knife and lituus to r.; mint-mark, RZ. Æ, 4.33 gm. ↓.
The form of issue mark carried over from the last coinage of Probus was still in use when Carinus was appointed Caesar.

1044 Aureus Rome, AD 282–284

Obv. CARINVS ET NVMERIANVS AVGG. Busts of Carinus and Numerian, jugate, laureate, bare but for drapery on l. shoulder.
Rev. VICTORIA AVGG. Victory advancing r., carrying trophy. N, 4.17 gm. ↓.

The presence of only two G's in the abbreviation AVGG indicates that this and the next two coins were issued after the death of Carus in the summer of 283.

1045 Denarius Rome, AD 283–284

Obv. As No. 1044.
Rev. VICTORIA AVGG. Victory advancing r., holding trophy in both hands. Æ, 2.97 gm. ↓.

1046 Aureus Rome, AD 283–284

Obv. IMP NVMERIANVS P F AVG. Bust, laureate, draped, cuirassed, r.
Rev. VIRTVS AVGG. Hercules standing r., holding club and lion skin. N, 5.99 gm. ↑.

1047 Antoninianus Rome, AD 283–284

Obv. IMP NVMERIANVS AVG. Bust, radiate, draped, cuirassed, r.
Rev. PRINCIPI IVVENTVT. Numerian standing l., holding wand and sceptre; in ex., KAΔ. Æ, 3.19 gm. ↑.

After the first coinage of the reign the antoniniani at Rome carried the value formula in Greek numerals KA, possibly because much of the coinage was intended for use in the East in the war against Persia.

1048 Denarius Rome, AD 283–284

Obv. As No. 1047, but laureate.
Rev. PAX AVGG. Pax advancing l., holding branch and sceptre. Æ, 2.37 gm. ↓.

1049 Medallion Rome, AD 283

Obv. IMP C NVMERIANVS P F AVG COS. Bust, laureate, mantled, r., holding Victory on globe, and eagle-tipped sceptre.
Rev. ADLOCVTIO AVGG. Carinus and Numerian accompanied by officer, standing l. on platform, haranguing four soldiers carrying a standard and two legionary eagles. Æ, 39.04 gm. ↓.

1050 Antoninianus Rome, AD 284–285

Obv. IMP CARINVS P F AVG. Bust, radiate, draped, cuirassed, r.
Rev. PIETAS AVG. Mercury standing l., holding purse and caduceus; in ex., KA. Æ, 3.37 gm. ↓.
The singular AVG of the reverse dates this issue to the sole reign of Carinus after the death of Numerian.

1051 As Rome, AD 284–285

Obv. As No. 1050, but laureate.
Rev. VICTORIA AVG. Victory advancing l., holding wreath and palm. Æ, 5.56 gm. ↑.
The reverse probably alludes to the defeat of Julian in Pannonia in 285.

1052 Aureus Rome, AD 283–285

Obv. MAGNIA VRBICA AVG. Bust draped, and with stephane, r.
Rev. VENERI VICTRICI. Venus standing r., raising robe over r. shoulder with r. hand, and holding apple in l. A', 4.73 gm. ↓.
Coinage of Magnia Urbica, wife of Carinus, is dated to the last two years of his reign.

1053 Quinarius Rome, AD 283–285

Obv. IMP CARINVS AVG. Bust, laureate-helmeted, cuirassed, with shield, and holding horse's head by bridle in r. hand.
Rev. MAGNIA VRBICA AVG. Bust, draped, and with stephane, r. Æ, 1.27 gm. ↑.

1054 Antoninianus Rome, AD 285

Obv. DIVO NVMERIANO. Head, radiate, r.
Rev. CONSECRATIO. Eagle standing r., head l.; in ex., KAA. Æ, 5.26 gm. ↑.
A consecration coinage for three deified members of the imperial family was included in the latest issues of Carinus.

1055 Antoninianus Rome, AD 285

Obv. DIVO CARO PERS. Head, radiate, r.
Rev. As No. 1054, but in ex., KAA. Æ, 5.04 gm. ↑.

1056 Antoninianus Rome, AD 285

Obv. DIVO NIGRINIANO AVG. Head, radiate, r.
Rev. As No. 1054. Æ, 4.21 gm. ↑.
An inscription records Nigrinian as a grandson of Carus, but it is uncertain who his parents were.

1057 Antoninianus Ticinum, AD 282–283

Obv. IMP C M AVR KARVS P F AV. Bust, radiate, draped, cuirassed, r.
Rev. SPES PVBLICA. Spes advancing l., holding flower and raising skirt; in ex., SXXI. Æ, 4.63 gm. ↓.
Unusually, especially at a western mint, K is substituted for C in the emperor's name.

1058 Aureus Ticinum, AD 283–285

Obv. IMP CARINVS P F AVG. Bust, laureate, draped, cuirassed, l.
Rev. FELICIT PVBLICA. Felicitas standing l., holding caduceus in r. hand, and leaning l. elbow on column. Ν, 4.44 gm. ↑.

1059 Antoninianus Ticinum, AD 283–285

Obv. MAGNIA VRBICA AVG. Bust, draped, and with stephane r., set on crescent.
Rev. VENVS CELEST. Venus standing l., holding apple and sceptre; in ex., SXXI. Æ, 4.29 gm. ↑.

1060 Aureus Siscia, AD 282–283

Obv. DEO ET DOMINO CARO AVG. Bust, laureate, draped, cuirassed, r.
Rev. VICTORIA AVG. Victory standing l. on globe, holding wreath and palm. Ν, 4.86 gm. ↑.

1061 Aureus Siscia, AD 282–283

Obv. M AVR CARINVS NOB CAES. Bust, laureate, draped, cuirassed, r.
Rev. As No. 1060. Ν, 4.06 gm. ↓.

1062 Aureus Siscia, AD 283–284

Obv. IMP C NVMERIANVS P F AVG. Bust, laureate, draped, cuirassed, r.
Rev. ABVNDANTIA AVGG. Abundantia standing l., emptying cornucopiae. Ν, 4.51 gm. ↑.

1063 Double antoninianus (?) Siscia, AD 282

Obv. DEO ET DOMINO CARO INVIC AVG. Busts of Sol, radiate, draped, r. and Carus, radiate, draped l.
Rev. FELICITAS REIPVBLICAE. Felicitas standing l., holding caduceus and sceptre, and resting l. elbow on column; in ex., ·X·I·I·. Æ, 5.18 gm. ↑.
A convincing explanation of the value formula in the exergue of the reverse has not yet been advanced (cf. No. 1037).

1064 Antoninianus Siscia, AD 285

Obv. IMP C M AVR CARINVS P F AVG. Bust, radiate,
  draped, cuirassed, r.
Rev. VOTA PVBLICA. Carinus and Numerian
  standing l. and r. respectively, sacrificing out
  of patera over tripod; behind, two
  standards; mint-mark, SMSXXIB.
  Æ, 3.91 gm. ↑.
The full signature of the mint S(acra) M(oneto)
S(isciensis) made its appearance on the last issue of
Carinus before the mint was seized by the usurper,
Julian.

1065 Antoninianus Cyzicus, AD 282–283

Obv. IMP C M AVR CARVS P F AVG. Bust, radiate,
  draped, cuirassed, r.
Rev. VICTORIA AVG. Victory advancing l., holding
  wreath and palm; in ex., B. Æ, 3.02 gm. ↑.
The first coinage at Cyzicus is for Carus alone.

1066 Aureus Cyzicus, AD 282–283

Obv. IMP M AVR CARINVS P F AVG. Bust, laureate,
  draped, cuirassed, r.
Rev. ADVENTVS AVGG NN. Emperors standing l.
  and r. respectively, together holding Victory
  on globe who crowns them; mint-mark, C.
  N, 5.27 gm. ↓.
Though the coin has the obverse of Carinus, the
two emperors who went to the East for the Persian
War were Carus and Numerian whose arrival at
Cyzicus is represented on the reverse.

1067 Antoninianus Antioch, AD 282–283

Obv. IMP C M AVR CARVS P F AVG. Bust, radiate,
  draped, cuirassed, r.
Rev. VIRTVS AVGG. Carinus standing r., holding
  sceptre, and receiving Victory on globe
  from Carus standing l., holding sceptre; in
  field and exergue, $\frac{B}{XXI}$.
  Æ, 3.64 gm. ↓.
The first coinage at Antioch includes Carinus,
possibly still as Caesar.

1068 Antoninianus Antioch, AD 282–283

Obv. IMP C M AVR CARINVS NOB C. Bust, radiate,
  draped, cuirassed r.
Rev. As No. 1067, but AVGGG; in field and ex.,
  $\frac{\epsilon\varDelta}{XXI}$.
  Æ, 4.33 gm. ↓.
The form AVGGG on the reverse indicates that by this
issue Numerian had also been appointed Caesar.

1069 Aureus Antioch, AD 282–283

Obv. IMP C M AVR CARVS P F AVG. Bust, laureate,
  draped, cuirassed, r.
Rev. VICTORIAE AVGG. Victory advancing r.,
  holding wreath and palm; mint-mark, SMA.
  N, 4.66 gm. ↑.
Gold at Antioch is also now marked with the full
mint-signature S(acra) M(oneta) A(ntiochensis).

1070 Aureus Antioch, AD 282–283

Obv. IMP C M AVR NVMERIANVS NOB C. Bust, laureate, draped, cuirassed, r.
Rev. CONSERVAT AVGGG. Sol standing l., raising r. hand, and holding globe in l.; mint-mark, SMA. *N*, 5.41 gm. ↑.

1071 Antoninianus Tripolis, AD 283–284

Obv. IMP C M AVR NVMERIANVS P F AVG. Bust, radiate, draped, cuirassed, r.
Rev. VIRTVS AVGG·. Numerian standing r., holding short sceptre, and receiving globe from Carinus standing l., holding long sceptre; mint-mark, $\frac{\text{TR}}{\text{XXI}}$.

R, 4.43 gm. ↑.
The dot at the end of the reverse legend probably distinguishes the second officina at this mint.

Julian, AD284-285

1072 Aureus Siscia, AD 284–285

Obv. IMP C IVLIANVS P F AVG. Bust, laureate, draped, cuirassed, r.
Rev. LIBERTAS PVBLICA. Libertas standing l., holding pileus and cornucopiae.
N, 4.48 gm. ↑.

1073 Antoninianus Siscia, AD 284–285

Obv. As No. 1072, but radiate.
Rev. PANNONIAE AVG. The two Pannoniae standing facing, head l. and r., respectively, each stretching out r. hand, and Pannonia on r., holding standard; mint-mark, XXIΓs.
R, 3.56 gm. ↓.
The mint at Siscia, which the usurper Julian controlled, signed its antoniniani with its initial s at the end of the formula in the exergue.

Diocletian and the First Tetrarchy (Pre-Reform), AD284-294

1074 Antoninianus Trier, AD 293

Obv. IMP MAXIMIANVS AVG. Bust, radiate-helmeted, cuirassed, r.
Rev. CONCORDIA AVGG. Diocletian and Maximian standing r. and l. respectively, clasping r. hands, and holding spear in l. hand; mint-mark, PT. *R*, 3.86 gm. ↓.
The date of the opening of a second mint in Gaul at Trier is determined by the participation in the first issue of Constantius and Galerius, appointed Caesars in 293.

1075 Antoninianus Trier, AD 293

Obv. IMP DIOCLETIANVS AVG. Bust, radiate, draped,
cuirassed, r.

Rev. CLARITAS AVGG. Sol standing l., r. hand
raised, and holding globe in l.; at foot l.,
captive; mint-mark, PTR. Æ, 4.16 gm. ↓.

The earliest mint-mark PT was soon changed to PTR,
presumably to avoid confusion with the signature
of Ticinum.

1076 **Antoninianus** Trier, AD 293–294

Obv. CONSTANTIVS NOB C. Bust, radiate, draped,
cuirassed, r.

Rev. PIETAS AVGG. Constantius standing r.,
holding spear, and raising turreted female
figure kneeling l., and holding cornucopiae;
mint-mark, $\frac{\text{C} \mid}{\text{PTR}}$.

Æ, 3.56 gm. ↑.

1077 **Antoninianus** Trier, AD 293–294

Obv. As No. 1070, but MAXIMIANVS NOB C.

Rev. AVSPIC FEL. Felicitas standing l., holding
tessera and cornucopiae; at foot l., child,
mint-mark, $\frac{\mid \text{D}}{\text{PTR}}$.

Æ, 3.30 gm. ↑.

1078 **Aureus** Lyons, AD 285

Obv. IMP C C VAL DIOCLETIANVS P F AVG. Bust,
laureate, draped, cuirassed, r.

Rev. MARS VICTOR. Mars advancing r., holding
trophy and spear. N, 4.40 gm. ↑.

1079 **Aureus** Lyons, AD 286

Obv. As No. 1078.

Rev. IMP C MAXIMIANVS AVG. Bust, laureate l., in
lion's skin, and holding club over r.
shoulder. N, 5.36 gm. ↓.

The occasion of this coinage was most probably the
co-option by Diocletian of Maximian as a fellow
Augustus.

1080 **Antoninianus** Lyons, AD 286

Obv. As No. 1078, but radiate.

Rev. IOVI CONSERVAT AVGG. Jupiter standing l.,
holding thunderbolt and sceptre; in field l.,
A. Æ, 3.47 gm. ↑.

From the earliest issue a frequent reverse pictures
Jupiter as the protector of Diocletian.

1081 **Antoninianus** Lyons, AD 289

Obv. IMP C MAXIMIANVS AVG. Bust, radiate,
cuirassed, l., with spear and shield.

Rev. HERCVLI INVICTO AVG. Hercules standing l.,
holding Victory on globe in l. hand, and
club and lion-skin in r.; in field l., s.
Æ, 4.24 gm. ↓.

Hercules is portrayed as the protector of Maximian.

1082 Antoninianus Lyons, AD 292

Obv. IMP DIOCLETIANVS AVG. Bust, radiate, draped,
      cuirassed, r.
Rev. P M TR P VIII COS III P P. Lion advancing l.,
      holding thunderbolt in mouth, in ex., A*.
      Æ, 3.49 gm. ↓.

1083 Denarius Lyons, AD 293–294

Obv. MAXIMIANVS AVG. Bust, laureate, draped,
      cuirassed, facing.
Rev. SAECVLARES AVGG. Elephant with mahout l.
      Æ, 2.12 gm. ↓.
This coin, unusual in its denomination, obverse
portrait, and reverse type, is linked by its reverse
inscription to antoniniani. Here SAECVLARES is
associated with *vota vicennalia suscepta*, appropriate
to Diocletian's tenth year, 293–4.

1084 Aureus Rome, AD 286

Obv. IMP C C VAL DIOCLETIANVS P F AVG. Bust,
      radiate, draped, cuirassed, r.
Rev. IOVI CONSERVAT AVGG. Jupiter standing l.,
      holding thunderbolt and sceptre.
      Ν, 5.68 gm. ↓.
Despite the radiate crown on the obverse this coin is
to be classed as a heavy aureus rather than a double
aureus.

1085 Aureus Rome, AD 286–287

Obv. As No. 1084, but laureate.
Rev. As No. 1084, Ν, 4.63 gm. ↑.
The light-weight aureus has a laureate obverse.

1086 Antoninianus Rome, AD 285–286

Obv. IMP DIOCLETIANVS AVG. Bust, radiate, draped,
      cuirassed, r.
Rev. IOVI CONSERVAT AVG. Jupiter standing l.,
      holding thunderbolt and sceptre; in ex., XXI.
      Æ, 4.64 gm. ↓.
The singular AVG of the reverse marks this as
coinage for Diocletian alone before the co-option of
Maximian.

1087 Denarius Rome, AD 285–286

Obv. As No. 1086, but laureate and P F.
Rev. As No. 1086. Æ, 2.92 gm. ↑.

1088 Quinarius Rome, AD 285–286

Obv. As No. 1086, but laureate.
Rev. As No. 1086. Æ, 2.05 gm. ↑.

1089 As Rome, AD 286

Obv. As No. 1086, but laureate.
Rev. As No. 1086, but AVGG. Æ, 6.60 gm. ↑.

1090 As Rome, AD 286

Obv. IMP MAXIMIANVS AVG. Bust, laureate, draped, cuirassed, r.
Rev. HERCVLI PACIFERO. Hercules standing r., head turned l., holding branch, club, and lion-skin. Æ, 6.75 gm. ↑.

1091 Dupondius (?) Rome, AD 286

Obv. DIOCLETIANVS AVG. Head, radiate, r.
Rev. MAXIMIANVS AVG. Head, radiate, r.
Æ, 7.27 gm. ↑.
The suggested denomination is based on the radiate portraits, and the higher weight, 7.30 gm.

1092 Quinarius Rome, AD 286

Obv. DIOCLETIANVS AVG. Jugate busts l. of Diocletian, laureate, cuirassed, with spear and shield, and of Sol radiate, holding whip.
Rev. FELICIA TEMPORA. The Four Seasons as four small boys. Æ, 1.76 gm. ↓.

1093 Medallion Rome, AD 285

Obv. IMP C C VAL DIOCLETIANVS P F AVG. Half-length bust, laureate, r. in cuirass decorated with Medusa head, with aegis on l. shoulder, and holding eagle in l. hand.
Rev. MONETA AVG. The Three Monetae standing facing, head l., holding scales and cornucopiae; at foot of each, l., a die? Æ, 44.10 gm. ↓.

1094 Medallion Rome, AD 286

Obv. IMP C M AVR VAL MAXIMIANVS P F AVG. Head in lion-scalp head-dress l.
Rev. As No. 1093, but AVGG. Æ, 74.59 gm. ↑.

1095 Medallion Rome, AD 286

Obv. IMP C C VAL DIOCLETIANVS P F AVG. Bust laureate r., in cuirass with Medusa head, and aegis on l. shoulder.
Rev. MONETA IOVI ET HERCVLI AVGG. Moneta standing front, head l., holding scales and cornucopiae; at foot l., a die?; to l., Jupiter, standing front, head r., holding sceptre and thunderbolt; to r., Hercules standing front, head l., leaning on club in r. hand, and holding lion-skin in l. Æ, 16.23 gm. ↑.

1096 Medallion Rome, AD 288

Obv. VIRTVS MAXIMIANI AVG. Half-length, bust, laureate, r., in cuirass decorated with Medusa head, holding horse's head by bridle in r. hand, and shield on l. shoulder.
Rev. As No. 1094. Æ, 38.43 gm. ↑.

1097 Aureus Rome, AD 288–293

Obv. IMP C C VAL DIOCLETIANVS P F AVG. Bust, laureate, draped, cuirassed, r.
Rev. IOVI FVLGERATORI. Jupiter standing r., hurling thunderbolt at snake-footed giant kneeling at foot r.; mint-mark, P R. Æ, 5.76 gm. ↓.

1098 Aureus quinarius Rome, AD 288–293

Obv. IMP DIOCLETIANVS P F AVG. Bust, laureate, draped, cuirassed r.
Rev. IOVI CONSERVAT AVGG. Jupiter standing l., holding thunderbolt and sceptre; mint-mark, PR. A̸, 2.32 gm. ↓.

1099 Aureus Rome, AD 288–293

Obv. VIRTVS MAXIMIANI AVG. Bust, laureate, r., draped, and in cuirass decorated with Medusa head, holding up spear in r. hand, and shield and two spears in l.
Rev. VIRTVS AVGG. Hercules standing r., strangling the Nemean lion; to l., club; mint-mark, PR. A̸, 5.91 gm. ↑.

1100 Aureus Rome, AD 288–293

Obv. MAXIMIANVS P F AVG. Head, laureate, r.
Rev. HERCVLI VICTORI. Hercules seated facing, head r.; to l., club; to r., quiver and bow; mint-mark, PR. A̸, 5.58 gm. ↑.

1101 Double aureus Rome, AD 293

Obv. IMP C C VAL DIOCLETIANVS P F AVG. Bust, radiate, r., with drapery on shoulders.

Rev. PERPETVA FELICITAS AVGG. Victory standing r., presenting globe to Jupiter standing l., holding thunderbolt and sceptre, r. foot on captive, seated l.; mint-mark PR.
ᴀᴠ, 12.92 gm. ↑.

Part of a special coinage on the occasion of Diocletian's decennalia.

1102 Double aureus Rome, AD 293

Obv. FL VAL CONSTANTIVS NOB CAES. Bust, radiate, r., with drapery on shoulders.
Rev. PRINCIPI IVVENTVTIS. Constantius standing r., holding spear and globe; mint-mark, PROM.
ᴀᴠ, 12.83 gm. ↑.

Part of a special coinage on the occasion of the appointment of Constantius and Galerius as Caesars.

1103 Aureus Rome, AD 293

Obv. DIOCLETIANVS P F AVG. Head, laureate, r.
Rev. IOVI CONSERVATORS AVGG. Jupiter standing l., holding thunderbolt and sceptre; mint-mark, PROM. ᴀᴠ, 5.12 gm. ↓.

1104 Antoninianus Rome, AD 293–294

Obv. IMP MAXIMIANVS P F AVG. Bust, radiate, mantled, l., holding eagle-tipped sceptre.
Rev. PRIMIS X MVLTIS XX. Victory standing r., inscribing VO/T X on shield on palm-tree; in ex., XXIє. ᴁ, 3.54 gm. ↓.

The reverse commemorates the celebration of Diocletian's decennalia in 293–294.

1105 Antoninianus Rome, AD 293–294

Obv. FL VAL CONSTANTIVS NOB C. Bust, radiate, draped, cuirassed, r.
Rev. PRINCIPI IVVENTVT. Constantius standing r., holding spear and globe; mint-mark, $\frac{\quad | \text{R}}{\text{XXIA}}$.

ᴁ, 3.10 gm. ↑.

1106 As Rome, AD 293–294

Obv. MAXIMIANVS NOB CAES. Bust, laureate, draped, cuirassed, r.
Rev. PRINCIPI IVVENTVTI. Galerius standing r., holding spear and globe. ᴁ, 6.39 gm. ↑.

1107 Antoninianus Ticinum, AD 285

Obv. IMP C C VAL DIOCLETIANVS P F AVG. Bust, radiate, draped, cuirassed, r.
Rev. IOVI CONSERVAT. Jupiter standing l., holding thunderbolt and sceptre; mint-mark, PXXIT. ᴁ, 3.72 gm. ↓.

1108 Aureus Ticinum, AD 286

Obv. IMP C M AVR VAL MAXIMIANVS P F AVG.
Bust, laureate, draped, cuirassed, r.

Rev. IOVI CONSERVAT AVGG. Jupiter standing l.,
holding thunderbolt and sceptre; mint-
mark, SMT. A̶, 5.23 gm. ↓.

Maximian appears here not with his own usual
Hercules reverse but with the Jupiter reverse
associated with Diocletian.

1109 Antoninianus Ticinum, AD 286

Obv. IMP C M AVR VAL MAXIMIANVS AVG. Bust,
radiate, draped, cuirassed, r.

Rev. HERCVLI CONSERVAT. Hercules standing r.,
holding club set on rock, and lion-skin;
mint-mark, SXXIT. Æ, 4.10 gm. ↑.

1110 Antoninianus Ticinum, AD 293

Obv. FL VAL CONSTANTIVS NOB C. Bust, radiate,
draped, cuirassed, r.

Rev. VIRTVS AVGG. Hercules standing r., holding
club and lion-skin; to r., apple-tree round
which is entwined a serpent; mint-mark,
XXIT. Æ, 3.34 gm. ↑.

The reverse pictures one of the labours of Hercules,
the securing of the apples from the Garden of the
Hesperides.

1111 Antoninianus Siscia, AD 288–289

Obv. IMP C C VAL DIOCLETIANVS P F AVG. Bust,
radiate, draped, cuirassed, r.

Rev. CONSERVATOR AVGG. Diocletian standing r.,
holding sceptre, and Jupiter standing l.,
holding sceptre, sacrificing out of pateras
over altar, in ex., •Γ• XXI•BI. Æ, 4.19 gm. ↓.

In series of antoniniani the products of the three
officinae are distinguished additionally by placing
the Greek letters, *I*, or *O*, or *βI* (the component letters
of IOVI) after the value formula on coins of
Diocletian.

1112 Antoninianus Siscia, AD 288–289

Obv. IMP C M AVR VAL MAXIMIANVS P F AVG. Bust,
radiate, draped, cuirassed, r.

Rev. CONSERVATOR AVGG. Maximian standing r.,
holding sceptre, and Hercules standing l.,
holding club, sacrificing out of patera over
altar; in ex., XXIB· *KOY*. Æ, 3.99 gm. ↓.

For Maximian Greek letters *HP*, or *KOY*, or *AI* (the
component letters of HERCVLI) are used as an
additional distinction of the three officinae.

1113 Antoninianus Heraclea, AD 291

Obv. IMP C M AVR MAXIMIANVS P F AVG. Bust,
radiate, draped, cuirassed, r.

Rev. CONCORDIA MILITVM. Maximian standing l.,
holding short sceptre, and receiving Victory
on globe from Jupiter, standing l., holding
sceptre; in field ε; in ex., XXI. Æ, 4.53 gm. ↓.

A new mint was established at Heraclea in Thrace in
291. The first coinage did not carry the initial letter
of the mint.

1114 Antoninianus Heraclea, AD 292

Obv. IMP C C VAL DIOCLETIANVS P F AVG. Bust,
   radiate, draped, cuirassed, r.
Rev. As No. 1109, but Diocletian standing r.;
   mint-mark, $\frac{H\epsilon}{XXI}$.
   Æ, 4.38 gm. ↑.
The initial H of Heraclea was placed on the reverse
in the second issue.

1115 Antoninianus Cyzicus, AD 285

Obv. IMP C C VAL DIOCLETIANVS AVG. Bust, radiate,
   draped, cuirassed, r.; below bust, ⦁.
Rev. CONCORDIA MILITVM. Diocletian standing r.,
   holding short sceptre, receiving Victory
   from Jupiter standing l., holding sceptre; in
   field, A; in ex., XXI. Æ, 4.48 gm. ↑.
The indication of officina by one or more dots
under the bust, a practice typical of this mint,
appeared on the early coinage of Diocletian.

1116 Aureus Cyzicus, AD 286

Obv. As No. 1115, but laureate.
Rev. FATIS VICTRICIBVS. The three Fates: the first
   standing r. facing the other two standing l.,
   each holding cornucopiae and together
   holding rudder; the third standing l.,
   holding cornucopiae and rudder; mint-
   mark, s c. N, 5.36 gm. ↑.
The signature on early gold issue includes the initial
C of the mint-name.

1117 Aureus Cyzicus, AD 286

Obv. IMP C MAXIMIANVS AVG. Bust, laureate,
   draped, cuirassed, r.
Rev. VIRTVTI HERCVLIS. Hercules standing r.,
   leaning on club set on rock, and holding
   lion-skin; mint-mark, s c. N, 5.30 gm. ↓.

1118 Aureus Cyzicus, AD 293

Obv. MAXIMIANVS AVGVSTVS. Head, laureate, r.
Rev. CONCORDIAE AVGG NN. Diocletian and
   Maximian seated l., each holding globe and
   short sceptre, and crowned by Victory
   poised between them. N, 5.31 gm. ↑.

1119 Antoninianus Antioch, AD 284

Obv. IMP C C VAL DIOCLETIANVS P F AVG. Bust,
   radiate, draped, cuirassed, r.
Rev. VICTORIA AVG. Victory standing r., holding
   palm and presenting wreath to Diocletian
   standing l., holding globe and sceptre; in
   field, B; in ex., XXI. Æ, 4.27 gm. ↑.

1120 Antoninianus Antioch, AD 285

Obv. As No. 1119.
Rev. IOVI ET HERCVLI CONSER AVGG. Jupiter standing r., holding globe and sceptre, facing Hercules standing l., holding Victory, club, and lion-skin; in field, š; in ex., XXI. Æ, 3.95 gm. ↓.

1121 Aureus Antioch, AD 285–286

Obv. IMP C C VAL DIOCLETIANVS P F AVG. Bust, laureate, draped, cuirassed, r.
Rev. VICTORIA AVGG. Victory advancing r., holding wreath and palm; mint-mark, SMA. N, 4.69 gm. ↑.
The first gold coinage continues to use the mark SMA employed on the gold of Carus and family.

1122 Aureus Antioch, AD 290

Obv. MAXIMIANVS AVGVSTVS. Bust, laureate, draped, cuirassed, l., with spear and shield.
Rev. HERCVLI VICTORI. Hercules standing l., holding club and lion-skin; in field, ≲; mint-mark, SMA. N, 5.16 gm. ↑.
The aurei of this issue are marked by the Greek numeral as being struck at 60 to the pound of gold.

1123 Aureus Antioch, AD 293

Obv. MAXIMIANVS AVGVSTVS. Head, laureate, r.
Rev. CONSVL IIII P P PROCOS M. Maximian standing l., in consular dress, holding globe in r. hand; mint-mark, SMA ≳*. N, 5.29 gm. ↓.

1124 Antoninianus Antioch, AD 293

Obv. FL VAL CONSTANTIVS NOB CAES. Bust, radiate, draped, cuirassed, r.
Rev. IOVI ET HERCVLI CONS CAES. Type as No. 1120, but in field S; in ex., XXI. Æ, 4.10 gm. ↓.

1125 Antoninianus Tripolis, AD 290

Obv. IMP C M AVR VAL MAXIMIANVS P F AVG. Bust, radiate, draped, cuirassed, r.
Rev. IOVI CONSERVATORI AVGG. Maximian standing l., holding sceptre, receiving Victory on globe from Jupiter standing l., holding sceptre; mint-mark, TR⤵/XXI. Æ, 4.07 gm. ↑.

10 The British Empire AD287-296

Carausius, appointed by Maximian to the command of the Channel Fleet, exploited his position to gain control of Britain and establish a separate empire, including control of at least the port of Boulogne on the coast of Gaul. He successfully resisted one attempt at invasion and reconquest, but in 293 Constantius wrested Boulogne from him, and in the same year he was assassinated and succeeded by his prefect, Allectus. In 296 Constantius mounted a successful invasion, defeated Allectus, and restored Britain to the empire.

Coinage was struck for Carausius at two mints at least in Britain. One, with mint initial L, is clearly to be identified as London; the other with mint initial C is most probably Colchester, though the form CL on some coins of Allectus leaves room for doubt. The identification of a large series of antoniniani without mint-mark is uncertain. Boulogne, as Carausius' original base, has been suggested, but against this is the dearth of finds of Carausian coins in its immediate hinterland. A series of antoniniani and rare gold in unusual style is attributed to a mint at the Channel port of Rouen.

Presumably because of lack of bullion Carausius produced only small issues of gold, and only late in his reign. To compensate, he instituted quite an extensive issue of silver denarii of good fineness at the beginning of his reign, anticipating in a way the silver coinage which formed part of Diocletian's monetary reform in 294. The formula XXI found on most antoniniani of the central empire was added to Carausian antoniniani only about 290 when Carausius was pursuing a policy of rapprochement with the central empire, to the extent of striking coins with the obverse portrait and titles of Diocletian and Maximian. The coinage of Allectus consisted only of gold and of antoniniani, always without the XXI formula. The last coinage of Allectus, apparently a reduced antoninianus, is marked by a Q placed before the mint initial.

Carausius, AD287-293

1126 Denarius London, AD 287

Obv. IMP CARAVSIVS P F AVG. Bust, laureate, draped, cuirassed, r.
Rev. EXPECTATE VENI. Britannia standing r., holding standard and clasping hands with Carausius, standing l., holding spear; in ex., RSR. Æ, 4.64 gm. ↑.

A possible explanation of the formula RSR is *rationalis summae rei*, the financial officer responsible for the coinage. The reverse inscription, a novel replacement for the more usual *Adventvs*, may be a Vergilian tag from the second book of the *Aeneid*, ll. 212–13.

1127 Denarius London, AD 287

Obv. As No. 1126.
Rev. RENOVAT ROMANO. She-wolf standing r., suckling the twins, Romulus and Remus, in ex., RSR. Æ, 4.01 gm. ↓.

1128 Denarius London, AD 287

Obv. As No. 1126.
Rev. VOTO PVBLICO. Wreath enclosing
MVL/TIS/XX/IMP; in ex., RSR. Æ, 5.12 gm. ↓.
In the third century, early coinage of a reign frequently carried reference to the *vota suscepta decennalia* but the vota here for Carausius are for the *vicennalia*.

1129 Medallion London, AD 287

Obv. IMP C M AV CARAVSIVS P F AVG. Bust, laureate, mantled l., holding eagle-tipped sceptre.
Rev. VICTORIA CARAVSI AVG. Victory in biga, r., in ex., I·N·P·C·D·A. Æ, 21.61 gm. ↓.
The consular portrait suggests that the consulship was one of the Roman institutions copied by Carausius. The formula apparent in the abbreviated letters in the exergue still awaits explanation.

1130 Antoninianus London, AD 287

Obv. IMP CARAVSIVS P F AVG. Bust, radiate, draped, cuirassed, r.
Rev. LEG I MIN. Ram standing r.; mint-mark, ML.
Æ, 4.22 gm. ↓.
An early series of antoniniani honoured the legions or vexillations of legions in Britain on whose support the emperor relied. The signature of the mint of London made its first appearance on this issue.

1131 Antoninianus London, AD 288–289

Obv. As No. 1130.
Rev. PAX AVG. Pax standing l., holding branch and sceptre; mint-mark, $\frac{\text{F}|\text{O}}{\text{ML}}$.

Æ, 3.34 gm. ↗.

1132 Antoninianus London, AD 291

Obv. As No. 1130 but IMP C.
Rev. As No. 1131, but mint-mark, $\frac{\text{B}|\text{E}}{\text{MLXXI}}$.

Æ, 4.49 gm. ↓.
Coinage from 291 onwards includes on the obverse the title *C(aesar)*. Between 290 and 292 antoniniani of Carausius carry the value formula XXI usually found on antoniniani of the Central Empire.

1133 Aureus London, AD 292

Obv. CARAVSIVS P F AVG. Bust, laureate, draped, cuirassed, r.
Rev. CONSERVATORI AVGGG. Hercules standing r., holding club, bow and lion-skin; mint-mark, ML. Ν, 4.30 gm. ↓.
An attempted rapprochement with the Central Empire is reflected in the use on the reverse inscription of AVGGG – the three emperors being Diocletian, Maximian, and Carausius himself.

1134 Antoninianus London, AD 292

Obv. As No. 1133.
Rev. COMES AVGGG. Minerva standing l., holding
spear in r. hand, and resting l. on shield;
mint-mark, $\frac{S\,|\,P}{MLXXI}$.

Æ, 3.96 gm. ↓.

1135 Antoninianus London, AD 292

Obv. IMP C DIOCLETIANVS P F AVG. Bust, radiate,
draped, cuirassed, r.
Rev. PAX AVGGG. As No. 1131, but mint-mark,
$\frac{S\,|\,P}{MLXXI}$.

Æ, 5.78 gm. ↓.

This issue of Carausius included coinage in the name
of the other two emperors, in this case Diocletian.

1136 Aureus London, AD 292

Obv. MAXIMIANVS P F AVG. Bust, laureate, draped,
cuirassed, r.
Rev. SALVS AVGGG. Salus standing r., feeding out
of patera, snake held in arms; mint-mark,
ML. N, 4.29 gm. ↓.

The shared coinage also included issues in gold, as
here for Maximian.

1137 Aureus London, AD 293

Obv. CARAVSIVS P F AVG. Bust, laureate, draped,
cuirassed, r.
Rev. CONSERVAT AVG. Jupiter standing l., holding
thunderbolt and sceptre; at foot r., eagle;
mint-mark, ML. N, 4.31 gm. ↓.

After the appointment of Constantius Chlorus as
Caesar on the West in 293 and his capture of
Boulogne, Carausius again coined in his own name
only.

1138 Antoninianus Colchester, AD 287

Obv. IMP CARAVSIVS P F AVG. Bust, bare-headed,
draped and cuirassed, facing.
Rev. SALVS AVG. Salus standing l., feeding out of
patera in r. hand a snake coiled round altar,
and holding sceptre in l.; mint-mark, C.
Æ, 3.90 gm. ↓.

Of the suggested identifications of the mint with
initial C, the most likely appears to be Camu-
lodunum (Colchester).

1139 Antoninianus Colchester, AD 292

Obv. CARAVSIVS ET FRATRES SVI. Busts, jugate,
radiate, cuirassed l. of (from l. to r.)
Carausius, Diocletian, and Maximian, with
r. hands raised.
Rev. MONETA AVGGG. Moneta standing l., holding
scales and cornucopiae; mint-mark, $\frac{S\,|\,P}{C}$.

Æ, 4.65 gm. ↓.

The unusual obverse is the fullest expression of
Carausius' rapprochement with the central
emperors.

1140 **Antoninianus** Colchester, AD 292

Obv. IMP C DIOCLETIANVS AVG. Bust, radiate, draped, cuirassed, r.

Rev. PAX AVGGG. Pax standing l., holding branch and sceptre; mint-mark, $\frac{S \mid P}{C}$.

Æ, 4.18 gm. ↓.

At this mint, as well as at London, Carausius issued coins in the name of the central emperors.

1141 **Antoninianus** Colchester, AD 293

Obv. IMP C CARAVSIVS P F AVG. Bust, radiate, draped, cuirassed, r.

Rev. PROVID AVG. Providentia standing l., holding globe and cornucopiae; mint-mark, $\frac{S \mid P}{C}$.

Æ, 4.73 gm. ↓.

With this issue Carausius resumed coinage in his own name only (cf. No. 1137).

1142 **Aureus** Rouen, AD 293

Obv. IMP CARAVSIVS AVG. Bust, laureate, draped, cuirassed, r.

Rev. CONCORDIA MILITVM. Carausius standing r., clasping hands with Concordia standing l. Ν, 4.53 gm. ↑.

After the loss of Boulogne in 293 coinage was issued briefly from a mint at Rouen.

1143 **Antoninianus** Rouen, AD 293

Obv. IMP C CARAVSIVS AVG. Bust, radiate, draped, cuirassed, r.

Rev. ECVITAS MVNDI. Aequitas standing l., holding scales and cornucopiae. Æ, 2.32 gm. ↓.

The odd spelling of the reverse inscription and the style are indicative of the emergency nature of this issue.

1144 **Antoninianus** AD 287–290

Obv. IMP CARAVSIVS P F AVG. Bust, radiate, draped, cuirassed, r.

Rev. PAX AVG. Pax standing l., holding branch and sceptre. Æ, 4.12 gm. ↓.

A plentiful coinage without mint-signature was issued in the early years of the reign. It has been suggested that the mint was at Gesoriacum (Boulogne) initially held by Carausius, but positive proof is lacking.

Allectus, AD293-296

1145 **Aureus** London, AD 293

Obv. IMP C ALLECTVS P F AVG. Bust, laureate, draped, cuirassed, r.
Rev. ORIENS AVG. Sol standing r., head l., raising r. hand, and holding globe in l.; at foot, l. and r., seated captive; mint-mark, ML.
N, 4.46 gm. ↓.

Allectus continued to coin at the mint of London opened by Carausius.

1146 **Antoninianus** London, AD 294

Obv. As No. 1145, but radiate.
Rev. FELICITAS AVG. Felicitas standing l., holding caduceus and cornucopiae; mint-mark,

$\frac{\text{S} \mid \text{A}}{\text{ML}}$.

R, 4.98 gm. ↓.

1147 **Aureus** London, AD 295

Obv. As No. 1145.
Rev. VIRTVS AVG. Virtus standing r., holding spear in r. hand, and resting l. on shield; mint-mark, MSL. N, 4.72 gm. ↓.

From the pattern of mint-marks on the antoniniani this form of the mint-signature on the gold is later than the mark ML.

1148 **Antoninianus** Colchester, AD 293-294

Obv. As No. 1146.
Rev. LAETITIA AVG. Laetitia standing l., holding wreath and rudder; mint-mark, $\frac{\text{S} \mid \text{P}}{\text{C}}$.

R, 4.46 gm. ↓.

The only other mint of Allectus was at Colchester.

1149 **Reduced antoninianus** Colchester, AD 295-296

Obv. As No. 1146.
Rev. LAETITIA AVG. Galley r.; mint-mark QC.
R, 3.25 gm. ↓.

The letter Q on the last coinage of Allectus here and at London suggests the denomination quinarius, but the obverse portrait is radiate, and the weight only slightly less than that of the antoninianus. If this new coinage is not simply a reduced antoninianus necessitated by economic circumstances, it may be some reaction to the new coinage of the central empire introduced by Diocletian's coinage reforms of 294.

Concordance

For Nos. 320–775 the reference given is to BMC (*Coins of the Roman Empire in the British Museum*, I–VI), and the heading, e.g. Augustus, gives the relevant catalogue section. For Nos. 776–1149 the reference is to RIC (*Roman Imperial Coinage*, III–V) with a heading, e.g. Gordian III, giving the relevant section. In a few cases where the members of an imperial family are given separate enumeration in RIC, e.g. Valerian I and family, the RIC number is preceded by the initial of the imperial name, e.g. V 41 = RIC Valerian I, No. 41. References to such medallions which are not included in BMC or RIC are given to Gnecchi, *I Medaglioni Romani*, I–III, abbreviated, e.g. G I, p. 51, I.

AUGUSTUS

320	617
321	633
322	647
323	655
324	316
325	345
326	319
327	334
328	357
329	372
330	I
331	13
332	69
333	91
334	104
335	110
336	171
337	159
338	170
339	247
340	224
341	659
342	664
343	671
344	702
345	705
346	722
347	288
348	295
349	298
350	447
351	450
352	467
353	478
354	498
355	533
356	506
357	565
358	576

TIBERIUS

359	28
360	2
361	24
362	35
363	70
364	75
365	76
366	79
367	82
368	98
369	88
370	92
371	99
372	95
373	125
374	151A
375	149
376	62
377	Cohen 97

CALIGULA

378	I
379	2
380	14
381	19
382	49
383	83
384	37
385	70
386	96
387	68
388	64
389	90
390	Tib 160

CLAUDIUS

391	8
392	23
393	40
394	124
395	224
396	149
397	cf. 152
398	180
399	227
400	32
401	237
402	99
403	159
404	109
405	166
406	218
407	219
408	73
409	231
410	92

NERO

411	6
412	I
413	7
414	14
415	405
416	29
417	52
418	82
419	102
420	67A
421	91
422	132
423	141
424	142
425	187
426	215
427	252
428	264
429	299
430	191
431	236
432	260
433	287
434	118
435	321
436	345
437	361
438	388

CIVIL WARS

439	37
440	31
441	8
442	46
443	13A
444	67

CLODIUS MACER

445	I
446	5

GALBA

447	271
448	214
449	170
450	178
451	84
452	156
453	186
454	257
455	29
456	94
457	4
458	17
459	44
460	57
461	144
462	20

OTHO

463	I
464	24

VITELLIUS

465	113
466	79
467	94
468	99
469	3
470	10
471	27
472	52

VESPASIAN

473	47
474	3
475	32
476	535
477	765
478	590
479	67
480	650
481	109
482	129
483	729
484	223
485	231
486	245
487	283
488	350
489	361
490	397
491	798
492	825A
493	414
494	427
495	433
496	443
497	450
498	465
499	474

TITUS

500	118
501	137
502	55
503	163
504	190
505	86
506	255
507	278
508	306
509	307A

DOMITIAN

510	39
511	62

512	251
513	288
514	73
515	83
516	125
517	318
518	490
519	130
520	419
521	431
522	410
523	191
524	250
525	517

NERVA

526	7
527	45
528	46
529	105
530	115
531	119
532	79
533	149

TRAJAN

534	8
535	64
536	137
537	155
538	674
539	702
540	847
541	786
542	793
543	385
544	395
545	829
546	378
547	404
548	853
549	863
550	976
551	484
552	454
553	509
554	554
555	960
556	978
557	526
558	649
559	659
560	507
561	503

562	613
563	1035

HADRIAN

564	5
565	45
566	47
567	50
568	57
569	1138
570	1159
571	1024
572	274
573	326
574	327
575	448
576	739
577	786
578	1655
579	856
580	1723
581	1689
582	868
583	cf. 1090
584	710
585	937
586	986
587	1017

ANTONINUS PIUS

588	7
589	30
590	32
591	44
592	1173
593	1185
594	124
595	1210
596	237
597	238
598	243
599	1298
600	1370
601	1314
602	1279
603	1273
604	239
605	276
606	263
607	1428
608	324
609	307
610	1494
611	1572

612	470
613	493
614	1637
615	606
616	548
617	678
618	1047
619	1083
620	2064
621	955
622	G II, p. 32, 44

MARCUS AURELIUS

623	12
624	31
625	70
626	133
627	953
628	200
629	238
630	1100
631	347
632	375
633	385
634	G II, p. 44, 1
635	443
636	500
637	1367
638	1373
639	564
640	583
641	637
642	682
643	704
644	1591
645	752
646	774

COMMODUS

647	10
648	25
649	52
650	543
651	128
652	550
653	G II, p. 51, 2
654	156
655	197
656	216
657	223
658	231
659	253
660	275

661	300	705	283
662	643	706	319
663	717	707	309
664	341	708	854
665	346	709	857
666	335		
667	G II, p. 55, 34		

661 300
662 643
663 717
664 341
665 346
666 335
667 G II, p. 55, 34

PERTINAX

668 18
669 2
670 40

DIDIUS JULIANUS

671 1
672 10
673 13

PESCENIUS NIGER

674 299A
675 303A
676 304

SEPTIMIUS SEVERUS

677 13
678 47
679 63
680 34
681 421
682 103
683 532
684 557
685 150
686 612
687 285A
688 284
689 622
690 226
691 463
692 207
693 458

SEVERUS, CARACALLA

694 115
695 676
696 244
697 184
698 255
699 265
700 731
701 417
702 333
703 47
704 845

705 283
706 319
707 309
708 854
709 857

SEVERUS, CARACALLA, GETA

710 821
711 217
712 33A
713 60

CARACALLA, GETA

714 26
715 28
716 18

CARACALLA

717 64
718 251
719 206
720 122
721 141
722 8
723 148
724 134
725 287
726 157
727 197

MACRINUS

728 5
729 18A
730 71
731 83A
732 95

ELAGABALUS

733 13
734 66
735 70
736 197
737 39
738 414
739 432
740 451
741 325A
742 273
743 148

SEVERUS ALEXANDER

744 11
745 156

746 242
747 325
748 380
749 472
750 537
751 546
752 591
753 634
754 750
755 1006
756 1055

MAXIMINUS I

757 4
758 63
759 118
760 127
761 184
762 213

GORDIANI

763 3
764 12
765 20
766 23

BALBINUS, PUPIENUS

767 1
768 5
769 35
770 42
771 71
772 79
773 94
774 96
775 64

GORDIAN III

776 1
777 80
778 131
779 252
780 G II, p. 89, 22
781 308A
782 326
783 147
784 213

PHILIP

785 36b
786 258c
787 209A
788 —
789 229

790 27c
791 G II, p. 96, 10
792 66
793 24
794 118
795 13
796 224
797 116b
798 8
799 223
800 167A
801 69

PACATIAN

802 4

JOTAPIAN

803 2b

TRAJAN DECIUS

804 4a
805 21b
806 115a
807 128
808 37b
809 58a
810 136a
811 148a
812 154
813 177a
814 44b
815 67c
816 158b
817 196d
818 77
819 90
820 191a

TREBONIANUS GALLUS

821 8
822 19
823 241
824 145
825 139
826 G II, p. 102, 4
827 71
828 206
829 89
830 225

AEMILIAN

831 3
832 14
833 31

URANIUS ANTONINUS		**MACRIAN**		**LAELIAN**		968	319
834	I	883	I	923	I	969	95
		884	II	924	6	970	110
VALERIAN I AND FAMILY						971	150
835	V 41	**QUIETUS**		**MARIUS**		972	151
836	V 143	885	10	925	I	973	S 8
837	V 75	886	13	926	18	974	192
838	G II, p. 105, 4			927	7	975	171
839	Mar. 1	**REGALIAN**				976	233
840	G 181	887	6	**VICTORINUS**		977	215
841	S 29			928	108	978	255
842	G 84	**DRYANTILLA**		929	113	979	258
843	G 236	888	I	930	101	980	260
844	V II 13			931	4	981	S 16
845	G I, p. 51, 1	**CLAUDIUS II**		932	96	982	327
846	V 241	889	9	933	118	983	368
847	M 6	890	16	934	126	984	366
848	G 397	891	128	935	25	985	374
849	V II 4	892	149	936	59	986	384
850	G 22	893	193			987	S 19
851	V 5	894	251	**TETRICI**		988	381
852	S 5	895	215	937	140		
853	V II 9	896	266	938	30	**VABALATHUS**	
854	Ss 1	897	264	939	135	989	3
855	V 213	898	267	940	2		
856	G 296			941	28	**TACITUS**	
857	S 63	**QUINTILLUS**		942	56	990	10
858	V II 34	899	18	943	259	991	63
859	Ss 35	900	45	944	126	992	209
860	V 294	901	79	945	Vict. 84	993	83
861	G 448			946	72	994	108
862	V II 49	**POSTUMUS**		947	71	995	172
863	Ss 36	902	87	948	9	996	121
864	S 67	903	18	949	90	997	174
		904	111	950	94	998	cf. 184
GALLIENUS (SOLE)		905	157	951	36	999	195
865	G 16	906	cf. 169	952	217	1000	cf. 206
866	G 395	907	172	953	270	1001	211
867	G 362	908	128	954	205	1002	212
868	G 447	909	144			1003	214
869	G 37	910	133	**AURELIAN**			
870	G 59	911	66	955	6	**FLORIAN**	
871	G I, p. 54, 25	912	75	956	S 1	1004	15
872	G 71	913	33	957	33	1005	23
873	G 346	914	277	958	15	1006	34
874	Vi, p. 361, 2	915	—	959	64	1007	55
875	G 74	916	267	960	S 4	1008	86
876	G 230	917	262	961	71	1009	cf. 90
877	G 324	918	341	962	73	1010	cf. Tac. 201
878	S 60	919	84	963	S 6	1011	116
879	G 471	920	307	964	A/S 1		
880	G 573	921	286	965	80	**PROBUS**	
881	G 586	922	378	966	S 7	1012	cf. 36
882	G 611			967	321	1013	11

1014	185	1066	319	1115	306
1015	cf. 140	1067	125	1116	294
1016	138	1068	208	1117	605
1017	147	1069	122	1118	615
1018	295	1070	373	1119	326
1019	249	1071	470	1120	323
1020	262			1121	320
1021	G II, p. 119, 32	JULIAN		1122	619
1022	307	1072	1	1123	611
1023	463	1073	4	1124	673
1024	336			1125	626
1025	590	DIOCLETIAN			
1026	703	1074 Cahn Sale xiii,		CARAUSIUS	
1027	766		225	1126	554
1028	585	1075	116	1127	571
1029	883	1076	654	1128	596
1030	828	1077	693	1129 BMQ xxxvii,	
1031	911	1078	2		p. 1
1032	914	1079	334	1130	156
1033	925	1080	43	1131	98
1034	927	1081	369	1132	98
		1082	5	1133	2
CARUS AND FAMILY		1083	NC 1870, 14	1134	M 21
1035	1	1084	137	1135	D 11
1036	cf. 138	1085	134	1136	M 32
1037	5	1086	161	1137	1
1038	390	1087	187	1138	400
1039	276	1088	cf. 193	1139 NC 1959, p. 10	
1040	33	1089	162	1140	D 26
1041	153	1090	532	1141	353
1042	—	1091	cf. 338	1142	624
1043	155	1092	189	1143	630
1044	330	1093	G II, p. 125, 3	1144	881
1045	332	1094	G II, p. 129, 12		
1046	407	1095	G II, p. 126, 30	ALLECTUS	
1047	420	1096	G II, p. 129, 18	1145	4
1048	435	1097	144	1146	18
1049	G II, p. 122, 1	1098	152	1147	13
1050	264	1099	500	1148	79
1051	286	1100	c. 305	1149	124
1052	340	1101	127		
1053	335	1102	G II, p. 13, 3		
1054	424	1103	cf. Cohen 279		
1055	48	1104	513		
1056	472	1105	659		
1057	81	1106	708		
1058	292	1107	222		
1059	345	1108	540		
1060	96	1109	552		
1061	190	1110	670		
1062	451	1111	263		
1063	99	1112	560		
1064	315	1113	595		
1065	120	1114	284		

Indexes

1 Emperors and their relatives, etc.

The references are to coin numbers, not page numbers.

Aemilian, 831, 832
Agrippa, 335, 355, 390
Agrippina I, 380, 383, 407
Agrippina II, 384, 412–13
Allectus, 1145–9
Annia Faustina, 740
Antonia, 404, 405
Antoninus Pius, 587–9, 592–604, 613–14, 616–17, 620–1; Divus, 625, 819
Aquilia Severa, 739
Augustus, 320–58, 442; Divus, 359, 373–5, 379, 389, 507, 533, 818
Aurelian, 955, 957–9, 961–2, 964–5, 967–72, 974–80, 982–7

Balbinus, 767, 771
Britannicus, 394, 508

Caligula, 378–90
Caracalla, 686, 692–4, 700, 704–5, 710, 712, 715, 717–18, 720–1, 723–7
Carausius, 1126–34, 1137–9, 1141–4
Carinus, 1036, 1039, 1041–5, 1050–1, 1053, 1058, 1061, 1064, 1066, 1068
Carus, 1035–7, 1040, 1057, 1060, 1063, 1065, 1067, 1069; Divus, 1055
Claudius I, 391–409; Divus, 411, 413
Claudius II, 889–96; Divus, 897–8
Clodius Albinus, 682–3, 687–9
Clodius Macer, 445–6
Commodus, 634, 641, 645–7, 650–67
Constantius Chlorus, 1076, 1102, 1105, 1110, 1124
Cornelia Supera, 833
Crispina, 649

Diadumenian, 731–2
Didia Clara, 673
Didius Julianus, 671
Diocletian, 1075, 1078–80, 1082, 1084–9, 1091–3, 1095, 1097–8, 1101, 1103, 1107, 1111, 1114–16, 1119–21, 1135, 1139–40
Domitia, 511

Domitian, 473, 482–3, 485, 491, 495, 499, 500, 505, 510, 512–23, 525
Domitilla, 501
Drusilla, 384
Drusus, son of Germanicus, 385
Drusus, son of Tiberius, 371–2
Dryantilla, 888

Elagabalus, 733, 736, 741–3

Faustina I, 591; Diva, 607–12
Faustina II, 618–19, 626–7; Diva, 643–4
Florian, 1004–11

Gaius, grandson of Augustus, 354–5
Galba, 447–62
Galerius, 1077–1106
Gallienus, 840–3, 845, 848, 850, 856, 861, 865–77, 879–82
Germanicus, 381–2, 406
Geta, 696, 711, 716
Gordian I, 763–4
Gordian II, 765–6
Gordian III, 775–8, 780–4

Hadrian, 564, 568–84; Divus, 590
Herennia Etruscilla, 810, 815
Herennius Etruscus, 811–12, 816
Hostilian, 813, 817, 820

Jotapian, 803
Julia, daughter of Augustus, 334
Julia, sister of Caligula, 384
Julia, daughter of Titus, 506, 524
Julia Domna, 678, 681, 703, 719, 722
Julia Maesa, 734–5
Julia Mamaea, 748, 750
Julia Paula, 738
Julia Soemias, 737
Julian Transpaduanus, 1072–3
Julius Caesar, Divus, 328

Laelian, 923–4
Livia, 362, 365–8, 374, 395, 457
Lucilla, 631
Lucius, grandson of Augustus, 335
Lucius Aelius, 586
Lucius Verus, 624, 628–30, 633; Divus, 637

Macrian, 883–4
Macrinus, 728–30
Magnia Urbica, 1052, 1059

Manlia Scantilla, 672
Marciana, 558
Marcus Aurelius, 605–6, 615, 622–3, 632, 635–6, 638–40, 642; Divus, 648
Mariniana, 839, 847
Marius, 925–7
Matidia, 559
Maximian, 1074, 1081, 1083, 1090–1, 1094, 1096, 1099, 1100, 1104, 1108–9, 1112–13, 1118, 1122–3, 1125, 1136, 1139
Maximus, 759, 762
Maximinus, 757–8, 761

Nero, son of Germanicus, 385
Nero, 410, 412–38
Nerva, 526–33
Nigrianus, 1056
Numerian, 1038, 1044–9, 1062, 1070–1; Divus, 1054

Otacilia Severa, 787, 794
Otho, 463–4
Orbiana, 746

Pacatian, 802
Paulina, 760
Pertinax, 668–9
Pescennius Niger, 674–6
Philip I, 785, 788, 790–3, 795, 798, 800–1
Philip II, 786, 789, 791, 796, 799
Plautilla, 701
Plotina, 557, 567
Poppaea, 417
Postumus, 902–22
Probus, 1012–34
Pupienus, 768–70, 772–4

Quietus, 885–6
Quintillus, 899–901

Regalian, 887

Sabina, 585
Salonina, 841, 845, 852, 857, 864, 878
Saloninus, 854, 859, 863
Septimius Severus, 677, 679, 680, 684–5, 690–1, 695, 697–9, 702, 706–9, 713; Divus, 714
Severina, 956, 960, 963–4, 966, 973, 981, 987
Severus Alexander, 744–5, 747, 749, 751–6

Tacitus, 990–1003
Tetricus I, 937–42, 944, 946–51, 954
Tetricus II, 943, 952–4
Tiberius, 473, 480, 484, 491–2, 495, 498; 502–4
Trajan, 534–56, 560–3; Divus, 565–7
Trajan Senior, 560
Trajan Decius, 804–8, 814
Tranquillina, 779
Trebonianus Gallus, 821–2, 826–7, 829

Uranius Antoninus, 834

Vabalathus, 988–9
Valerian I, 835–8, 845–6, 851, 855, 860
Valerian II, 844–5, 849, 858, 862; Divus, 853
Victorinus, 928–36; Divus, 948
Vitellius, 465–72
Vitellius Senior, 470
Volusian, 823–5, 828, 830

II Mints

The references are to coin numbers, not to page numbers.

'Africa', 447
Antioch, 674–6, 742–3, 775–6, 784–5, 801, 815–17, 829–30, 855–9, 882, 895, 922, 985–7, 1001–2, 1032–3, 1067–70, 1119–24
'Asia', 583

Bilbilis, 377
Byzantium, 497

Caesarea Cappodociae, 401, 405
Carnuntum, 887–8
Carthage, 445–6
Colchester, 1138–41, 1148–9
Cologne, 465, 921, 925–6, 928–33, 937–44
Cyzicus, 860–4, 883–6, 894, 898, 982–4, 1000, 1011, 1031, 1065–6, 1115–18

'East', 323, 341–6, 494–6, 571
Emerita, 347–9
Emesa, 680–1, 834, 989
Ephesus, 409, 498–9, 512, 583

'Gaul', 439–40

Heraclea, 1113–14

Laodicea-ad-Mare, 691, 693, 695, 700
London, 1126–37, 1145–7
Lyons, 350–62, 378–80, 435–8, 448–54, 466–8, 488–92, 509, 525, 687–9, 923–4, 927, 934–6, 945–56, 990–1, 1004, 1012–13, 1035–9, 1078–83

Milan, 877–9, 892, 897, 900, 969–71
'Moesia', 802

Pergamum, 532
Poetovio, 493

'Rhineland', 444
Rouen, 1143
Rome, 320–2, 330–40, 363–76, 380–400, 402–8, 410–14, 416–34, 455–64, 469–87, 500–8, 510–11, 513–24, 526–31, 533–70, 572–82, 584–673, 677–8, 682–6, 690, 692, 694, 696–9, 701–41, 744–54, 757–83, 786–800, 804–14, 818–28, 831–3, 835–45, 865–76, 889–91, 896, 899, 957–68, 992–4, 1005–7, 1014–21, 1040–56, 1084–1106

Serdica, 979–81, 999, 1010, 1029–30
Sirmium, 881
Siscia, 880, 893, 901, 974–8, 996–8, 1009, 1025–8, 1060–4, 1072–3, 1111–12
'Spain', 324–9, 441–3
'Syria', 803

Ticinum, 972–3, 995, 1008, 1022–4, 1057–9, 1107–10
Trier, 849–54, 902–20, 1074–7
Tripolis, 1003, 1034, 1071, 1025

'Western', 846–8

III Types

The references are to coin numbers, not to page numbers.

Abundantia, stg. l., 1062; stg. r., 752, 873

Achaea, kneeling r., 582

Aeneas, advancing r., 596

Aequitas, stg. l., 790, 814, 830, 886, 888, 934

Aesculapius, stg. r., 979

Aeternitas, stg. l., 568, 610

Africa, stg. l., 577; stg. r., 707

Agonistic table, 429

Altar, 339, 357–8, 375–6, 399, 436, 818–19, 897

Annia Faustina, stg. l., 740

Annona, stg. l., 509

Antoninus Pius, crowning Armenian king, 603

Antoninus Pius, with Marcus Aurelius and Lucius Verus, in quadriga l., 604

Apollo, bust of, r., 517, 931; stg. l., 353, 822; stg. r., 431, 660, 837

Aqua Traiana, 550

Arabia, st. l., 556

Augustus, stg. l., on platform, 350; in quadriga r., 320; Divus, std. l., 364

Arms, pile of, 642, 645

Armenia. std. l., 629

Aurelian, stg. l., 965, 967, 976, 983–4; stg. r., 977, 980–1, 987

Arch, triumphal, 400, 402, 405

Ba'al, stone of, 834; in car l., 736, 742

Basilica Ulpia, 554

Bonus Eventus, stg. r., 674

Bow, club and quiver, 920

Branch, olive, 518

Branches, laurel, two, 326

Bridge, 540, 709

Britannia, std. l., 580, 614, 653; stg. r., 1176

Bull, butting r., 351

Caduceus, 919; between two cornua-copiae, surmounted by busts, 372

Caligula, stg. l., 387

Cappadocia, stg. l., 593

Capricorn, l., 325; r., 342, 344

Capricorns, two, 676

Car, drawn by elephants, r., 637

Caracalla, advancing r., 712; stg. l., 692–4, 723, 725; stg. r., 704

Carausius, stg. l., 1126; stg. r., 1142

Carinus, stg. l., 1042, 1064, 1071; stg. r., 1067–8

Carinus and Numerian, stg. l., 1049

Carpentum, 365, 383

Carus stg. l., 1067–8

Castor, stg. by horse, l., 646

Ceres, std. l., 498; stg. l., 506, 611

Chariot, drawn by four elephants, l., 413

Circus Maximus, 548, 706, 718

Claudius, in quadriga, r., 401

Clementia, std. l., 466

Club, 603

Club, bow and quiver, 664

Colosseum, 504, 745, 780

Column, 321, 552, 625, 793

Comet, 328

Commodus, stg. l., 641, 657, 666; with four soldiers, stg. l., 655; ploughing r., 662

Concordia, std. l., 459, 585, 738, 746, 779, 824, 857, 956; std. r., 701; stg. l., 671, 739, 900, 960, 973–4, 977, 1024, 1142

Congiarium, 424

Constantia, stg., facing, 404

Constantius I., stg. r., 1076, 1102, 1105

Cornuacopiae, crossed, surmounted by small busts, 617

Crocodile, r., 323

Cybele, std. l., 703; std. r., 626

Dacia, std. l., 541, 555; stg. l., 808

Dacian, std. r., 543

Danuvius, 542, 544

Dea Caelestis, 702

Diadumenian, stg. r., 731

Diana, bust of, 334, 931; advancing l., 855; stg. r., 883

Diana, of Ephesus, 409, 583

Diocletian and Maximian, std. l., 1118

Domitian, std. on platform, r., 520; stg. l., 522; sacrificing l., 521

Dove, r., 619

Eagle, 507, 558, 592, 896, 945, 1054–5; carrying Diva Faustina I, r., 607; carrying Divus Hadrian, r., 590

Eagle, legionary, 636, 677, 687, 869

Elagabalus, stg. r., 740–1

Elephant, advancing, l., 810, 1083; advancing r., 650

Emerita, view of, 347

Fates, three, 1116

Faustina I, Diva, in biga of elephants, l., 609

Faustina II, Diva, std. l., 643; in biga, r., 644

Felicitas, stg. l., 571, 574, 627, 632, 683, 732, 806, 854, 926, 982, 998, 1058, 1063, 1077, 1146; std. r., 821; bust of,

jugate with Victory, r., 916

Fides, std. l., 733, 922; stg. l., 758, 776, 846, 868, 892, 899, 908, 928, 946, 1017–18

Florian, stg. l., 1009–11; stg. r., 1007

Fortuna, stg. l., 501, 755, 1036; std. l., 658, 688, 715, 802, 975

Forum Traiani, 553

Galba, on horseback, r., 462

Galerius, stg., r., 1106

Gallia, bust of, r., 443; stg. r., 449

Galliae, Tres, busts of, r., 448

Galley, l., 1038; r., 445, 909, 1149

Gallienus, advancing l., 856; stg. l., 842

Genius, stg. l., 427, 686, 804, 970

Germania, std. l., 516, 534

Geta, stg. l., 716, 796

Gordian I, stg. l., 763

Gordian III, std. l., 782; stg. r., 781; on horseback, r., 777

Hadrian, std. on platform, l., 570; on horseback, r., 581

Hands, clasped, 444, 465, 526, 687, 771–3, 925

Heifer, walking, l., 341

Herald, stg. l., 332; advancing l., 519

Hercules, std. r., 1100; stg. l., 661, 667, 679, 704, 910, 918, 1081, 1112, 1120, 1122, 1125, 1137; stg. r., 572, 665, 831, 865, 911, 1028, 1046, 1090, 1094, 1096, 1099, 1109–10, 1117, 1133; bust of, jugate with Postumus, r., 916

Herennius Etruscus, stg. l., 811

Hilaritas, stg. l., 615, 673

Hippopotamus, stg. r., 797

Hispania, bust of, r., 443; stg. l., 449; advancing l., 458

Honos, stg. l., 606; stg. r., 454

Janus, standing facing, 609; temple of, 435

Judaea, std. l., 475–7; std. r., 502; stg. l., 578

Juno, stg. l., 585, 672, 719, 734, 840, 966; stg. r., 737

Julia Mamaea, std. l., 750

Jupiter, bust of, l., 539; std. l., 726; stg. l., 573, 659, 675, 729, 836, 859, 880, 980, 989, 1000–2, 1034, 1080, 1084–9, 1098, 1101, 1103, 1107, 1111, 1113–14; stg. r., 935, 1097, 1120; stg. facing, 850; as child, on goat, r., 844

Justitia, bust of, r., 366; std. r., 527

Laetitia, stg. l., 618, 785, 835, 949, 1006, 1148

Liber, stg. l., 679, 704

Liberalitas, stg. l., 616, 743, 767
Libertas, bust of, r. 441; stg. l., 460, 528, 871, 1072
Lion, stg. r., 795; advancing l., 1082
Livia, stg. l., 457; (as Pax) std. r., 362, 374
Lucius Verus, std. l., 630; on horseback, r., 628
Luna, in biga, l., 722
Lyre, 517

Macellum, 430
Macrinus and Diadumenian, std. l., 730
Marcus Aurelius, on horseback, r., 638
Marcus Aurelius and Lucius Verus, std. l., 623; clasping hands, stg. l. and r., 624
Mars, stg. l., 333, 807, 891, 993, 1003; stg. r., 984; advancing l., 468, 472, 488, 508, 525, 957; advancing r., 492, 600, 783, 813, 950, 958, 994, 1012, 1078
Maximian, stg. l., 1074, 1113, 1123; stg. r., 1112–13, 1125
Maximinus, stg. l., 761
Maximus, stg. l., 762; stg. r., 761
Mercury, bust of, r., 539; stg. l., 640, 915, 1050
Minerva, bust of, r., 439, 518; std. r., 515; stg. l., 514, 1134; stg. r., 523; advancing r., 396–7, 505, 510
Minos, std. l., 720
Minotaur, stg. facing, 720
Modius, 398, 530
Moneta, stg. l., 513, 912, 921, 1095, 1139
Monetae, Tres, stg. l., 788, 1021, 1093
Mules, two, with cart, 531

Neptune, stg. l., 390, 622
Nilus, reclining, l., 579
Nobilitas, stg. r., 656, 756, 798
Numerian, stg. l., 1047; stg. r., 1038, 1064, 1071
Nymphaeum, 747

Ops, std. l., 668
Ostia, harbour of, 422

Palm tree, 529
Pannonia, stg. r., 816
Pannoniae, the two, standing facing, 805, 1073
Parthia, std. r., 633
Parthian, kneeling r., 331, 485
Panther, stg. l., 875
Pax, std., 774; stg. l., 463, 478, 757, 801, 827, 933, 948, 1131–2, 1135, 1140, 1143; advancing l., 1037, 1048
Peacock, facing, 524, 612, 839; flying r.,

bearing emperor, 853; bearing empress, 760, 847
Pegasus, stg. r., 876
Perpetuitas, stg. l., 749, 1008
Pertinax, std. l., 670
Philip I and Philip II, in facing quadriga, 791
Philip II, stg. l., 786
Pietas, bust of, r., 368; stg. l., 589, 735, 936; stg. r., 588
Pileus, 388, 441
Postumus, std. l., 914; stg. l., 905; stg. r., 904
Praetorian camp, 392
Priestly vessels, 605, 685, 759, 775, 849, 943, 1043
Probus, stg. l., 1019; stg. r., 1016, 1024, 1034; on horseback, r., 1029; in quadriga, r., 1032
Providentia, stg. l., 765, 769, 913, 999, 1141
Pudicitia, std. l., 787, 817; stg. l., 631, 809–10
Puellae Faustinae, 608
Pulvinar, 469, 502
Pyre, funeral, 648, 714, 819, 897

Ram, stg. r., 1130
Rhea Silvia, reclining l., 600
Rhine, river-god reclining l., 902
Roma, std. l., 434, 456, 766, 829, 864, 884, 990, 992, 997, 1009, 1015; std. r., 418, 484, 569; stg. l., 416, 451, 453; advancing r., 450
Romulus, advancing r., 584, 597

Saeculum frugiferum, std. l., 682
Salonina, std. l., 877
Salus, bust of, r., 367; std. l., 421; stg. l., 458, 848, 944, 951, 1138; stg. r., 870, 991, 996, 1039, 1136
Seasons, four, 634, 1020, 1092
Securitas, std. l., 728, 764, 1030; std. r., 436, 439; stg. l., 820; stg. r., 965
Segetia, stg. facing, 987
Severina, stg. l., 987
Severus, on horseback, r., 684, 708
Severus Alexander, on horseback, r., 754; in quadriga, l., 744
She-wolf and twins, 575, 595, 1026, 1127
Shield, inscribed, 327
Ship, l., 705
Siscia, std. l., 1027
Spes, stg. l., 863, 1040; advancing l., 394, 483, 680, 952, 1056
Sphinx, std. r., 344
Sol, bust of, l., 696; r., 932, 968; three busts of, 903; with globe, stg. l., 724, 753, 784, 882, 885, 890, 999, 1070,

1075; with globe, stg. r., 985, 1022, 1025, 1145; with globe, advancing l., 986; with globe, advancing r., 971–2; with whip, stg. l., 691, 887; with whip, advancing l., 929, 955, 1004; in quadriga, l., 721; in quadriga, r., 690; in facing quadriga, 1031
Soldiers, two, stg. l. and r., clasping hands, 493
Sow, stg. r., 599
Stars, seven, in crescent, 681

Tacitus, stg. r., 1000–2
Tellus, stg. l., 576; reclining l., 704
Temple, distyle, 532; tetrastyle, 512, 826; hexastyle, 329, 345, 794, 815, 1014; octastyle, 549, 602, 620
Tetricus I, stg. l., 940–1, 953
Tetricus II, stg. r., 954
Throne, ornamented, 591
Tiberis, reclining l., 601
Tiberius, std. l., 363; in quadriga, r., 480
Trajan, seated on platform, l., 562; stg. l., 546–7; stg. r., between Euphrates and Tigris, 563; on horseback, r., 536; ploughing, r., 545; in quadriga, l., 537; in quadriga, r., 566
Trophy, 561, 647, 894
Tripod, 469

Uberitas, stg. l., 872, 893, 901

Valerian I and Gallienus, std. l., 838, 841
Valerian II, stg. l., 862
Venus, stg. l., 778, 963, 1059; stg. r., 649, 1052
Vespasian, in quadriga, r., 479, 490
Vesta, std. l., 386, 557; stg. l., 748, 833; temple of, 419, 481
Via Traiana, 551
Victory, bust of, jugate with Felicitas, r., 916; bust of, jugate, with Mars, r., 917; std. l., 487; std. r., 352, 361, 651, 727; stg. l., 322, 330, 442, 454, 486, 839, 851, 881, 995, 1060–1; stg. r., 320, 348, 440, 489, 613, 635, 639, 651, 828, 858, 889, 895, 1005, 1010–1, 1101, 1104, 1119, 1121, 1147; advancing l., 426, 438, 464, 467, 654, 695, 699, 700, 713, 792, 803, 866–7, 906–71, 937, 962, 1051, 1065; advancing r., 415, 717, 812, 924, 927, 938, 942, 969, 1013, 1044, 1045, 1069; flying r., 324; kneeling r., 343; in biga, r., 1129
Victories, two, stg. l. and r., 710, 860
Vitellius, children of, 471
Volusian, stg. l., 823, 825

Wreath, oak, 336–7, 414, 455, 494; enclosing inscription, 874, 1023, 1128

IV General

The references are to page numbers.

Actium, battle of, 7, 8, 12
Agricola in Britain, 37
alimenta, 49
Antonine wall, 61
antoninianus, introduction of, 72, 82;
  mark of value on, 124
Augustus, deification of, 13
Arabia Petraea, annexation of, 50
Armenia, client kingdom, 11; conquest
  by Corbulo, 23; new province, 52
Antoninus Pius, consecration of, 64

Ba'al, cult of, brought to Rome, 85–6
Britain, conquest of, 20; Caledonian
  invasion of, 68–9; Severan campaigns
  in, 79–81; separate empire of, 153

Carus, consecration of, 141
Cistophoric tetradrachm, 7, 45, 55
Civil War, AD 68–9, 28–34; AD 193,
  73–6
Claudius I, consecration of, 22
Claudius II, consecration of, 113–14
Coinage system: Augustus, 7; Nero, 7;
  Domitian, 35; Trajan, 45; Caracalla,
  72; mid-third century, 89; Aurelian,
  124; Diocletian, 124
Contemporary copies, 20
Cremona, battle of, 34

Dacia, new province, 50
Dacian War, 47–8
Danube, bridged by Trajan, 48
denarius, decline in fineness, 57
double-sestertius, introduced by Trajan
  Decius, 89; resumed by Postumus,
  115
drachm, 7

Faustina I, consecration of, 60
Faustina II, consecration of, 67

Hadrian, consecration of, 57; travels of,
  45; visits to provinces of, 54–5
Hadrian's Wall, 55
Hercules, cult of (Commodus), 70–1;
  (Postumus), 118

Imperial post service, 46–7

Jewish revolt, suppressed by Vespasian
  and Titus, 36, 40

Livia, consecration of, 19–20
Lucius Verus, consecration of, 66
Ludi Saeculares, *see* Saecular Games

Marciana, consecration of, 51
Marcommanic War, 66, 68
Marcus Aurelius, consecration of, 68
Marks of value on coinage, 7, 25
Mesopotamia, new province, 52

Nigrinian, consecration of, 141

Officinae, first marking of, 89

Piso, conspiracy of, 24
Praetorian Guard, 18, 19, 28
Princeps Inventutis, title of heir, 13, 22

quadrans, latest instance of, 57–8
quindecimviri sacris fuciundis, 33

remissa ducentesima, 18
remissa quadragesima, 30
Raetia, conquest of, 12
'restored' coins, 31, 41, 45–6

Saecular Games, 9, 43, 79, 96–7
Sarmatian War, 67
Septimius Severus, consecration of, 81
standards, return of, by Parthia, 9
semis, revived by Trajan Decius, 89, 99

Tetrarchy, First, 124, 144
Trajan, conquests of, 45; consecration
  of, 52
Trajan Senior, consecration of, 51
'tribute' penny, 14

Valerian II, consecration of, 106
Vespasian, consecration of, 40
Vesuvius, eruption of, 40
Victorinus, consecration of, 122
Vindex, revolt of, 78